OONA STRATHERN is a journalist who has worked for fifteen years as a trend and future consultant for many international companies. She writes a regular column about the latest consumer and socio-economic trends in London for one of Europe's leading future and trend consultants, the Zukunfts-institut. She currently lives in Vienna with her husband and two sons whose visions of the future include 'sweets growing on trees' and 'homework writing machines'.

D1440072

Other titles in this series

A BRIEF HISTORY OF
THE FUTURE

How visionary thinkers changed the
world and tomorrow's trends are
'made' and marketed

OONA STRATHERN

ROBINSON
London

Constable & Robinson Ltd
3 The Lanchesters
162 Fulham Palace Road
London W6 9ER
www.constablerobinson.com

This edition published by Robinson,
an imprint of Constable & Robinson Ltd, 2007

A copy of the British Library Cataloguing in
Publication data is available from the British Library.

ISBN-13: 978-1-84529-218-8

Printed and bound in the EU

1 3 5 7 9 10 8 6 4 2

To Matthias

*If you do not think about the future,
you cannot have one.*

John Galsworthy

CONTENTS

INTRODUCTION

The future enters into us in order to transform itself in us long before it happens.

Rainer Maria Rilke, poet and writer

When the novelist Iris Murdoch died in 1999, cognitive neuroscientists took a special interest in her last novel, *Jackson's Dilemma*. The book was about a mysterious disappearance, but for the scientists it told another, much more interesting, story. Following an analysis of word use in comparison with her earlier novels, they retrospectively established evidence of the onset of Alzheimer's disease. Unbeknown to her, at the time of writing, the author was in a so-called pre-symptomatic period which can precede the clinical onset of a disease by many years. It was a stage at which the disease had not yet manifested itself in her day-to-day behaviour, yet was still having an impact on cognition.

The future, as Rilke pointed out, is rather like that too. It is in fact already here, buried somewhere in the past, and germinating in the present, there to be revealed by those with the desire or the talent to do so. Poets and neuroscientists do not belong to the kind of professions one would naturally associate with those trying to predict the future, but predictions have, over the centuries, occupied everyone from historians and hack porno writers to politicians and rocket scientists. The people who set themselves this magnificent and not immodest task are today generally known as futurists, but they were not always known as such; utopians, prophets, charlatans, magicians, or even liars are some of the more repeatable names that have been used over the years. After the term 'futurology' was invented in the 1940s, they were, for a while known as futurologists, but this quickly and thankfully fell out of favour for being unpronounceable and sounding suspiciously similar to an unpleasant branch of medicine. For the purposes of this book, in general I have not differentiated between the various terms used in futurism such as prognosis, forecast, vision and projection. This is because over the years thanks to different practitioners, methods and interpretations the terminology has become a bit of a methodological muddle, and therefore the term 'prediction' is used here as the general or umbrella term for what these futurists do when working with the future. Furthermore, the terms 'futurist' and 'futurism' are used liberally from the start – i.e. well before they were actually invented.

This book explores the lives, works and mindset of some of the most important futurists, who are united here not only by a deep desire to predict the future, but to prepare us for it, and in doing so, help shape the way we live. Some of them are unashamed, stubborn optimists, others miserable misanthropic pessimists, but they are all heralds, riding bravely out to see what is ahead, and galloping back with advice, ideas or warnings. Sometimes they are bearers of good news who want to altruistically push progress and civilization forward on a safe and stable path. Others are mischievous mavericks who have earned an outrageously good living pointing out all the nastiest pitfalls and playing on our deepest fears for the future.

Some of them mentioned here are bona fide futurists with a proper paid job to predict the future. However, many of the most interesting and influential ones were accidental futurists (those never recognized as such but who made monumental contributions to our perception and thinking about the future), frustrated futurists (those with the imagination but not the power) and closet futurists (those who do not know they are futurists). Many of their predictions were of a practical, technical and scientific nature – Leonardo's flying machines, Darwin's evolutionary theory, Mendeleyev's periodic table. Some were political – from Marx's political futurism to von Neumann's game theory that nearly led to a Third World War. Some of the most interesting were sociological – bold ideas about the future of love, relationships and the role of men and women in society from people such as H. G. Wells and Charlotte Perkins Gilman. Along the way, prediction became an integral part of business and politics, too – the multinational company Shell used scenario planning against oil shocks in the 1970s, cool-hunters prowled the streets in the 1990s and today Nokia has a thrusting 'foresight' department. Even the government of Liechtenstein has a shiny new futures department.

As well as attracting a huge range of personalities and professions over two millennia, the methods of looking at the future have ranged from the use of drugged virgins to more conventional, systematic employment of computers and simple common sense.

This book begins with the formative years of futurism, shows how it evolved into a respectable discipline and explores how it later branched out to adapt to the changing needs and greed of civilization. In trying to predict how we would live, work and even love, some of these futurists were spectacularly right, some were embarrassingly and hilariously wrong, and some really gave the future a run for its money. There are of course plenty of diligent and hard-working futurists whom I have not mentioned, but I hope that in leaving some out I have left room for others that you may not have heard of or seen as such. All of them in this book have, however, had something interesting and poignant – if not controversial or unusual – to say about what was and is to come, and in doing so many of them have risked their lives, reputations and sometimes even their marriages.

Futurism is often called the second oldest profession. Not because of any affinity to the oldest but because it was the early astronomers who were the first to think systematically and scientifically about the future. Looking at the stars they could successfully predict the positions of the sun, moon and planets, first for the calendar, and later for scientific and navigational purposes. What they could not, however, have predicted was the extent to which their activity would be appropriated by astrologers who claim they can foretell human events and destinies by observing the sky. Astrology first originated in Mesopotamia around 3000 BC and, despite every scientific proof that has since appeared to the contrary, horoscopes are still the most popular method for the laywoman (and sometimes man) to predict their future. While astronomy is not futurism in the sense of this book, astrology is definitely not futurism in any sense, although the obstinate belief in it provides us with a poignant warning. Scientist Richard Dawkins tells an apocryphal tale in *Unweaving the Rainbow* of a modern-day journalist who was ordered by his newspaper to write the day's horoscopes. Driven to boredom, he wrote under one star sign, 'All the sorrows of yesteryear are as nothing compared to what will befall you today.' Desperate readers phoned the newspaper offices in panic, and the poor journalist was promptly sacked. For the journalist who wrote that fateful line, it is a wonderful case of a self-fulfilling prophecy (which unfortunately only goes to affirm people's belief in such things).

Similarly, before I had even considered a career in futurism, my own first professionally paid 'predictions' were made while working for a well-known London weekly newspaper group. As one of several sub-editors, my job was to check and rewrite copy, and the most fought-over sections were the horoscopes, sent to the office in fat batches by one of Britain's best-loved and highest-paid astrologers. The horoscopes of whoever was lucky enough to win the draw to edit them would suddenly look remarkably positive for the week – regardless of whether the original horoscope was meant for the previous month or the following week. The funny thing was that many of the journalists still believed in their horoscope, despite having tailor-made it to suit themselves! I certainly would not want to claim that this practice is regularly repeated in newspaper and magazine offices throughout the world, but it might nevertheless be worth bearing in mind next time you reach for that section of the newspaper.

A far more admirable attempt to influence the future with horoscopes was reported to have taken place during the Second World War, when the British Secret Service tried to destabilize Hitler with pessimistic predictions. Hitler was apparently a great believer in horoscopes and was terrified of dying before he had completed his life's work. The British tried to create a self-fulfilling prophecy by sending out astrological predictions that he would suffer a massive defeat and die in 1942. Unfortunately, this did not work; later Hitler would even have his own personal astrologer sent off to a concentration camp when his prophecies proved wrong.

Michael Wood, author of *The Road to Delphi* points out, 'It's not that the horoscope, for all its avuncular advice, can remedy our helplessness, or really tell us what to do – no oracle can do that. But there is a definite thrill in the chance that the words of a stranger will, once in a while, offer an echo or an image of one of our most intimate fears or hopes, as if we had lost it and coincidence had found it.' The same sentiment can often be applied to futurism, as many people or companies will automatically seek out a future or a futurist that fits or simply reaffirms their beliefs, hopes or point of view. The danger of this is swiftly demonstrated by the legend of the Sultan and the soothsayer. When a soothsayer was once asked by a Sultan to predict his future he peered into the globe and declared, 'I have great news. All your relatives will die before you.' The Sultan was horrified and ordered the man to be killed immediately. Another soothsayer was dragged in and he declared, 'I have great news for you. You will outlive all your relatives.' The sultan rewarded him handsomely. The predictions were the same – it is just that the delivery was somewhat different.

Along with astrologers and soothsayers, religious prophets are also conspicuously absent from this book as I do not believe they played a significant role in the development of futurism as we know and use it today. Their case was not helped by a technique used to boost their reputation, *Vaticinium ex eventu* (prophecy from the event). This was the devious practice of writing down a prophecy after the event that it supposedly foretells. Along with prophets, weather forecasters also get short shrift. Despite many advances in short-term forecasting, weather forecasting is a misnomer as far as many people are concerned. Even Britain's much-loved television weather forecaster Michael Fish never really recovered his reputation following that fateful day in October 1987 when he confidently assured a woman viewer that there would be no hurricane, only for one to sweep the country some hours later, leaving the most catastrophic trail of damage on record. Luckily, Fish was working for the BBC, which forgave him; state meteorologists in Moscow were not so lucky. In 2005 they were warned by the mayor that they would have to compensate businesses that suffered financial losses resulting from any faulty forecasting.

Accountability is one of the biggest and most obvious hazards of predicting the future, but another compelling matter to bear in mind while reading this book is what writer Bruce Sterling terms the futurists' monkey puzzle. The classic monkey trap involves placing something tempting inside a jar with a narrow opening. When a monkey puts its hand in and grips the prize, its fist gets stuck and it is caught in a dilemma between letting go and hanging hopelessly on to the prize. 'The lesson for the futurist here is simple,' explains Sterling, 'out in the wilderness of delightful trends, conjectures and happenstances is the one you can't resist. That is your monkey puzzle. It is the one futuristic curiosity that proves unbearable to your heart . . . It is the scheme that you champion against all odds . . . It is generally something rather trivial, silly and goofy. You may find yourself longing to have your head frozen for millennia inside a tub of liquid nitrogen . . . It might suddenly occur to you that UFOS might really and truly exist. The monkey puzzle is almost never based on a sober, rational analysis.

Instead, it speaks to some underfed, sugar-starved part of the victim's personal psyche.'

After fifteen years of working as a researcher, writer and consultant in the trend and futures business, I now have an in-built radar for such traps, which functions pretty reliably when at conferences or meetings or talking to futurist friends and colleagues. While I often become aware of a potential peccadillo or obsession that a particular colleague or futurist might be peddling, it doesn't unfortunately work so well for myself. Hence, in the chapter on the business of futurism today, I reluctantly look back and squirm in embarrassment at some of the trends I predicted for particular clients. Although it may contribute to a minor part of a major futurist's repertoire (or in my case to a major part of a very minor futurist's repertoire), the point is that the monkey puzzle is potentially very danger-ous. As Sterling soberly says, 'it doesn't feel like a trap. It feels heroic.' Umberto Eco pointed out a similar truth when he warned: 'Never fall in love with your own airship.' What he was referring to was the fact that for fifty years nobody believed that aeroplanes would play a role in aviation. It seemed so obvious to people at the time that the Zeppelin, elegant and lighter than air, would be the way to travel in the future – not by ugly, noisy aeroplanes! Even as recently as in the 1960s a prominent futurist in Slovenia predicted that in the future everyone would travel about in small flying objects and that therefore there was absolutely no need for the government to invest in motorways, garages, parking lots, tramways, trains and buses. Today the sorry state of the public transport and road system in the capital Ljubljana is a testament to his predictions, and to the suspicion that he read too many science-fiction comics as a child.

When it comes to weird and wonderful promises for the future, science fiction has a lot to answer for. Novelist Kingsley

Amis once amusingly pointed out that people do not read science fiction to discover scientific truths, any more than they read Westerns to learn about ranching. But do they read it to find out about the future? In *What Futurists Believe*, Joseph Coates and Jennifer Jarratt gloat that 'Sci-fi is of little, or no, value . . . is usually so barren of plausible psychological, social, or institutional sophistication as to fall into one of three categories: entertainment, fantasy or cautionary tales.' Even the renowned science-fiction writer Ursula Le Guin recommends that the business of prediction is best left to futurists, because 'a novelist's business is lying'. The point these critics all choose to ignore is not only that science fiction is frequently rather good prediction masquerading as fiction, but that much of it is actually written by respectable scientists and futurists (albeit sometimes shamefully under a pseudonym).

Because the future hasn't happened yet, when futurists make a prediction, they are in the privileged position of not yet being proven wrong. This is the conceit of the future (not always inseparable from the conceit of some futurists) that makes futurism both so fascinating and so potentially powerful. With all their privilege, futurists are also often considered to be in a unique position to create and control the future. One school of thought says that if you can really predict something, you are in effect helping to invent or create it. This is common in the field of technology, where the forecasting of inventions is often indistinguishable from the invention process itself. Thinking about what the future will bring is also, however, about learning and accepting how much control we do or do not have over it. As the brilliant quantum physicist Nils Bohr once admitted, 'It's very difficult to predict – especially about the future.' And that from a man who hung a horseshoe above the entrance to his house because, as he famously explained to a friend, 'they say it works even if you don't believe in it'.

Welcome to the future. Some of it, as they say, is already history.

Oona Strathern, Vienna, 2006

CHAPTER 1

SEX, DRUGS AND HEADS THAT ROLL . . .

Sometimes the sheer feel of prophecy is more significant than what is prophesied.

Michael Wood, *The Road to Delphi*

Drugs, virgins, trances and sacrifice – the forecasting methods used by the oracles of ancient Greece were rather unconventional by today's standards. But for over a thousand years, from as early as the eighth century BC to the third century AD, when an edict was issued against them, the oracles had an important and influential role to play in many people's lives. In their role as political think tanks the oracles had a reputation and power that reached far beyond the dreams and ambitions of most futurists today. This is essentially where the business of futurism began and despite the unusual packaging of the predictions, many of the underlying principles of how and why it worked have continued to be an inspiration for futurists to the present day.

There were several oracles in ancient Greece, but the greatest of all was at Delphi on the slopes of Mount Parnassus. It was here, the legendary spot where Zeus discovered the centre of the world, that peasants, statesmen and leaders travelled to consult the oracle. Making their way over the rocky mountain paths the pilgrims usually brought with them a nice plump sheep or goat as payment along with the ritual *pelanos,* a flat honey cake. Unless the enquirer was to be given preferential treatment, he would have to wait upon arrival, rather like in a doctor's surgery, for his turn to pose his question to the resident god, Apollo. The temple of Apollo with its statues and columns was formidably designed as befitting such an important consultant. Inscribed on the walls were the oracle's snappy and inspiring slogans such as, 'know thyself' and 'nothing in excess'. These provided food for thought for those patiently waiting their turn to submit queries that ranged from the banal to the bold – from such things as 'should I attack my enemy?, to 'should I marry?' or more famously 'who is the wisest among the Greeks?' (answer, Socrates).

Unfortunately, with such oracles there were no short cuts or direct access to the 'boss' or the results. Not unlike the case with many top futurists and consultancies today, you were entirely at the mercy of their availability (Apollo, for example, took a generous three months off in the winter). Not only was there blatant sexual discrimination – only men were allowed to ask questions – but the questioner had to wait patiently as his question was passed from the priests to a Pythian priestess, whose job it was to consult the great god himself. Though much sought after and highly respected, the job of Pythia was not ostensibly an enviable one. She was typically over fifty and a virgin, and she spent much of her time in a drug-induced trance in her damp basement 'office' which was split by a deep fissure. Having first bathed and purified herself in a nearby spring the Pythia would dress in regulation white robes. Briefed by the priests, she would then take up position on a tripod amid the intoxicating sweet-smelling vapours that rose from bituminous limestone in the chasm. These rather unusual working conditions induced a state of euphoria as well as delirium and the tendency to thrash wildly about. When the gases ceased to appear after an earthquake, the priestesses munched laurel leaves instead and waved a laurel branch about for full hypnotic effect. It was in this trance-induced state of ecstasy that the Pythia would proclaim the prophecy in a garbled form – which then had to be deciphered by the priests. Given the circumstances this was not an easy task, and one that lent itself to a variety of interpretations, and naturally to accusations of bribery and corruption.

The Pythias were an exciting and impressive part of the packaging of the predictions – or as Henry Adams wrote in 1898, 'Delphi . . . a transparent and elegant fraud that no one more than half believed in except when it suited them, but that was artistically satisfactory and socially perfect.' The real work lay with the priests, who, behind the scenes, used their intelligence as well as a wide network of contacts, gossip and messengers to gather relevant information that would provide astute or 'useable' answers, thus maintaining customer satisfaction. Despite this (or essentially because of this), ambiguity was always the trademark of the prophecies, and one of the secrets of the oracle's long-lasting success lay in a special kind of ambiguous double speech (amphibology) enabling the oracle to be right whatever the outcome. Michael Wood, in *The Road to Delphi*, likens this special kind of ambiguity to 'a dual-voltage electrical appliance . . . with a switch for its use in different locations or on different occasions'.

This optimizing strategy is best illustrated by the big political prediction made by Delphi for King Croesus of Lydia.

Croesus, whose name has come to be synonymous with the wealthy, was justly wary of invading the Persian Empire, and consulted the oracle. It famously told him that if he went to war, he would destroy a great empire. Encouraged by this, he promptly attacked the Persians, who proceeded to thrash the Lydians, capture their capital and throw Croesus into prison. Fuming in his cell, Croesus sent a delegation to Delphi, demanding to know why the oracle had deceived him. The reply? She had not deceived him. Croesus had indeed destroyed a great empire: his own. As Wood puts it, 'in oracle stories the promise or the prediction needs only to have a chance of having been right, needs only not to have been unequivocally wrong. Faith, enthusiasm and ingenious interpretation will do the rest.' Or perhaps Croesus should have read the advertising slogans a little more carefully.

The key lesson that has been learnt by some futurists from the oracles is something that is often and judiciously forgotten by those who keenly request their services. It is that the best predictions simply provide a mirror, and that the customer actually has to work too. This crucial point is neatly illustrated by Wood in a dialogue between two figures who are chatting nervously on their way to consult an oracle. One asks the other, 'What if it doesn't say anything?' The other says, 'It won't say anything; it won't just give us simple instructions' . . . The first figure asks, 'What if it says just what we want to hear?' The other replies, 'What do we want to hear?'

Another poignant and timeless example of the problems and pitfalls of prophecy is the so-called curse of Cassandra. Cassandra appears in Greek mythology as the daughter of Priam, the last king of Troy. She was so desired by the god Apollo that he promised her the power of prophecy if she would comply with his wishes. Having received this great gift of foresight, she then refused him her favours and was promptly cursed to a life in which no one would believe her prophecies. Not only was she considered dreadfully melodramatic, but her predictions were laden with doom and gloom – she predicted the fall of Troy and the death of Agamemnon. The moral here is certainly not that one should accept sexual advances of powerful men if you want your prophecies taken seriously (though that hasn't stopped some people), but that it is immeasurably hard to separate possible truth from disbelief when looking into the future. As Bruce Sterling puts it in *Tomorrow Now,* Cassandra's greatest contribution to futurism is 'in facing her harsh truth; that treasured things and circumstances will die and rot. People pay futurists to predict glittering novelties, not to mourn the solemn doom of the obsolete and the overthrown.'

Plato's *Republic*, written in around 360 BC, was another formative – and indeed more informative – Greek contribution to futurism, as it is one of the first surviving European utopias, and it was to set a standard for many to come. Utopia literally means 'no place', and Plato's vision of a future society was, by our standards, actually more of a dystopia (a negative utopia).

Plato (428–348 BC) was primarily a philosopher but also a man of mathematics, as well as a rather well-known wrestler in his younger days. For him life and work was not so much about knowing thyself, but knowing thy numbers (he was deeply impressed by Pythagoras' famous saying, 'All is number'). Over the door to Plato's Academy near Athens was said to have been inscribed the warning, 'No one shall enter who knows no geometry'. And indeed much of his life was characterized by a failed pursuit of an idealized world of order run by even-tempered logicians. Plato's fantasies for an ideal future were played out in *The Republic* in the form of a dinner-party dialogue between Socrates and other worthy male characters in a tycoon's palace. Among the hot topics of discussion in this sumptuous setting were the principles of a just society, private ownership, feminism and birth control.

Plato's *Republic* is true to his character, a controlled, logical place, ruled by a philosopher-king with a solid background in pure mathematics who uses nothing less than knowledge, wisdom and truth to maintain strict order. He is aided by a regulated and ruthless system of eugenics to ensure the best offspring, with the state organizing jolly nuptial festivals to make the necessary matches. Soon after birth, the results of these unions are then conveniently shipped off to be educated communally in the art of gymnastics and uplifting music until the age of twenty. At this point they are then progressively weeded out according to their abilities and inabilities, and if they do not happen to show any talent for even the most basic skills, they are sent off to perform menial tasks and support the community as farmers or businessmen. The rest go on to study arithmetic, geometry and astronomy (as Plato had done). In his ideal world, those who fail mathematics at the age of thirty are promptly dispatched to the military, and those who succeed are permitted the great privilege of studying philosophy for another five years. Only at the age of fifty, after fifteen years of practical study of government are citizens then deemed fit to rule (naturally as a 'philosopher ruler'). According to Plato's ideals, 'justice in the state means that each of the three classes found within it is performing its proper function . . . each of us is just and does his duty only when each part of us performs its proper function' (*The Republic*, Book IV).

The Republic, like many utopias, is both a product of its age and of the writer's personal obsessions or monkey puzzle. His vision of the future is, by our standards, a totalitarian nightmare run by a megalomaniac philosopher. But Plato could be forgiven a little if one remembers that this was a rough time when neither democracy nor tyranny had provided order, and there was a desperate need for a vision of a government that could. Athens had just been defeated in the Peloponnesian War by Sparta, an economically backward but strictly controlled philistine society, and one-third of the population at the time were slaves with no rights. However, *The Republic* was not just a product of its political age, it also revealed something about the writer himself. As well as making bodily health a basic life requirement for the inhabitants of this utopia (he was, remember, a prize-winning wrestler), Plato based the academic preferences and requirements to make it to the top of the food chain entirely on his own strengths (artists, poets, dramatists and lawyers were summarily banned from this utopia). Furthermore, the revolutionary ideas about families and bringing up children ('wives are to be held in common by all, so too, are children') reveal the fact that Plato was the product of a broken home, and is said to have been brought up in a number of households. Moreover, according to Diogenes Laertius, Plato's father failed 'to win' his mother after making 'violent love' to her, and she took a second husband.

However miserable the prospect of such a life may seem today, Plato clearly thought deeply and carefully about a new and improved society for the future, and his ideas were to inspire many a utopia to come. Like many influential futurists he was provocative, but his ideas were not, it could be argued, outside the realms of a sharp imagination of the time. The same could not, however, be said of Englishman Roger Bacon, a Franciscan monk who lived around 1,500 years later. Pitifully little is known about Bacon's private life, let alone the exact place and date of his birth and death, but what has survived from the thirteenth century are some of his remarkable predictions and his reputation as one of the forerunners of experimental science.

Bacon was, even by today's standards, a likely candidate for a futurist. Born into a wealthy family, he was, by his own admission, possessed with a prodigious energy and curiosity. He both studied and taught philosophy and mathematics at Oxford and Paris but also took a keen interest in the new sciences of optics, alchemy and astronomy. Bacon was initially rich enough to enable him to not only concentrate on his studies while at Oxford, but also to experiment indulgently with his ideas. According to one report, 'from love of experiment he neglected teaching and writing, and made two mirrors in the University of Oxford: by one of them you could light a candle at any hour, day or night; in the other you could see what people were doing in any part of the world' (from *Roger Bacon*, by W. Woodruff). Students were apparently so distracted by these inventions, lighting candles or seeing 'their relations dying or ill or otherwise in trouble' that there were fears it would lead to the ruin of the university, and both mirrors were promptly destroyed.

Bacon not only appears to have carried out early systematic observations with lenses and mirrors but also had some sort of a laboratory for experiments that he believed to be the only true path to scientific knowledge. His experiments, however, cost him a fortune, and he admitted in his writings to a weakness for spending large amounts of money not only on constructing instruments and paying for assistants but also on acquiring 'secret' books of knowledge. It was such research that enabled Bacon to get his hands on the directions for making gunpowder before anyone else in the West, and helped establish his reputation as knowing what the future would bring. Having got his hands on the recipe, he wrote how 'the sound of thunder may be artificially produced in the air with greater resulting horror than if it had been produced by natural causes'. Among the other extraordinary possibilities he dwelled upon was the potential for flying in a machine with flapping wings: 'It is possible that a device for flying shall be made such that a man sitting in the middle of it and turning a crank shall cause artificial wings to beat the air after the manner of a bird's flight . . .' Other things he foresaw were a vehicle 'which will move with inestimable speed, and the motion will be without the help of any living creature . . . It is possible also that devices can be made whereby, without bodily danger, a man may walk on the bottom of a sea or of a river . . .'

As far as most people were concerned in those medieval times, what Bacon envisaged was not the future, but magic. Through this work Bacon may have acquired the title of *doctor mirabilis* (wonderful teacher), but he was seen by many as a charlatan and a conjurer. In the interests of survival, ego and education, Bacon took great intellectual pains to separate what he saw as the future, from magic. Of his inventions he said, these are 'marvels wrought through the agency of Art and of Nature . . . in these there is no magic whatsoever because . . . all magical power is inferior to these works and incompetent to achieve them' (from *The First Scientist*). Such was Bacon's belief in the future of science that when he entered the Franciscan order in about 1257, he appealed to his patron Pope Clement IV to give sciences an improved status in universities. Exactly why Bacon became a monk at the peak of his futurist career remains unclear, for he did not display an overtly monastic temperament. As one writer pointed out, 'poverty and chastity he could manage intermittently, but obedience was quite beyond him.' Some have suggested it was because he was by now completely broke, but it is equally likely he needed a safe place with peace and quiet to write his life's works, such as the modest little idea he had for an encyclopaedia containing all human knowledge. While he failed with the latter, he managed at the Pope's request, to produce an impressive three large volumes of an encyclopaedia of all known sciences.

As many a futurist has subsequently found out, it is not simply risky, but downright dangerous, to be ahead of your time. In the thirteenth century it was almost unheard of, and following the death of his patron, Bacon was at the mercy of his enemies; his books were largely destroyed, and he languished in a Parisian jail for fifteen years before his death. Three centuries later, much the same fate was to befall another forward-thinking Englishman, Thomas More. More is frequently considered to be the true creator of the utopian genre. His book, called simply *Utopia*, was written almost 2,000 years after Plato's *Republic* and is widely considered to be a benchmark for positive utopian visions. In many ways More's vision could not have been more different to Plato's. Written in 1516, this is a vision of an island inhabited by healthy happy communists where work is required for only six hours a day, and leisure time is spent sensibly in brain-challenging pursuits such as playing board games or attending lectures (Plato would have approved there). In Utopia there is no poverty, there are no idle rich, and certainly nothing as degrading as overt exploitation. To the starving, desperate, exploited European peasants at the time, this would have read more like Paradise than a simple utopia (though reading was not an option for the majority of peasants then). But times change, and from our privileged point of view More's Utopia seems a spectacularly boring place to live. Everyone wears the same simple functional clothes and lives in similar houses. There are no taverns and no gambling, and all the inhabitants appear to go sober to bed at 8pm. And if the good life gets too much or someone gets an incurable disease, there is even a form of voluntary euthanasia that even by today's standards is advanced: 'Let's face it, you'll never be able to live a normal life,' say the priests and officials to the afflicted ones. 'You're just a nuisance to other people and a burden to yourself . . . say the word, and we'll arrange for your release. It's only common sense to cut your losses' (*Utopia*, translated from the Latin by Paul Turner).

But behind all the smokescreen of equality and forward thinking lay many contradictions and unresolved problems. There is the tricky question of the slaves who do the dirty work, and of the mercenaries hired from another land to fight for the Utopians: 'You see, the Utopians are just as anxious to find wicked men to exploit as good men to employ.' Furthermore, when it comes to marriage, adultery is not condoned (though divorce was permitted). The first time you strayed got you penal servitude, and the second offence carried the death penalty. Indeed all round, women and children got a pretty raw deal in this, as in most utopias. Plato parted mothers from their children shortly after birth, and More had surplus children farmed off to less fertile families. Neither visionary was, it seems, very keen on close parental bonding or marriages made for love. 'When they are thinking of getting married . . . the prospective bride . . . is exhibited stark naked to the prospective bridegroom by a respectable married woman, and a suitable male chaperon shows the bridegroom naked to the bride.' More's procedure for choosing a partner is reduced to that of buying a horse at the time – whereby you always whipped off the saddle to inspect for sores. Given that disease, deformity and undernourishment were rife, it was probably considered by his contemporaries as not such a bad idea (indeed, today most of us would admit to having seen our partners naked before marriage). Less egalitarian was the fact that More had Utopian women down on their knees confessing their faults once a month to their husbands.

As with Plato, these extreme measures make you wonder about their private lives. More himself was married twice – the second rather hastily and conveniently after his first wife died leaving him to raise their four children. As John Carey in *The Faber Book of Utopias* tactfully puts it, 'human complexity is born out of the oppositions we harbour within ourselves. We know from More's book some of those that harboured within him.' Or rather we can imagine all too well. It has also been suggested that More's vision of a perfect future was actually a product of his infamous deadpan humour, and that he didn't actually mean it to be taken seriously. However, as John Carey points out, 'this could be More's double bluff, simulating jocularity as self-defence, in a society where spreading new ideas could be dangerous.' In More's case it did not prove to be just dangerous, but fatal. He was of course *the* Sir Thomas More, advisor to Henry VIII, executed in 1535 for refusing to accept the king's supremacy over the Church of England, and from a futurist's viewpoint for being a dangerous visionary.

This period of history saw rumblings of progress, and also the rise of the Renaissance and visionaries like More who were prepared to risk their lives and reputations for their ideas. One of the greatest of this era was Leonardo da Vinci, who as 'the most relentlessly curious man in history', was well qualified to be a futurist. Leonardo was not just a brilliant painter but a restless universalist whose lines of scientific inquiry and mechanical inventiveness were centuries ahead of his time.

Leonardo said that his earliest memory was of a kite settling on him in his cradle and pushing its tail into his mouth. Although Freud claimed that this provided the key to Leonardo's relationship with his mother ('What the fantasy conceals is merely a reminiscence of sucking – at his mother's breast', from *Leonardo de Vinci, A Memory of His Childhood*), futurists would interpret this somewhat differently, pointing more pragmatically to the origins of Leonardo's life-long obsession with flight. His first sketches of a flying machine, made between 1478 and 1480, seem rather disappointing at first glance. 'No more than a doodle' on a scruffy-looking page, remarks Charles Nicholl in his biography of Leonardo, 'but quite unmistakeable.' It shows wings unfurled like a bat's, attached to a cockpit-like frame, and is accompanied by a more detailed drawing of a mechanism for manoeuvring the wing. It was more of a hang-glider than a plane, and may well have flown had he managed to construct it. Other visions of flight included a four-man helicopter, which would not have worked, and a parachute which did.

Over 500 years after he had first sketched a design for the world's first-known parachute, Leonardo's construction was built true to his description and with period tools. His instructions were clear: 'If a man has a canopy of coated linen 12 braccia (24 feet) wide and 12 long, he can jump from any great height whatsoever without injury.' In June 2000, ignoring all expert advice, a British man called Adrian Nicholas followed what he hoped was 'Da Vinci's promise that it would work' and parachuted down from a hot air balloon in an 85-kilo heavy wood and canvas construction. It was a beautiful sight – the top of a white pyramid sailing smoothly down to earth. Only at 600 metres did Mr Nicholas have to cut himself free and deploy a modern parachute to ensure Leonardo's device did not crush him upon landing. After the adventure he said 'It took one of the greatest minds who ever lived to design it, but it took 500 years to find a man with a brain small enough to actually go and fly it.'

It took somewhat less time (and possibly more brains) for

Leonardo's other inventions and futuristic visions to be realized. His catalogue of fighting military hardware for the Duke of Milan included 'armoured cars, totally unassailable', and his sketches show nothing less than a prototype of the modern army tank. Leonardo is also credited as having designed the first humanoid robot in 1495. A direct result of his anatomical studies, his remarkable sketch for a robot was an armoured knight with cords to simulate the tendons and muscles. It was designed to sit up, nod its head and wave its arms. Not one to miss a trend, Leonardo also turned his hand to designing the ideal city, as was highly fashionable during the Renaissance. Drawings and notes from the late 1480s revealed his vision for a futuristic city built on two levels. The upper level was envisioned as a pleasant pedestrian zone of piazzas, whereas the lower level was designed for animals, traders and the transportation of goods. As well as these extraordinary flights of the mind into the future, he also turned his thoughts to the more immediate issue of designing the perfect toilet. 'The seat of the latrine should be able to swivel like the turnstile in a convent,' he wrote enthusiastically.

Leonardo's legacy to the history of futurism is perhaps not so much in the inventions and visions *per se*, but in *saper vedere* – 'knowing how to see'. He was, it could be said, a natural futurist, who set a high visionary standard that would remain unrivalled for many decades to come. The sixteenth century saw no serious threats to his supremacy as top futurist, but it did see the appearance of one curious challenger, a certain Michel de Nostredame. Commonly known as Nostradamus, he was born in 1503 and became a highly respected doctor, rising to the rank of court physician to Charles IX of France. Most usefully, he helped prevent the spread of the plague by recognizing that sufferers should be isolated, and that masks and hygiene were imperative during an epidemic. For all his later faults and fancies, this was a bold and admirable suggestion at a time when superstition reigned and the Church propagated the belief that the black death was a punishment for bad Christians.

While his medical knowledge and advice was promptly forgotten for the next 300 years, his predictions – sadly – were not. Nostradamus published the first edition of these, called the *Centuries*, in 1555, when he had already gained widespread trust and respect as a doctor. These prophetic cryptic verses, which have never been out of print since, consist of 1,000 rhymed quatrains. They are a canny blend of astrological, biblical and literary lore embellished by 'insights' he gained using a few of the tried-and-tested 'tricks' borrowed from the Delphic oracle. During late-night bouts Nostradamus would apparently perch Pythia-like on a tripod staring into water or flames, most probably aided by a little self-prescribed herbal stimulant. In a letter to his newborn son Nostradamus admitted that he deliberately wrote 'in nebulous rather than plainly prophetic form'. As well as adding to his mystique, it was also partly to keep attention away from the Inquisition, which had called for his arrest following a 'fulfilled prophecy' that Henri II would die following a jousting incident (given that this was a popular and dangerous pastime, it was not an unlikely way to go at the time).

The devious and ultimately redundant function of his predictions is that they can, like horoscopes, be interpreted at will – and naturally best – with the benefit of hindsight. Take almost any tragic, traumatic or significantly grim event in history – optimism does not appear to be a popular option – and someone, somewhere will fish out a line or two in which Nostradamus 'predicted' it happening. The rise of Hitler, the Great Fire of London, 9/11 and even the Challenger disaster were all supposedly 'predicted' – though not unfortunately prevented – by Nostradamus. Take for example, the tragic Asian tsunami of Boxing Day 2004, which was, according to one V. F. Hewitt, predicted in Quatrain X.74. In his 'proof', Hewitt first adjusts the original French verse to 'reveal' the allusion to an earthquake. He then translates it into English, helpfully interpreting it on the way, and brings us, 'Seven, the year past of the great earthquake'. The number seven does not, by any stretch of the imagination, bear any relation to 2004, so he advises 'we have to look for a significant event seven years earlier'. In this case he triumphs: it is the death of Princess Diana in 1997. There is thankfully not, he reassures us, any causal relationship between the two events, and this type of 'reading' of the quatrains is something anyone can try for entertainment at home on a wet Monday night. As Jay Leno, the American TV chat-show host, said in the wake of the absurd discussions as to whether Nostradamus really had predicted 9/11, 'If he were alive today his name would be "Miss Cleo" and he'd be charging $2.99 a minute!' Or as one futurist likes to jeer, 'his jam recipes are better than his predictions.' Apparently the recipes are not only reliable but delicious.

In the grand scheme of the history of futurism, Nostradamus is symbolically, but not prophetically, important. His writings have no real predictive function in either preventative or evolutionary terms (the CIA and MI5 are not, I am reliably informed, scanning his books for tip-offs). But importantly what we are left with is a stern warning about the potential for exploitation, since if we take prevention out of the equation, we are left with a perfect breeding ground for people's fears and uncertainty about the future. Nostradamus is clearly not taken seriously by professional futurists, though some, it has to be said, would give their right arm and even some right predictions for his publishing sales record and lifetime of fame and fortune.

Working as a 'consultant' for politicians, the monarchy or even the general public was often a thankless task. The oracle at Delphi had to deal with customer dissatisfaction from the likes of King Croesus, and Thomas More was simply and brutally silenced. Francis Bacon (no relation to Roger), Lord Chancellor of England from 1618–21, had rather more luck in his role as advisor to King James I in that his career ended simply in disgrace rather than death. While his policies were questionable, he was, as he said himself, 'no mountebank in the King's services'. One of the things that carried him through was not only his notorious confidence, but also the sheer precociousness of some of his ideas – perfect qualifications in fact for a futurist. Bacon is remembered not only intellectually as a man who claimed all knowledge as his province and coined the phrase 'knowledge is power', but also for advocating and predicting new ways by which man might reorganize the sciences to establish command over nature. It was the latter which was to form the central idea of his scientific utopian book *The New Atlantis*, written while he was Lord Chancellor, but printed only in 1627, a year after his death.

Bacon's utopia was located, as is still the fashion, on an imaginary island. Here on Bensalem, Bacon's citizens were all directed towards one ultimate objective: 'the enlarging of the bounds of human empire to the effecting of all things possible'. The inhabitants are, naturally, exemplary Christian citizens, which is more than could be said of Bacon (his extravagance led him into debt, and a spell in the Tower of London for taking bribes). Bacon was clearly inspired by More's 'Feigned Commonwealth', especially the part about seeing a prospective bride or groom naked. 'This they the Bensalemites dislike;

for they think it a scorn to give a refusal after so familiar knowledge: but . . . they have a more civil way; for they have near every town a couple of pools (which they call Adam and Eve's pools) where it is permitted to one of the friends of the men, and another of the friends of the woman, to see them severally bathe naked.' This is not so much splendid prediction of the popularity of nude bathing and voyeurism, but a worrying projection of Bacon's sexual frustrations (his wife was barely fourteen when he married her, and he later disinherited her in his will). Those who suggest that Bacon was really homosexual often point paradoxically to his vehement dismissal of it in his utopia: 'as for masculine love, they have no touch of that'.

While the sexual revolution was clearly beyond his imagination, Bacon did, however, admirably predict the results, though not the means, of scientific advancement and genetic engineering. At the heart of his utopian island is Solomon's House, a kind of command control from where all scientific research is directed: 'We make . . . trees and flowers to come earlier or later than their seasons; and to come up and bear more speedily than by their natural course they do. We make them also by art greater much than their nature; and their fruit greater and sweeter and of differing taste, smell, colour, and figure, from their nature.' The same gene-splicing procedure is applied in Bensalem to animals. 'We find means to make commixtures and copulations of different kinds; which have produced many new kinds . . . Neither do we this by chance, but we know beforehand . . . what kind of those creatures will arise.'

Four centuries before the discovery of DNA, Bacon was pushing the boundaries of the imagination in a way that was to bring a new consciousness about what was possible. These are the kind of predictions that differentiate someone with simply a good imagination from what we now call a futurist. He did also admittedly have more common dreams of flight and the usual Freudian male fantasies for more powerful weapons, explosives and submarines. One more surprising prediction in *The New Atlantis* is of modern-day science theme parks – 'houses where we imitate and demonstrate meteors'. In other rooms the inhabitants can listen to sound synthesizers, smell synthetic perfumes, or taste different flavours.

If sexuality could be said to be a blind spot for Bacon, so too was the future of medicine. His personal physician for a time was Sir William Harvey, who discovered the circulation of the blood, yet Bacon appears uninspired by this in his writings and imaginings. Furthermore, he rather carelessly died as the result of an experiment to see if refrigeration could stop the putrefaction of flesh. Having purchased a chicken he then stopped to stuff it with snow, and caught a chill which then developed into a fatal pneumonia. Brilliant idea though it was, it was over 250 years before freezing methods that worked on the principle of mixing salt with ice were introduced commercially for storing poultry. Like many utopian writers of the seventeenth and previous centuries, Bacon concerned himself with aspirations rather than anticipations. They were caught, as I. F. Clarke puts it in *The Pattern of Expectation*, 'between an eagerness to demonstrate their theories of social improvement and an inability to foresee the consequences of the technological developments they so earnestly desired.'

It was to be nearly two centuries before there came another significant player in future thinking and planning. Thomas Robert Malthus was the English Cassandra of his generation, gaining a reputation as a predictor of gloom and doom. During the years that separate Francis Bacon and Malthus, much had changed. By the early years of the eighteenth century, the scientific revolution and the Enlightenment were leading to great industrial and intellectual advances. There was a growing sense of expectation and change. Astronomy, for centuries the popular choice of 'futurists', had entered a new era. Comets, once thought to be erratic signs of imminent flood, famine and death, were shown in 1705 by Edmund Halley to be entirely predictable. Halley's work was highly influenced by his friend Isaac Newton, who had meanwhile revolutionized scientific thinking with the publication of his three laws of universal motion in 1687. Advances in medicine were also significantly changing the 'rules' and perceptions about the future of mankind. One of the most significant discoveries at this time was the smallpox vaccine, introduced by Dr Edward Jenner in 1798. Not just a medical break-through, it also changed perceptions about a possible future, and was noted by the British Parliament at the time as 'un-questionably the greatest discovery ever made for the preser-vations of the human species'. Following centuries of decimating plague and pestilence, this would almost have been comparable today to the discovery of the secret of eternal life. The celebrations were not, however, to last for long, for the very same year that Jenner was hailed a hero, economist Thomas Malthus published his *Essay on the Principle of Population as It Affects the Future Improvement of Society*, in which he claimed all hopes for happiness are in vain.

Malthus was to influence, inspire and ultimately corrupt generations of thinking about prediction of population growth and planetary resources. The crux of his theory, outlined in the 50,000-word essay, was really quite straightforward; hence its hold on people's imagination. According to it, the fate of the future of mankind basically comes down to food and sex. Malthus believed that while the population was liable to increase in geometric progression (i.e. 2, 4, 8, 16, 32 . . .), the food supply would increase only in arithmetic progression (i.e. 2, 4, 6, 8, 10 . . .). The population will be able to expand only to the limit of the means of subsistence, whereby it is regulated by the ensuing sickness, war and famine. 'The power of population is so superior to the power of the earth to reproduce subsistence for man, that premature death must in some shape or other visit the human race,' he stated. The only hope of rescue for mankind was, therefore, strict limits on reproduction. In his role as a Reverend, that meant for Malthus the 'vices' of contraception and abortion, as well as 'misery' and 'self-restraint'. He even toyed with the idea of selective breeding as a future solution to the population problem: 'As the human race could not be improved in this way, without condemning all the bad specimens to celibacy, it is not probable that an attention to breed should ever become general; indeed, I know of no well-directed attempts of this kind, except in the ancient family of the Bickerstaffs, who are said to have been very successful in whitening the skins and increasing the height of their race by prudent marriages, particularly by that very judicious cross with Maud the milkmaid.'

Messing with milkmaids aside, Malthus' theories not only went against the general optimism of the time but, worse still, against his father's beliefs. A wealthy philanthropist, his father believed in the possibility of ameliorating the lot of the poor, whereas Malthus argued that any well-meaning attempt could only make things worse. The poor laws, he claimed, 'alleviated a little the intensity of individual misfortune,' but 'it has spread the evil over a much larger surface.' If their living standards improved, he reasoned, they would produce more children, thus impoverishing themselves once more. 'If every man were sure of a comfortable provision for a family, almost every man would have one; and if the rising generation were free from the fear of poverty, population must increase with unusual rapidity.' From today's Western point of view, where the opposite tends to be true – the higher the standard of living, the lower the birthrate – we see how precarious prediction can be. To be fair, it would have been difficult then to predict today's Western 'birth strike', but on the other hand the full-scale repercussions of the agricultural revolution were not beyond the imagination or the possibilities of the time.

Malthus was, in true futurist tradition, considered ahead of his time, but this alone does not guarantee improvement or progress for civilization. The legacy of his ideas could be seen in the politics of future British social policy – his attitude to the poor paved the way for the repressive mores and poorhouses of the Victorian era. Not only were his theories provocative, so was his hairdo – Thomas Malthus apparently wore his golden locks hanging loose, lightly dusted with pink powder. His 'incontrovertible logic' and 'empirical science' were also, unfortunately, coated with a little decorative dusting. The first census did not take place in Great Britain until 1801, and prior to this the population could only be roughly estimated. Furthermore, in his calculations of the rapidly expanding American population, he failed to take into account the effect of immigration. The controversy surrounding his ideas and his methods was such that, as the witty US economist Todd Buchholz pointed out, when Malthus died in 1834 'some came to mourn, others to make sure he really was dead'.

Long after his death, Malthus' simplistic predictive methods were still finding favour with the doom-and-gloom brigade. A typical example is Paul Ehrlich, who in 1968 published *The Population Bomb* in which he claimed that commodities and sources of energy would become scarce, and prices would rise inexorably. Luckily someone had the foresight to challenge these presumptions, and in 1980 the economist Julian Simon waged a bet with 'the modern-day Malthus'. Ehrlich was asked to choose $1,000 worth of any world commodities and wait for ten years. If the price went up – an indicator that the commodities were becoming more scarce – Simon would pay Ehrlich the difference. If the price went down, Ehrlich would have to pay him the sum of the decrease. By 1990 the value of the stocks of five metals had sunk to $424, and 'doom-slayer' Simon won $576. The supply of some of the metals had diminished as Ehrlich had predicted, but prices fell rather than rose because of the discovery of vast new oil fields and the arrival of new synthetic materials such as plastics. Furthermore, recent United Nations figures show that population growth is tailing off, and that the planet will most likely reach a population peak of 8.95 billion by 2060, rising from 6.5 billion in 2005. Other intriguing future bets, so-called accountable predictions aimed at improving long-term thinking, including a prediction that by 2060 the total human population will be less than it is today, can be found on www.longbets.org.

One of the lesser-known legacies of Malthus' theories was his influence on Charles Darwin. Darwin initially read Malthus 'for amusement', but quickly realized that it described the conditions in which the survival of the fittest could take place. Darwin even gives him due credit in his autobiography. 'In October 1838, that is, fifteen months after I had begun my systematic inquiry, I happened to read for amusement Malthus on *Population*, and being well prepared to appreciate the struggle for existence which everywhere goes on from long-continued observation of the habits of animals and plants, it at once struck me that under these circumstances favourable variations would tend to be preserved, and unfavourable ones to be destroyed. The results of this would be the formation of a new species. Here, then I had at last got a theory by which to work.'

Darwin was an accidental futurist. His contribution to futurism was to define a principle to which any theories of evolutionary science will be eternally compared, and from which many are drawn. He is part of the permanent wallpaper that lines the halls of discussion about the future, and his basic idea of the 'survival of the fittest' is one of the most plagiarized, misinterpreted and misused ideas in the whole of the history of futurism. The 'theory of evolution by natural selection' echoes around many hollow utopias, 'legitimizes' visions of eugenics and selective breeding (see H. G. Wells), and regularly rears its head in the realm of science fiction. Unlike Malthus, Darwin was at least an optimist about the future; he rounded off *Origin of the Species* with 'a prophetic glance into futurity'. He reassured readers that past evidence showed there would be further development of life, and that mankind could 'look with some confidence to a secure future of equally inappreciable length.' He even had some interesting and positive points to make about forthcoming globalization. 'As man advances in civilisation, and small tribes are united into larger communities, the simplest reason would tell each individual that he ought to extend his social instincts and sympathies to all the members of the same nation, though personally unknown to him. This point being once reached, there is only an artificial barrier to prevent his sympathies extending to the men of all nations and races.'

Such sympathies were not, in Malthus' time, extended across the channel between England and France. Debate, however, was, as reflected in the remains of the laborious title of Malthus' defining essay . . . *With Remarks on the Speculations of Mr. Godwin, M. Condorcet and other writers.*

To call the Marquis de Condorcet's ideas mere 'speculations' is somewhat unfair, as he was, by anyone's standards, a key mover and shaker during the French Revolution. Born in 1743, Condorcet was a brilliant mathematician, a qualification that was still proving to be one of the most popular for progressive thinkers and potential futurists. Condorcet made his name as a philosopher in the Paris salons, and also as an economist and educational reformer. While his ground-breaking mathematical work on probability in collective decision-making was ignored for over 200 years, the French wisely took his essays on economic and educational reform as being of more practical and immediate use for the purpose of 'liberty, equality, fraternity'.

Despite – or maybe even as the result of – his minor aristocratic lineage, Condorcet was apparently a man of very little social sophistication. He was described by friends as a 'volcano covered with snow' for his coolness of manner and a tendency to become highly passionate when discussing ideas or falling in love. When he did erupt emotionally, it was with such apparent intensity that the ladies in question fled. One that stayed and married him was Sophie de Grouchy. Not only considered the most beautiful woman in Paris, she had more than a passing interest in reform and economics. Her previous lover was the Marquis de Lafayette, the French hero of the American Revolution, and she produced the first, and the best, translation of Adam Smith's *Theory of Moral Sentiments*. The Condorcets were a kind of model futurist couple running a famous salon for the liberal and intellectual elite of Paris at the Hotel des Monnaies ('Money Mansion'), a large townhouse that came with his job as Inspector of the Mint. It was here, in this intellectual think tank, that many of the ideas for the future of France were formed. Condorcet was a member of the National Convention, elected to provide a new constitution for the country after the overthrow of the monarchy, drawing up legislation on public education and constitutional reform. His proposals for a state education system were aimed at reducing the inequality between people and increasing the supply of scientists, and these plans provided the basis of what was ultimately formed. In presenting his ideas for the 'Reorganis-ation of Public Instruction' he said, 'I long considered these views as dreams that could only be realised in an indeterminate future, and in a world in which I no longer exist.' He saw that he was ahead of his time in these fields of public institutions and also in advocating free trade and the abolition of slavery. When it came to women he boldly declared, 'we must number the complete annihilation of the prejudices that have brought about an inequality of rights between the sexes,' and even proposed birth control. Some of his inspiration can be traced to his reading of Francis Bacon's utopia written 150 years previously. In *Fragment sur l'Atlantide* Condorcet proudly claimed that the world was within reach of *The New Atlantis* in terms of improved longevity and a centralized government programme of scientific research.

A staunch anti-monarchist (though notably against the execution of the king), Condorcet even wrote a satirical future vision of how France could replace the monarchy with a more economical 'mechanical king'. This royal automaton would be programmed to perform ceremonial functions, greet visiting dignitaries and naturally to automatically sanction all decrees passed by the legislature. As well as causing no trouble (unless of course programmed to), this robot would be much cheaper to run than a traditional monarchy. No extravagant royal balls, no ten-course banquets, and certainly no expensive, time-consuming mistresses.

In his more serious role as a political advisor, Condorcet's proposals for a new French constitution were in line with the views of the moderate Girondists, but behind all his ideas was the essential notion of 'progress and reason', crucial to any solid thinking about the future. But advocating progress, reason and moderation in turbulent times can be dangerous, and he was forced to flee for his life. It was during the Reign of Terror, when he hid on the outskirts of Paris, that Condorcet found time to work on his most famous essay, *Sketch for a Historical Picture of the Progress of the Human Mind*. His fundamental idea was 'that the perfectibility of man is absolutely indefinite' and limited only by the laws of nature, which could, however, be overcome with technological and political progress. Facing certain death, he still wrote optimistically and in exemplary futurist fashion.

> The friend of humanity cannot receive unmixed pleasure but by abandoning himself to the endearing hope of the future . . . If man can predict, almost with certainty, those appearances of which he understands the laws; if, even when the laws are unknown to him, experience of the past enables him to foresee, with considerable probability, future appearances, why should we suppose it a chimerical undertaking to delineate with some degree of truth, the picture of the future destiny of mankind from the results of history? . . . Our hopes as to the future condition of the human species may be reduced to three points: the destruction of inequality between different nations; the progress of equality in one and the same nations; and lastly, the real improvement of man.

By the late-eighteenth century all the basic foundations, principles and inspiration for futurism as we understand it today had essentially been established. Delphi had not only laid down some useful ground rules for the gathering and processing of the necessary information but had also shown how a unique selling point could work wonders for a consultancy's success and reputation. Moreover, utopias were by now established as a socially and politically provocative literary platform from which to discuss the future of society, and there was a range of pessimistic and optimistic options on the future to suit the taste and temper of even the fussiest futurist. Futurists came in all shapes, guises and even disguises, and for the most part played a significant, if sometimes subtle, role in helping push forward political, social and technological progress.

The first person in this pre-industrial era to really popularize futurism was Louis Sebastian Mercier. Like his contemporary and countryman Condorcet who died in suspicious circumstances following his arrest in 1794, Mercier was a determined revolutionary idealist. He saw himself as 'the true prophet of the Revolution' and voted bravely against the execution of Louis XVI. He was later imprisoned for his views, but was narrowly saved from the guillotine by the fall of Robespierre. Mercier did not, however, entirely agree with Condorcet's belief in progress. He was much more impressed by the romanticism and social idealism of Jean Jacques Rousseau. This is cruelly revealed by Mercier's nickname – 'Le Singe de Jean-Jacques' (Jean Jacques' ape) – and also by his translation of *Romeo and Juliet* in which he took a little artistic licence (it had a happy ending). To be honest, Mercier did not do much justice to *King Lear* either – reducing it to a bourgeois soap-opera of household quarrelling – but his real contribution to literature in general, and more specifically to futurism, was a novel called *L'An 2440* (*The Year 2440*). This marked the beginning of a great tradition of the *roman de l'avenir*, the *tale of futurity* as this new fiction was called. First published in 1770, when the author was 31 years old, it tells the story of a

man who goes to sleep and wakes up in Paris nearly 700 years
in the future. Subtitled 'A dream if ever there was one', his
book represented not just a new awareness of the far-off
future, but introduced – albeit in a very unscientific way –
the idea of time travel. The book was immediately banned.

Printed clandestinely and published anonymously, it sold
like hot cakes, and was to become one of the most widely read
books in the latter part of the eighteenth century. It boasted
over twenty French editions, was honoured with several
English, American, German and Dutch translations, was ad-
mired by Goethe and inspired many imitations. The Spanish
monarchy was less impressed, and in 1778 the King of Spain
issued an edict that banned the sale of the book on the grounds
that it was blasphemous and anarchic. 'This impious writer . . .
describes the supposed state in that time 2440 of the . . .
Monarch of France, Europe and America – affecting disillusionment and supposing changes to have taken place in all
ecclesiastical, civil and political government.'

What was so threatening about Mercier's 'predictions' that
prevented him from claiming authorship for twenty years? Not
much by today's standards. But in pre-Revolutionary France,
the futuristic dream of a peaceful, happy, orderly, clean,
salubrious city in which the citizens, and even a king, could
walk safely around, was clearly too much. In Paris of 2440, no
one is ostentatious or vain. People wear ordinary, loose-fitting,
comfortable clothes, and simple hairstyles have replaced
elaborate powdered wigs. There are no traffic jams, much
of the city is pedestrian-only (the long-term dream of the
mayor of Paris in 2004–5 too) and the Louvre is completed.
Finding inspiration on his famously long walks round the city
of his birth, Mercier had a vision of 'the flat roofs filled with
flower-pots. And of all the houses of the same height, which
formed a spacious garden. The whole city appeared, from an

eminence above, to be crowned with flowers, with fruit and
with verdure.'

Although Mercier did not have the imagination or the
knowledge to describe the details of technological and scientific inventions in the way that Leonardo did, like Thomas
More, he tried instead to envisage the results of them. Mercier's time traveller discovers an optical cabinet where all kinds
of landscapes, palaces, rainbows, meteors and food are displayed. By pressing buttons he is transported into a virtual
world – to a forest with the roar of lions, tigers and bears.
Interestingly, Mercier's theme parks do not foresee a Disney-
like commercial purpose. These sound-and-light shows have a
profound moral and political purpose – if someone shows
signs of wanting to wage war he is taken to a room called 'hell',
where he has to listen to the horrors of battle, the screams of
rage and pain and the howls of the dying. If he is not moved to
change his mind, he is condemned to listen to it for the rest of
his life. What Mercier was in effect envisaging were the
potential psychological and therapeutic uses of virtual reality.
The power of such 'worlds' is apparent today not just to
parents of children who are addicted to brutal computer
games, but also to the Pentagon. In 2005, the Pentagon was
reported to have spent $4 million creating virtual-reality
games that simulate combat situations to help treat trauma-
tized soldiers. In a strange echo of Mercier's thoughts, a
psychologist working on the project explained, 'We want
the virtual reality environment to be enough to trigger the
thoughts and feelings so they can control those.'

When it came to physical as opposed to mental health,
Mercier predicted great leaps in medical progress, with cures
for pneumonia and tuberculosis and an abundance of doctors
with time to examine every patient. One idea that would cause
a few ripples in the medical establishment even today was his

prediction that when somebody dies, 'to the name of the dead person is affixed the name of his physician, who is obliged to give an account of all his prescriptions and justify the course he has followed with him from the beginning'. But this being 2440 and a perfect society, 'every person knows how to watch over his own health and preserve it . . . We have taken the trouble to study our own constitutions.'

When it came to women in the future, Mercier's views, while certainly not scandalous for the time, differed sharply from Condorcet (who, remember, had an intellectual equal as a wife). In the dream, the narrator finds that, 'Restored to the duties of the state . . . women attended to their children, comforted their husbands in various calamities incident to human life, and were never seen out of their proper sphere.' Furthermore, he proposes that women should not try to be funny, because it irritates men. Over two centuries later, *plus ça change*, and the French President Jacques Chirac admitted that his ideal woman is one who 'served the men at table, never sat down with them, and never spoke'.

Moving swiftly away from any presumptions about the nature of Mercier's (or indeed Chirac's) personal life, one of the predictions that lay close to his heart was a free press and no censorship. Strangely enough, he proposes that in the twenty-fifth century an author who is deemed by the public to have written an immoral book must wear a mask of shame till he has written something more rational (another rewrite of Shakespeare perhaps?). A more welcoming prospect for the future is that children are no longer expected to 'waste away ten of the most precious years of their lives' learning Greek and Latin. This is the heart of Europe, where presumably alongside French 'the four most useful languages taught are English, Italian, German and Spanish'.

Mercier's book being a novel, he had to concern himself

with day-to-day details of living in the future. But the crux of his motivation was that he was deeply concerned with the political future of France and optimistically predicted 'a rational government, calculated for men'. He solves the tricky subject of taxes with a large donation box for voluntary contributions in the public squares. Taxpayers throw in 'little sealed-up packages' with 'cheerful countenance', and payments are left to honesty since 'every citizen knows that when he gives part of his revenue to the state, he is serving himself'. But behind the façade of egalitarianism and unbounded happiness, we discover that there is a highly sophisticated surveillance system, checking who has paid. In order to function, this society is strictly organized, and Mercier's vision of the future has not only been celebrated as a liberal utopia, but also condemned as a prescient preview of totalitarianism and Nazism.

When the world discovered the joys of ballooning, and Paris became the Cape Canaveral of France, Mercier rewrote *L'An 2440* to include a new chapter on *L'Aerostat*, in which huge flying machines 'move from one climate to another in 24 hours'. The first balloon ascents took place in 1783, and a whole wave of romantic plays, comedies and even a German space operetta were performed across Europe. In Germany the term *Aeropetomanie* (air mania) was even coined to describe the new euphoria. The conquest of the air, like the discovery of the New World 300 years earlier, represented a very real promise of things to come. It was comparable to when Neil Armstrong stepped on to the moon over 200 years later and famously declared, 'That's one small step for [a] man, one giant leap for mankind.' All three events represented a shift not just in the perception of the physicality of the planet, but the whole way in which people perceived the future. As German writer Christopher Wieland said in the 1780s, 'The marvels of our century seem to press ever more closely on one another, and the nearer we come to the end of the century, they seem to become ever greater and ever more wonderful' (from *The Pattern of Expectation*).

CHAPTER 2

FANCY'S SEVEN-LEAGUED BOOTS

The very essence of man is being aware that tomorrow will exist.

Albert Jacquard, French philosopher and scientist

As the nineteenth century loomed, there was a growing sense of optimism about the future, and possibly for the first time in history a real hope there might actually be a worthwhile long-term future, and not just an imaginary one. In particular there was a shift in the expectation of what science and technology could bring and a growing realization that some of it could actually be predicted.

For Jules Verne, science, technology and exploration was where the future was happening. It was, in fact, his great dream to be an inventor, but he eventually resigned himself to writing fiction because no one took his ideas and predictions seriously. The fact that he eventually became a great and inspirational futurist is partly because in his formative years his parents did not take him seriously either. Verne was born in 1828 in the port of Nantes, and talked from an early age about visiting exotic countries far beyond the Brittany coast. At the age of eleven he took his chance. Hanging around at the port he managed to wangle himself a position as cabin boy on the merchant ship *Coralie* which was bound for the West Indies. When Mr and Mrs Verne realized what had happened, a red-faced Verne junior – whose exciting adventure had consisted almost entirely of mopping floors and carrying dirty dishes – was collared at the next port. After he got a thorough spanking, his wanderlust was confined for much of the rest of his life to his imagination.

Verne left Nantes when he was twenty, and rather than pursuing his law studies as instructed and financed by his father, he hung out at Parisian salons meeting writers such as Victor Hugo and Alexandre Dumas. After a mildly successful career as a playwright Verne returned to his passion for science and travel, and wrote a worthy but dull book on the mechanics and history of ballooning. It was rejected by several publishers until one spotted some vague potential (and possibly a way to stop Verne pestering him), and suggested he go away and try to turn it into an adventure story. The resulting work, *Five Weeks in a Balloon,* published in 1863, was an immediate bestseller and launched his career as a successful writer of 'science fiction' as opposed to 'science fact'. That very same year he proudly presented his by now very keen and attentive publisher with his one and only work that was actually set in the future. Not only was *Paris in the Twentieth Century* one of his most futuristic works, but also his most pessimistic and unpopular. It was unceremoniously and brutally rejected with the dreaded words scribbled on the manuscript, 'no one today will believe your prophecy'.

Legend has it that the manuscript was rediscovered over a century later by his grandson in an abandoned safe. It was finally published for the first time in France in 1994. Although it predicted a world where science took precedence over art and culture, it had some of the best descriptions of daily life in the future of any of his works. In it he foresaw Paris in 1960 with an efficient metro, splendid large bookshop chains and – extraordinarily – even a 500-foot high electric lighthouse near where the Eiffel Tower was eventually erected, twenty-six years later. Verne also saw 'boulevards illuminated with a brightness equal to that of the sun . . . thousands of vehicles circulating soundlessly on the muffled asphalt . . . stores rich as palaces, from which light spreads as bright rays.'

The real potential of electricity and telecommunication was beginning to grip the common imagination, thanks to extravagant illustrations by one of Verne's contemporaries, Albert Robida. In his book *Le Vingtième Siècle, La Vie Électrique (The Twentieth Century, The Life Electric)* published in 1890, Robida foresaw all sorts of wonders for the use of electricity as it becomes a slave to man. 'It is the final conquest of electricity,' he wrote, 'which has enabled man to change what seemed unchangeable . . . to take on the deputy role of creation, to change that which seemed for ever and eternally beyond the power of man.' His detailed drawings of life in the twentieth century were often humorous and even featured a prototype test-tube baby which a manic scientist appears to be trying to cook rather than create. Another of his spectacular foresights was the use of the videophone, and he drew delightful domestic situations such as a man in army uniform commanding his bored-looking wife via a life-size screen. Other more pleasant uses he envisaged for the so-called téléphonoscope were long-distance learning, shopping and gossiping. Strangely enough, what Robida and many of his contemporaries could not, or would not, foresee was any change of manner, dress or décor. Even as part of his imagined 'Generation Artificielle', the ladies of the 1950s are still in their restrictive whale-boned ankle-length dresses and wear impossibly impractical hats as they stand at the counter of the pharmacist trying to decide between an elixir that would guarantee twins or a girl or a boy. Robida's success was due largely to the fact that the differences between the realities of the late-nineteenth century and what might happen in the twentieth were still big enough to provide amusement rather than provoke despair and fear.

While Robida had a playful and generally optimistic vision of the future, Verne's vision of Paris in the twentieth century ruminated less on how the coming technological wonders would illuminate the streets and more on their darkening effect on the human spirit. The narrator of his book, a failed and suicidal poet, rumbles on gloomily about an 'American spirit' of haste that is driving the inhabitants on without 'respite or mercy'. Whether he really predicted the continuation of a European anti-American sentiment regarding progress and commercialism is debatable, as is his apparent coup in describing the *télématique photographique*, or fax as we call it. In *Paris in the Twentieth Century* he described how 'the facsimile of any form of writing or illustration . . . and letters of credit or contracts could now be signed at a distance of five thousand leagues.' For all his acclaimed predictive talents, the first demonstration of a facsimile transmission had actually already taken place over ten years earlier at the first Great Exhibition in London. While he was clearly describing rather than predicting a technology that was in its infancy, what he *did* predict was the extent of the usage and the popularity of the fax machine, something that was still being underestimated 100 years later. Following the rejection of *Paris in the Twen-*

tieth Century, Verne from then on avoided fiction set in the future, but satisfied his need to champion technological progress by setting it in his own time. This way he did not frighten off the readers, time stayed still, and that which was carried forward was aspirations and enthusiasm.

Verne's methodology was not, as we shall see, so very different to that of a modern-day trend researcher. He was a hunter and gatherer of interesting ideas, and as part of his researches a frequent visitor to such events as the Paris Universal Exhibition of 1867. Emperor Napoleon III's World Fair brought the wonders of the machine age to his door. Then as now, these exhibitions were a matter of national pride, whose objective was not merely to promote rivalry amongst businesses, but 'to forward the progress of industrial civilisation'. France was of course determined to outdo the resounding success of London's Great Exhibition, and Napoleon III saw his mission as employing the best talents of France to show the world that his country was leading the way for the future of the human race. To prove his commitment to improving the physical and moral conditions of the people, the Emperor entered – and naturally won – a design competition for a future workers' housing project. Second prize for sheer audacity must, however, go to the automatic bunny-to-hat device that was on display. 'They put a live rabbit at one end of the machine, and it emerged at the other end as a trimmed, embellished, and garnished hat,' observed one startled visitor.

Some of the prime exhibits were the central Gallery of the Machines designed by Gustave Eiffel, and America's pride and joy, the telegraphy exhibit under the supervision of Samuel F. B. Morse. Verne would also have seen the heavy machinery pavilion that boasted a 50-ton steel cannon capable of firing 1,000-pound shells. Another visitor, the writer Victor Hugo, lamented, 'These enormous shells, hurled from the gigantic Krupp cannons, will be no more effective in stopping progress than soap bubbles blown from the mouth of a little child.' Ironically, it was these very cannons that just three years later during the Franco-German war pounded Paris into defeat. Not one to let a good adventure story or a good invention pass, Verne wrote *The Begum's Fortune*, which told the eternally popular tale of a fight between a good Frenchman and a bad German. The evil figure of Professor Schultze was an attack on Alfred Krupp, the cannon-king and founder of the dynasty that armed the victorious Prussians. Published in 1879, ten years before Hitler was born, it could not have, as some have tried to suggest, predicted the rise and fall of the Führer. What it did foresee was the power and influence of the industrial steel dynasty which, in 1943, became the centre of German rearmament.

As well as having a youthful enthusiasm and curiosity, Verne was a reader and recorder of everything interesting that came his way. Even towards the end of his life he would go every afternoon to the reading room of the Société Industrielle in Amiens and scan the magazines as long as his failing eyesight would allow him. This was how he picked up a 'great number of scientific odds and ends'. All his life he displayed a remarkable curiosity and instinct for picking up and recycling information that would capture the popular imagination. Sitting in a cafe one day, Verne read a report in *Le Siècle* that claimed a man could travel round the world in eighty days. After storing and playing around with the idea in his head for a while he worked it into the theme of one of his most popular and bestselling novels. Similarly, he did not invent or predict the submarine *per se*, but convincingly described and promoted the real potential for underwater transportation and travel. Indeed, the name *Nautilus*, which he gave to the submarine in *Twenty Thousand Leagues Under The Sea*, was actually borrowed from one of the earliest submersibles built in 1800 by British inventor Robert Fulton in France with a grant from Napoleon I. Verne has been attributed as saying 'the future of the submarine ... is to be wholly a war future ... submarine fleets are in the near future and they will, I believe ... cause war to cease between the nations' (*Popular Mechanics Magazine*, 1904). He also suggested that one day 'electricity for their propulsion may ... be gathered from the sea itself.' To his credit, Verne told one interviewer 'I do not in any way pose as a scientist, but I esteem myself fortunate as having been born in an age of remarkable discoveries, and perhaps still more wonderful inventions.' He also admitted to using the privilege of fiction to 'spring over every scientific difficulty with fancy's seven-leagued boots, and create on paper what other men were planning out in steel and other metals.' As well as the potential for undersea travel, Verne could not ignore the fact of the growing importance and influence of steam power on people's lives in the nineteenth century. A lesser-known work, *The Steam House*, published in 1880, produced one of his more eccentric inventions. Set in India, it featured a huge clunking mechanical steam-powered elephant that was strong enough to pull a train. It didn't actually appear to be much of an improvement on the animal itself, and wasn't ever seriously proposed as a replacement.

When it comes to Verne's place in the futurists' hall of fame, there is always something of a debate surrounding him. More than anything Verne popularized the *idea* of the future – which is paradoxical, given that his stories did not actually take place there. The 'grandfather of science fiction' is not considered, for example, by Edward Cornish, current editor of *The Futurist* magazine and founder of the World Future Society, to be a real futurist. This he claims is because 'science fiction, though often drawing on science, consists of fantasies that make no claim to being forecasts.' More brutally he simply says, 'fiction is not prediction.' But fiction is inspiration, and Verne's reputation as a forecaster is based on the fact that many of his readers were inspired to realize the inventions he dreamed about. Even Mr Cornish can be worn down, and at some point concedes, 'it can be argued that Verne did more than any other single individual to make the moon landing of 1969 a reality.'

Konstantin Tsiolkovsky, the pioneering Russian rocket scientist and 'father of aeronautics', was just seven years old when Verne published *From the Earth to the Moon* in 1865. At the age of nine Tsiolkovsky lost his hearing and, following the death of his mother four years later, withdrew into a fantasy world of books. At the time Verne was the most popular foreign writer, having judiciously authorized the translation and retelling of his books for a Russian audience. As a teenager Tsiolkovsky began to speculate on space travel, and later confessed the 'great fantastic author Jules Verne . . . directed my thought along certain channels'. Similarly, American zoologist William Beebe, one of the first men to explore the ocean in a bathysphere in 1930, was inspired by Verne. *Twenty Thousand Leagues Under the Sea*, confessed Beebe, was his guide for what was then a very risky operation. This ability of Verne's fiction to generate optimistic expectation was summed up by the science-fiction author Ray Bradbury, who wrote with great admiration that, 'without Verne there is a strong possibility that we would never have romanced ourselves to the moon'.

Verne's *From The Earth To The Moon* describes a post-Civil War society in which members of an American Gun Club are left frustrated with nothing to fire their weapons at. To relieve their feelings of boredom and impotence, the club's president proposes a plan to use a giant gun to fire a manned projectile to the moon. The suave, young – and naturally French – hero reassures the crowds, 'As for the mode of locomotion adopted, it simply follows the great law of progress.' It is these very laws of progress that enabled NASA to land men on the moon on what has been described as a meagrely tested tower of high explosives and equipped with a navigational computer boasting less memory than a modern mobile phone. To give Verne a little credit, he *did* foresee the use of aluminium in cabin construction despite it being prohibitively expensive at the time, and proposed a launch site in Florida remarkably near Cape Canaveral.

Verne's talent for foresight was based on a fortuitous and enthusiastic extrapolation of the progress that was incubating around him. But in the case of lunar travel, it also followed a long tradition of male fantasy, from Lucian of Samosata's *True History* in the second century to the real-life Cyrano de Bergerac's *Voyages to the Moon and Stars* in the seventeenth. Verne's lunar adventure was, nevertheless, an instant success, and he was quite forgiven for overlooking a few small scientific details such as the problems of weightlessness, and more devastatingly the fact that the travellers – and not just the sweet dog Satellite – would be crushed to death on take-off. Arthur C. Clarke, who also shares the 'grandfather of science fiction' mantle, suspects that Verne himself did not take the idea of the monster-sized cannon seriously. 'It seems unlikely that he seriously imagined that any of the occupants would have survived the shock of take-off,' said Clarke. Astronaut Frank Borman was a little more generous. After his historic lunar orbit in 1968 he wrote a letter to Verne's grandson, joyfully pointing out that his capsule 'splashed down in the Pacific a mere two-and-a-half miles' from the position mentioned in Verne's *All Around the Moon*. Ironically, Verne died in 1905, the year that Einstein published his special theory of relativity, which revolutionized our notion of space and time. In a small but significant tribute to Verne's legacy, a crater has been named after him on the official map of the moon.

What more, you ask, could a frustrated futurist like Verne have wished? Well, probably that someone took him seriously during his lifetime. Indeed, as he got older and was unable to write prolifically owing to ill-health, Verne got grumpier and grumpier. In a severe case of sour grapes, or possibly extreme megalomania, he predicted the end of the fantasy novel as he knew, and more or less invented, it. In a comment for the *Pittsburgh Gazette* in 1902 he claimed that in the future writers would work with actual facts, newspapers would replace books, and in fifty or a hundred years the novel would be dead. Verne was at this point working on his hundredth book.

One of the exhibits that Verne would have seen at the Paris Exhibition was the Russian Pavilion, organized by the Russian scientist Dmitri Mendeleyev. Like Verne, Mendeleyev used the exhibition to gather information and inspiration for his own work. Both were fascinated by the mechanics and science of aeronautics, and during the summer and autumn of that year they could admire the sight of the hydrogen-filled balloons that floated passengers over Paris. Unlike Verne, Mendeleyev himself made several balloon ascents during his lifetime, and encouraged his colleagues to pursue the possibilities of heavier-than-air flight. His own professional pursuits and predictive talents were, however, much more down to earth.

Mendeleyev was not a typical futurist. He was an eccentric, bad-tempered chemist whose idea of a haircut was to call in the local farmer with his sheep shears once a year. Yet he predicted things that most futurists would never even dream of trying to do. In fact, Mendeleyev did literally that. On a snowy February night in 1869, after several sleepless nights of struggling to find a system to classify the chemical elements, he slumped with exhaustion on to his desk and dreamt of how they all fitted together. 'I saw in a dream,' he later recalled, 'a table where all the elements fell into place as required. Awakening, I immediately wrote it down on a piece of paper.' This table, the Periodic Table of the Elements as he called it, is the cornerstone of chemistry. Not only was this system a great advance on previous attempts at classification according to atomic weight or chemical properties, most significantly it enabled Mendeleyev to predict the existence of several undiscovered elements. Better still, he could predict their exact properties. At the time of his dream only 63 elements had been discovered. The table, which was hastily published two weeks later, shows a series of question marks that to the unimaginative eye were simply gaps. To the critics they were a bold guess, but to Mendeleyev they represented the future – the elements that he knew existed (modesty was not one of his talents) and were just waiting to be discovered. Three were in fact discovered within twenty years, and they did indeed possess the properties he had predicted.

Mendeleyev did for chemistry what Darwin had done for evolution and what Newton had done for physics, and together their theories changed forever the way we see and foresee the world. But while they were busily pushing forward the boundaries of scientific understanding, one man had been doing nothing less than foreseeing a new political landscape for the world. Karl Marx is the most influential political futurist there has ever been. His qualifications were more than suitable; as well as being a difficult character, he had studied law, and believed firmly that 'philosophers have only interpreted the world in various ways. The point is to change it.'

(Ironically he was voted Britain's most revered philosopher in 2005.) Writing on progress in the *Communist Manifesto* he asked, 'Subjection of nature's forces to man, machinery, application of chemistry to industry and agriculture, steam navigation, railways, electric telegraphs, clearing of whole continents for cultivation, canalisation of rivers, whole populations conjured out of the ground – what earlier century had even a presentiment that such productive forces slumbered in the lap of social labour?'

Contrary to Marx's belief, some of these things had actually been foreseen a century earlier, and even some of his own revolutionary socialist ideals do not look quite so fresh next to Plato's *Republic* or Thomas More's *Utopia*. Naturally Marx did not approve of such fancies as utopias. He referred to them disdainfully as 'castles in the air' and complained that in order to realize them one is 'compelled to appeal to the feelings and purses of the bourgeois'. What really concerned Marx was the feelings and future of the world's working classes, and to this purpose he drew up plans for the ultimate socialist utopia of all time. The blueprint for this utopia was, of course, the *Communist Manifesto*, published in 1848 when he was just thirty years old. In it he famously predicted that communism was a necessary and inevitable product of the historical development (and demise) of capitalism.

His contribution to political thinking was, in the words of Frederick Engels, 'As Darwin discovered the law of evolution in organic nature, so Marx discovered the law of evolution in human history.' Marx had been commissioned to write the manifesto with Engels, who was to become not only a key intellectual collaborator but a close friend of the family as well as most importantly the one to keep the Marx family's purse full from his own pocket. From the outset, the whole commission was vague to say the least, and it is a wonder that it ever

got written, let alone that it went on to become a world
bestseller. Marx had just been expelled from France for his
radical ideas, and had moved to Brussels with Engels following
close on his heels. Together they joined the newly formed
Communist League and with their journalistic reputation were
promptly given the monumental task of writing a manifesto
for a party that did not actually exist (at the time there was no
unified Communist Party as such, and the League was simply
one of several disparate groups who referred to themselves as
Communists).

It was every futurist's dream – a blank page on which to
write a manifesto for the future of society. They rose dramatically to the occasion, writing some forty pages of dark and
passionate text peppered with juicy sound bites and superb
slogans. The opening line was legendary rabble-rousing stuff:
'A spectre is haunting Europe – the spectre of communism.' In
the manifesto they argued that humanity has been dehuma-
nized by an industrial urban lifestyle. The sins of the bour-
geoisie were not just the exploitation of the working class, but
that they have 'reduced the family-relation to a mere money-
relation', and 'turned the doctor, the lawyer, the priest, the
poet and the scientist into its paid wage slaves'. More famously, he wrote that the emancipation of the proletariat
would be achieved by 'the elimination of private property
and its replacement by community of property'. The dire
consequences of such consequent communist policy is (almost)
history, but to their credit it has to be said that Marx and
Engels also offered a list of reforms for capitalism (for before it
was to be abolished in favour of communism) that were
actually quite sensible and forward-thinking. Among these
was the abolition of child labour, free education for all
children and progressive income tax. One of his less popular
recommendations that has since been pushed discreetly under

the carpet of political correctness is the 'confiscation of the property of all emigrants and rebels' (a somewhat strange suggestion coming from an emigrant rebel). Controversial to the last, the manifesto ends as dramatically as it begins: 'Let the ruling classes tremble at a communist revolution. The proletariat have nothing to lose but their chains. They have a world to win. Workers of the world, unite.' While it did not have an immediate effect, it showed exceptionally good foresight and timing: 1848 was the year of the revolutions in Europe that spread from Sicily to Paris and Germany, and Marx had captured the zeitgeist perfectly.

Marx was a victim of his own success. The failure of the revolutions across Europe had him on the run again and the following year he took refuge in London, where he lived in various lodgings as an emigrant rebel until his death in 1883. Life in London was not easy for the Marx family. The man whose name is synonymous with the vision of an organized and effective communist society had great difficulty keeping his life in order and handling the household finances. Marx was appallingly bad at budgeting, and the family was held back from the brink of bankruptcy by the occasional newspaper fee and regular handouts from his loyal, rich friend, Engels. The jolly nature of their friendship, and Marx's dependency on Engels' Robin Hood-like generosity, can be seen in their correspondence which was regularly interspersed with the scribblings of his children and various unsavoury details of his hypochondria. 'Dear Frederick,' he wrote to Engels in December 1858, 'thou hast triumphantly snatched me out of the clutches of the Exchequer, praised be thy name – halleluiah!' Indeed, much of their correspondence begins with either a thank you for a gratefully received £5 or a long-winded plea for more. As well as providing unconditional financial and intellectual support for a struggling futurist,

Engels even went so far as to cover for Marx's indiscretions by claiming responsibility for the family maid's pregnancy so as not to upset his long-suffering wife. The family were so broke at times that Marx was forced to admit to Engels that, 'the situation as regards the children's summer dresses is subproletarian', and confessed that he had pawned his only pair of trousers in order to buy a cigar. Such were the priorities of a bourgeois intellectual married to an aristocrat, and who probably earned less in his lifetime than one of his beloved proletarian workers.

Appropriately it was here in London that he wrote his other greatly remembered and plagiarized work, *Das Kapital* (Capital). Even his mother saw the irony and commented, 'What a shame little Karl doesn't make some capital, instead of just writing about it.' And write about it he did. The first volume, published in 1867, consisted of over 1,000 pages that revealed the full extent of the appalling conditions in which the workers of the most industrially advanced nation in the world lived. While England was leading the way to the future in terms of industry, Marx was intent on pointing out that this very success would be its ruin. The solution for the future of mankind he offered was put most concisely in *Critique of the Gotha Program* with the memorable motto: 'from each according to his ability, to each according to his needs.'

This was to become the mantra of many egalitarian utopias and communist regimes over the years. It is perhaps not surprising that the intellectual snob in Marx did not approve of utopias – they are after all literally 'no place'. But what is surprising is that he so poetically described one in which following the revolution and the falling away of the state he foresaw a life of blissful individuality. 'No one is limited to any single sphere of activity. Each individual can become accomplished in any activity he chooses. Society itself regulates the general production, and in this way it makes it possible for me to take up one thing today and another tomorrow. I can hunt in the morning, fish in the afternoon, rear cattle in the evening, and offer my own critical opinions after dinner. I can do all this, depending upon how I feel, without ever having to become a hunter, fisherman, herdsman, or critic.'

If this sounds like champagne socialism, his cavalier attitude to prediction about other people's political matters was also quite surprising. When asked by the editor of the *New York Daily Tribune* to predict the outcome of the Indian Mutiny, he confessed to a little Delphi-style ambiguity. 'It's possible that I shall make an ass out of myself,' he told Engels, 'but in that case one can always get out of it with a little dialectic. I have of course worded my proposition as to be right either way.' Like many great and difficult futurists he was frustrated that not enough people took him seriously during his lifetime. Writing to Engels he often complained about dealing with editors at the newspapers: 'It's often three months before the asses discover that we've foretold events for them, whereupon they print the relevant articles.'

Marxism was one of the most ambitious and yet catastrophic attempts at shaping the future of all time. By the middle of the twentieth century approximately a third of the world was run by leaders who followed Marx's vision and, worse still, many of them believed it to be merely a short interlude to world domination. One classic declaration came from the Soviet leader Nikita Khrushchev during his reign of 1953 to 1964. 'Speaking of the future it seems to me that the further development of the socialist countries will in all probability proceed along the lines of the consolidation of a single world socialist economic system. The common economic foundation of world socialism will grow stronger, eventually rendering pointless the question of borders' (from *The City of Man*, W. Wagar).

It was not just such large-scale megalomania that was doomed to fail, but also smaller, more modest, attempts at creating a real-life utopia such as Icaria, dreamt up by a French politician, Étienne Cabet. In 1840, just a few years short of the publication of Marx's *Communist Manifesto*, Cabet publicized his ideas for the future in *Le Voyage en Icarie* (*Travels in Icaria*). These were dangerous times in France, and Cabet – a radical Republican – not only initially used a pseudonym, but unlike the more radical and principled Marx, disguised his ideas in the form of a romantic novel so as not to violate the strict laws against subversive writings. Inspired chiefly by Mercier's *L'An 2440* and More's *Utopia*, *Travels in Icaria* is the fictional story of a young English nobleman who travels to an island in the Indian Ocean where he hopes to find 'a people that resembles the human race as I would like to see it'. Much to his delight, Lord William Carisdall discovers a true haven from the evils of nineteenth-century capitalism, where there is complete egalitarianism, no money and private property, and even equality for the sexes. The visiting lord is shocked to learn that the leader, Icar, has banned domestic servants, and declares 'I could not stop admiring the republic's deep concern for making housework free from any sort of fatigue or repulsion.' In fact, the task is simply left to women and children, and one mother declares dutifully, 'Sweeping up is hardly any trouble.' Carisdall is naturally charmed by this, but rather less by the idea that people from the noblest of families are working as lowly locksmiths, dressmakers and house painters instead of taking up their rightful titles. The means of production have been rationalized and mechanized to the point that not only are they humane, efficient and clean, but they enable the workers to knock off at 1pm to pursue worthy leisure activities and enjoy good clean fun provided by the state (there are no such diversions as brothels, gambling dens, graffiti or crime).

Within the framework of turbulent political times in France with increasing labour and political unrest, this was not simply intended as a romantic adventure story, but as the real promise of a possible future earthly paradise. Despite the fact that it was dripping with finger-wagging morality (strict chastity for the young and absolute fidelity in marriage) and its literary merit was highly questionable, it became a bestseller. It was the book (and the future) that everyone was talking about, and in 1848 an awed English reviewer noted: 'It has already gone through five editions – there is not a shop or stall in Paris where copies are not in readiness for a constant influx of purchasers – hardly a drawing room table on which it is not to be seen.' By then it had become much more than just a cult book – it had become the veritable bible of one of the country's biggest non-religious utopian movements ever.

The extraordinary thing about this tale of the perfect future society was not only that it became a reality but that, unlike Marx, the writer actually for a while lived in it. As interest grew, the *Populaire* newspaper, of which Cabet was editor, proclaimed in May 1847, 'Allons en Icarie' (let's go to Icaria) and wooed readers with the promise of realizing a terrestrial paradise for 600 francs per person. At the time the average unskilled worker earned little over 10 francs per week, but enough interest was generated, and the paper soon announced 'C'est au Texas!' (it's Texas!). The American location for the very first Icarian colony was chosen judiciously for its climate and its physical and psychological distance from France, but mainly for the fact that Cabet learnt he could get the land for free if he could rustle together 1,000 colonists. An eager advance party left without Cabet for America in March 1848 and following a series of blunders eventually managed to put up a few rough cabins and plant some basic crops on the promised land. By July they officially and optimistically proclaimed 'Icaria is founded'. But a paradise it wasn't. August was mosquito season, their doctor went completely mad and disappeared, several more died of cholera, and their leader was still in Paris.

By the time Cabet finally arrived six months later, the colony had, in effect, collapsed. It had divided into two rival factions – the 'dissidents', who wanted their money back, and the 'loyalists', who despite enduring hardship and misery, were devoted to 'Papa' Cabet. After a tense and hastily convened meeting, 218 bitterly disillusioned Icarians voted to return to France with their refund and pledged to sue Cabet, who they branded a charlatan and cheat. The thin majority of 280 devotees who had decided to stay on moved to an abandoned Mormon town near St Louis in search of a new start. By 1855 the population had risen to a rather meagre 469 members and for the first time the community, with its schoolhouse, shops, mill, library, workshops and laundry, was beginning to resemble the 'real' Icaria. Not only was it beginning at last to look like the book, but it was *run* to the book. A blast from a bugle roused the inhabitants to work at 6am, and communal breakfast was served on the dot of 8am. There were even the promised public concerts and theatre performances, the success of which they could read about in their very own French language newspaper, *Revue Icarienne*. The paper also boasted about the education system that resembled Plato's Republic for its stringent discipline and segregation of children from their parents. The price of translating this picture of perfect equality from the page to the people was nothing less than the tyranny of uniformity over individuality, and a strictly centralized communist system run by a dictator.

Just when things seemed to be running to his liking, Cabet, who was in charge of teaching morality, was called back to France to answer the charges of deceit and theft that the returnees had brought against him. Cabet was eventually pronounced not guilty, but it was to be over a year before he got his affairs in order and returned to his faithful flock in America. A year is a long time in utopia, and much to his horror Cabet discovered upon his return that, as historian Sylvester Piotrowski put it, 'the Icarians conducted themselves as school-boys on a holiday.' And what a holiday it was. The women slapped on contraband make-up, men hunted and fished for fun rather than for food, and the workshops were such a scene of merriment that production plummeted. This was all too much for Cabet, who decided to put an immediate stop to it with a set of tyrannical measures designed to curb once and for all any swaying from his socialist and moral ideals. Silence was intro-duced into the workshops, the simple pleasures of hunting and fishing were prohibited, and whisky and tobacco were forbid-den. A fog of gloom quickly settled on the majority of the community, and after a nasty power struggle, Cabet plus 179 loyal followers were thrown unceremoniously out of the colony. Cabet's attempt at resuscitating the colony proved too much for even his dictatorial determination, and in November 1856 he died of a stroke at the age of 68. Without a leader the remaining colonies slowly but surely unravelled, and in 1895 the last surviving eight members voted to disband their community and with it the dream of realizing a real utopian future.

Not everyone was discouraged by such spectacular failure. At the very time that the remaining Icarian communities were collapsing in America, writer Edward Bellamy was doing his best to promote his own vision of the perfect future. Unlike Cabet, or even Marx, Bellamy was almost single-handedly instrumental in spreading the idea of socialism across America. His defining book, *Looking Backward,* was the last of the great optimistic utopias of the nineteenth century. First published in 1888, it was, like many a utopia before it, an instant hit and became the third bestselling book in America after *Uncle Tom's Cabin* and *Ben-Hur.*

Looking Backward stars Julian West, a Bostonian who goes to sleep in 1887 and wakes up in a socialist paradise, 113 years, three months and eleven days later in the year 2000. The book was yet another futurist manifesto disguised as fiction, 'intended in all seriousness as a forecast, in accordance with the principles of evolution, of the next state in the industrial and social development of humanity.' Bellamy originally set the novel in the year 3000, but as well as admitting to a conceit that his predictions would be realized earlier than that, he was probably wary of direct comparisons with Mercier's *L'An 2440* from whom he had taken the idea of the dream. For prior to the 'invention' of the time machine by H.G. Wells in 1895, this sleeping-beauty method of time travel was still proving to be the most popular and convenient way of getting to the future.

Young West awakens in the home of a fine gentleman called Dr Leete, who conveniently has a beautiful and unattached daughter. Here in the year 2000 we find many of the superficial delights of modern-day society. For a start there is abundant electric lighting and everyone can enjoy 'music by telephone' or even listen to a sermon from the comfort of their armchair. 'There are some who still prefer to hear sermons in church,' explains Dr Leete, 'but most of our preaching, like our musical performances, is not in public, but delivered in acoustically prepared chambers, connected by wire with subscribers' houses.' Many of the technological advances, and even possibly the TV evangelists that Bellamy predicted, were foreseeable in his day. What would have been harder to predict were the subtle details of such things as the interior design and decoration, and the shopping centres of the future. Bellamy's description of the malls sound uncannily like those of today: 'A vast hall of light . . . the walls and ceiling were frescoed in mellow tints calculated to soften . . . Around the fountain was a space occupied with chairs and sofas, on which many persons were seated conversing.' He also noted that these 'distributing establishments' would, for the sake of convenience, all sell exactly the same goods. Julian West is understandably rather puzzled that the shop assistants, or 'clerks' as they are called, are not badgering people to buy things they don't want. He explains to a shocked Ms Leete that in the nineteenth century 'they were hired for the purpose of getting rid of the goods, and were expected to do their utmost, short of the use of force, to compass that end.'

What he miscalculated in the psychology of shop assistants of the future, Bellamy made up for in his vision of an efficient delivery service. Bringing to mind the speed and advertising slogans of courier services today, Ms Leete boasts to West that 'my order will probably be at home sooner than I could have carried it from here'. The young lady naturally does not pay in the future in cash, but with 'an American credit card' which is available to everyone and can conveniently be used abroad. Unlike the credit cards of the twenty-first century, Bellamy's are used to distribute 'surplus wealth (which) . . . all enjoy in equal degree,' and as a result, selfishness and 'excessive individualism' have been all but eradicated.

As well as the classic socialist dream of complete financial equality for all, Bellamy also fell foul of the futurists' monkey trap. His brief experience as a lawyer had left him bitter and disenchanted, and consequently he had these 'public bloodhounds' banished, along with politicians, by the year 2000.

The 'female question' is a trickier matter for many (male) futurists. While it was dealt with boldly and surprisingly well by Mercier a century previously, beyond shopping and flirting, Bellamy finds it harder to foresee how women would live, think and want today. Where he fails, as many before and after him, is to envisage the more subtle social and moral shifts in society. Bellamy for example, still envisions the ladies politely retiring after dinner, and leaving the men to discuss more important matters. Unmarried women – even in the twenty-first century – are, according to Bellamy, poor specimens to be pitied, though on a more positive side he foresaw that the independence of women means that 'there can be no marriages now except that of inclination'. Bellamy himself was happily married to his adopted sister, with whom he had two children. As a well-off writer and subsequently a speaker much in demand, he would have been able to afford domestic help, and his wife would, as he hoped for women of 2000, have been released from domestic drudgery. Indeed, women in the future would not need to cook as every household would be able to eat à la carte in a community dining hall.

As with any of these visions or hopes for the future there are always a few logical loopholes to fill. There is always, for example, the tricky question of dogsbody work. If everyone is going to be treated fairly and equally in the future, who is actually going to clean the loos and do the dishes? The answer for Bellamy lay with a strict social and educational structuring that echoed Plato's ideals. All men and women would be made to join Bellamy's compulsory industrial army at the age of twenty-one, when they finished their basic education. From then on they are allocated jobs according to their abilities until they are allowed to retire at forty-five. Only then are they considered sensible and incorruptible enough to get the vote. Women are generously let off early for childbearing, but otherwise are expected to do their duties as equals to men.

Another of Bellamy's predictive preoccupations was with efficiency. Among other things he deplored 'the waste from idle capital and labor', 'the waste by mistaken undertakings' and 'the waste from the competition and mutual hostility of those engaged in industry'. He found the solution in the up-and-coming theories of management science. These were the brainchild of Frederick W. Taylor, who, in the 1880s, developed ways to enhance industrial output using efficient movement of workers and their tools. Bellamy was quick to latch on to the potential of what became known as Taylorism. In *Looking Backward* he described how rationalization, or a 'prodigious increase of efficiency', could be employed in everything from shopping centres to centralized kitchens. What he did not, in his enthusiasm, foresee was the modern-day backlash against the mass production that Taylorism eventually spawned.

The root of many of Bellamy's obsessions for a future society can be traced back to his childhood. The son of a Baptist minister, he had an austere but educated Calvinist mother who denied herself and her family all pleasures. Selfishness was simply not an option as he grew up – hence individualism, which Bellamy described as 'the animating idea of society' in his day has, in his future, been replaced by 'common interest'. As well as endlessly trying to please women in his writings (his mother thought novels were a waste of time), he was also obsessed with physical health and the discipline brought by military training. This is largely due to the fact that he was a sickly man who was rejected by the military training college at West Point. However, Bellamy's vision of the future was not only a projection of his own physical and maternal hang-ups: it was the result of the grim general conditions of late-nineteenth century America, and in particular those of Chicopee Falls, Massachusetts, where he lived all his life. As Dr Leete explains to West how the bloodless revolution brought about Nationalism: 'You must, at least, have realized that the widespread industrial and social troubles, and the underlying dissatisfaction of all classes with the inequalities of society, and the general misery of mankind, were portents of great changes of some sort.'

If this sound suspiciously like thinly disguised Marxism, it is because it was. At the age of eighteen Bellamy had been reluctantly packed off on an educational trip to Germany, financed by a rich aunt. It was here, in the bourgeois comfort of a cousin's house, that the worldwide plight of the urban poor first really hit him. It was 1868, a few years before unification, and a turbulent time in Germany when the social democratic movement was growing fast. It was already twenty years after the publication of Marx's *Communist Manifesto*, but *Das Kapital* had just appeared and would have been a hot topic of discussion among German intellectual and student circles. When it came to 'selling' these ideas to his readers, Bellamy was careful to avoid heavy dialectic – or lumpen jargon as it has also been called – as it would have alienated the ordinary readers he aimed at converting to 'Nationalism'. He quite sensibly stuck to a tried-and-tested pseudo-romantic adventure style that was popular at the time, and claimed instant fame, fortune and, better still, effect. *Looking Backward* not only sold over 500,000 copies in the first few years, but started a political mass movement. By 1890, over 160 'Bellamy Clubs' had been established all over the United States, all for the purpose of discussing and propagating the book's ideas. Bellamy became an active propagandist for the nationalization of public services, his ideas inspired political groups as far afield as the Netherlands and impressed Tolstoy, and he was banned by the Tsarist authorities of Russia. Even as late as 1948 the British Labour Prime Minister Clement Attlee told Bellamy's son Paul that English socialism was 'a child of the Bellamy idea'. Bellamy's book is still remembered as one of the most remarkable books ever published in America.

A great fan of Bellamy's and an enthusiastic member of the Nationalist movement was the writer Charlotte Perkins Gilman. A compatriot and contemporary of Bellamy, Gilman referred to *Looking Backward* as 'that great modern instance', even if half of the inhabitants of that 'instance' were poorly represented by her tough feminist standards. Celebrated more in feminism than futurism, she was, however, one of the first significant female futurists even though the details of her life and death were so miserable that one would seriously think twice before reading her vision of any future. Charlotte's father abandoned the family shortly after her birth, and she grew up in poverty with a repressive mother who, like Bellamy's, deprived her, as a matter of principle, of maternal love. As an adult she suffered severe postnatal depression, and was ordered to take to her bed and avoid intellectual excitement. This led to a complete nervous breakdown, and when she eventually recovered she promptly divorced her husband, then scandalized society further by sending her daughter to live with him. Three years after she was diagnosed with inoperable breast cancer in 1932 she killed herself, preferring 'chloroform to cancer'.

But do not let that put you off. There is no Cassandra-like doom and gloom in her writings, and her two main futuristic works are – at least from a woman's point of view – funny and prophetic in unexpected ways. Admittedly Gilman had a very distinctive feminist-driven vision of the future, and confessed that she only 'wrote to preach'. Bellamy on the other hand, wrote to teach, and his quaint, somewhat stilted, literary style seems old-fashioned compared to Gilman's lively satirical humour. Strangely, her predictions are interesting not because they were wildly wrong, nor because they have come true, but because nearly a hundred years later, some fundamental questions and concerns have not changed. Answers are all very well, but asking the right questions at the right time is one of the founding principles that sets an interesting futurist apart from a mediocre one. One of Gilman's most prophetic and funniest scenes is from her 1911 book *Moving the Mountain,* when explorer John Robertson returns to America after being lost in Tibet for thirty years and asks his sister, 'Now tell me the worst – are the men all doing the housework?' She reassures him they are not. He thinks a bit, and then still wondering where the catch is, inquires nervously, 'they still wear trousers don't they?'

In the fictional America of 1940 he is, however, disappointed to find that there are no more dutiful and desperate housewives. Robertson, who is treated like an extinct species, finds it hard to adjust and notes wistfully how a house without a housewife seems 'altogether empty'. Gilman was looking ahead to a time when the mountain had been moved, when 'the women woke up', have become economically independent, and work like men, according to their abilities and talents. Interestingly, Gilman does not insist – as some feminists do – on equality in everything in the future. In *The Home: Its Work and Influence* she reassures readers that everyone will work according to their human talents. Men do not have to change nappies (unless they really, really want to), but should do the heavy, 'violent plain' work as that is what they actually are best at. So while the men are busy digging and hammering, women she predicts, will prefer the administrative and constructive jobs. To cover for that predictive blind spot as to who then actually does all the dirty work, it is the women in *Moving the Mountain* who have naturally found the solution. In a forerunner of the work-life balance and domestic services that are widely on offer today, the women set up the superbly named Home Service Company. This is a successful business that among other things manages the new food industries, centralized cooking and home-delivery services. As well as the housework and cooking being taken care of, the women are further liberated by the fact that there are childcare services available everywhere.

As mentioned above, Gilman herself had a complete nervous breakdown when she was first married and faced with a small screaming baby and a dreary domestic routine. So although these predictions were in many ways a personal projection, they still represented the dream of a better future for many women of her generation. At the time, ideas such as the kitchen-less house were shocking for the social shifts they represented. Another classic personal concern that pops up with suspicious frequency in futurist works is the fate of the novel in the future. 'Don't you have novels any more?' queries Gilman's explorer. 'Oh yes plenty; better than were ever written,' he is relieved to hear.

In her preface to *Moving the Mountain* Gilman said, 'One of the most distinctive features of the human mind is to forecast better things.' Better things for her meant not only better novels, but also a 'new social consciousness'. She christened the book a 'baby utopia' as it involves 'no other change than a change of mind, the mere awakening of people, especially the women, to existing possibilities. It indicates what people might do . . . in thirty years.' Even by the most utopian of utopian standards, thirty years represents pretty optimistic thinking for deep social shifts. *Herland* published four years later, was an altogether bigger and bolder vision of the future and hence a much more frightening proposal. Set in a remote mountain area, it tells the story of three male explorers who stumble across an all-female society. Herland, they discover, has emerged triumphant from the ashes of a civilization destroyed, rather predictably, by reckless male behaviour. The women they encounter are of enviable Amazonian proportions – athletic, strong and with cropped hair – and sexless, though one of the men reports, 'when I see them knit, I can almost call them feminine'. But as the hapless three soon discover, far from fulfilling every clichéd male fantasy, the place has serious disadvantages. Although the men are treated kindly, they are kept locked up or under guard for much of the time – not so much to protect the women from the 'gentlemen', explain the Herlanders, but vice versa. Not only are the men bewildered by the absence of either recreational or procreational sex, they are also surprised to find that the literature lacks any erotic or even clichéd romantic elements.

Compensation is not to be found in the usual realm. There is no smoking or drinking, and even a good juicy steak is out of the question as the Herlanders are all vegetarian. Despite this being a sexless race, the women have survived and multiplied thanks to the discovery and development of procreation by parthenogenesis. The scientific details of virgin birth are not one of Gilman's strong points, and the women manage re-markably well to produce female offspring without the benefit of test-tubes and other modern advances. Far from devalued, motherhood in Herland is seen as the highest social service. But in an all-too-transparent reflection of her own desires and experiences, babies in Gilman's utopia never cry, and are not brought up by home-bound depressed mothers, but by all mothers collectively. Given that child-rearing is so easy, it is not surprising that Herland periodically has a population problem. 'There soon came a time when they were confronted with the problem of the "pressure of population" in an acute form,' explains one of the men. 'There was really crowding, and with it, unavoidably, a decline in standards.' The solution we learn, was not a 'struggle for existence' nor 'predatory excursions to get more land from somebody else', but a good old-fashioned form of family planning. Women practise 'negative eugenics' – forgoing motherhood for the good of the country. When it reaches crisis point, the women sit down and discuss just how many people they can make, 'with the standard of peace, comfort, health, beauty, and progress we demand'. Malthus might not have been welcome in Herland, but he would have been proud. If they do not want to conceive during their fertile period, they simply abstain – from thinking about it. The best method of contraception, is, they say, to distract themselves with hard physical labour. Furthermore, they happily adopt a Mao-like one-child policy, and in times of need, the less desirable social types are encouraged to abstain altogether.

Despite the obvious differences of opinion on certain basic sexual needs, two of the men fall in love with Herlanders. Terry, the macho one of the trio, marries and decides to stay in this pollution-free, advanced civilization with its park-like cities and speedy electric cars. All is well until he demands his 'marital rights'. After an ugly struggle he is humiliatingly overpowered and anaesthetized, put on trial and banished from Herland forever. Van, the softy social scientist, meanwhile resigns himself to the fact that 'much of what I honestly supposed to be a physiological necessity was a psychological necessity – or so believed'. Gilman's vision of how to solve what was known as the 'female question' in the second half of the nineteenth century was clearly not everybody's idea of a good time. Even Gilman herself gives in, and in the sequel *With*

Her in Ourland the narrator returns to Herland with his son, and both sexes learn to live happily ever after. Well, almost.

At this point in the history of the future, women still were not recognized officially as writing utopias, but simply as writing in a utopian fashion. This was a convenient distraction from the fact that there were some frustrated female futurists looking for a medium in which to express themselves. This was also the case with the English writer and fin-de-siècle feminist campaigner, Elizabeth Burgoyne Corbett. Her book *New Amazonia, A Foretaste of the Future*, published in 1889, represented a sharp departure from her usual derring-do boys'-own hack-style detective novels. Ironically and rather shamefully for a book advocating a feminist future, it was published under the name Mrs George Corbett, though in her prologue she complains of women who 'have husbands who regard them as . . . personal property, and who treat them alternately as pets or slaves'.

The ladies of *New Amazonia* would naturally never let a thing like that happen to them. The story starts à la Mercier and Bellamy, with the female narrator falling asleep and waking up in the future. Given the competitive nature of futurists to occupy a time and place in the future, it cannot just be any random date, and in Corbett's case she opts for the year 2472, edging cheekily a few decades beyond Mercier's *L'An 2440*. The adventure begins when the female narrator falls asleep while reading a trashy women's magazine of the type that Corbett particularly dislikes, and wakes to the voice of a man exclaiming 'By jove! But isn't this extraordinary? I say, do you live here, or have you been taking hasheesh too?' The garden of Eden in which they both happen to awake is Ireland following a war that has wiped out most of the original population. The British government has generously offered to repopulate the island and the capital Andersonia (the name is a homage to Elizabeth Garrett Anderson, a physician who campaigned for the admission of women to medicine) with a choice selection of its female surplus. Far from being an inclusive, egalitarian utopia, only the healthy and well-off are chosen for a place in this female future. The inhabitants, who over a period of 600 years have evolved to 7-foot tall, are the embodiment of beauty and fitness. Their waists, unrestricted by the corset, have 'thickened' to twenty-six inches. Complete freedom from the psychological and physical constraints of the clothing of the nineteenth century was also one of Gilman's obsessions for the future and she has her heroines dressed in horribly practical, sexless outfits. Corbett's complete distaste for the fashion of her time is revealed when she has corsets – 'one of the maddest and silliest fashions ever instituted . . . in order that she might meet with the favour of some idiot of the opposite sex' – put on display in a museum for educational purposes.

The women of the future may not care for sexy clothes and stilettos, but they do still worry about their wrinkles. In Corbett's future 'wrinkles are not necessary evils' and you simply do not have to worry about 'the gradual decay of all physical beauty'. As with many futuristic novels, the delights are in the details, and Corbett's detailed descriptions of the whole beauty business are predictions that would not look out of place on the pages of *Vogue* magazine today. When in need of a little perking up, the ladies of New Amazonia go to the Andersonia Physiological Hall. The 'renewing rooms' are naturally all marble and pillars, a 'perfect dream of taste and splendour'. Here the ladies lounge around on sumptuous settees sipping coffee and reading books while waiting for their treatments. The surgeons are naturally 'of splendid physique, elegantly dressed, and of dignified, yet gentle and calm demeanour'. Among the aged or debilitated the most popular treatment is nerve rejuvenation, which involves being injected with 'the nerves of young and vigorous animals'. While today the animal-protection league would be outside defacing the statue of the inventor of 'nerve-rejuvenation', the New Amazonians have no such reservations about killing animals for the benefit of beauty. 'One of the dogs was coaxed from the hearth, and given a dainty and appetizing meal, afterwards springing upon the bassinet to enjoy a quiet nap.' Seconds later he is zapped by a stun gun, and killed painlessly. 'In a few minutes more some of the dog's nerve force was being transferred to my own arm,' explains the newcomer, who leaves the building feeling 'ten years younger and stronger'.

The cult of health, beauty and fitness even among the elderly that she foresaw must be seen in the context of Corbett's times, when society was just waking up to 'the benefits and beauties of science'. Corbett herself lived to the age of seventy-six, but she was born at a time when the average life expectancy in England was in many places less than half of that, and crippling and deforming diseases were still rife. The New Amazonians speak for a common nineteenth-century hope for the future, when they explain that 'science has succeeded in affording us absolute protections against scarlet fever, measles, yellow fever, cholera, whooping cough and many other dreadful ailments which formerly decimated nations'.

Thanks to this new technology people in her utopia live to be well over a hundred years old, which is, according to current trends, most likely by the twenty-fifth century, i.e. exactly when her book is set. Less conservative estimates say that the average life expectancy will be between ninety-five and a hundred by the end of this century, which is likely given that in almost all countries in the world, life expectancy is estimated to be rising by around a month every year. Interestingly,

Corbett envisaged that in the future 'we are individually and collectively enormously benefited' by the benefits of a state-organized rejuvenating system. 'It is due to the benefit we derive here that much of our national prosperity is due,' explains a guide to the narrator. Corbett's ideas for state support in the future take a strange and not uninventive turn when it comes to keeping fit. The narrator learns that when the people started to show 'rapid signs of deterioration' they looked for the causes of this 'unfortunate falling back'. It was found to be the result of 'the mania for saving labour and exercise of every possible sort'. Corbett thought ahead to a time where 'lifts were abolished, and substantial staircases erected in their stead'. Recently, the Austrian Ministry of Health and Women's Affairs introduced a countrywide campaign to discourage the use of elevators under the motto 'take the stairs and live longer'.

While healthy-eating campaigns are backed by many governments of the twenty-first century, they seem distinctly wimpy when compared back (or forward) to New Amazonia, where all indigestible or 'innutritive' foods are banished. Corbett even 'predicted' the health benefits that are currently being discovered and declared in tea, when her heroine discovered the drink 'was not condemned as entirely useless'. Nor, thankfully, is sex condemned as entirely useless, as unlike in Herland it is used for the pleasure of procreation with the few lucky men that are permitted to live in the country. Although they are barred from government office, men are allowed to marry following a Plato-style inspection and the issuing of a 'medical certificate of soundness'. Where Bellamy frowned upon unmarried women, Corbett clearly hoped that in a female-dominated future 'as much public homage is paid to married women as to single ones'. The state of Corbett's own marriage can only be speculated upon but something of it is perhaps revealed in the New Amazonian experience that 'all our most intellectual compatriots, especially the women, prefer honour and advancement to the more animal pleasure of marriage and re-production of species'.

While this appears to be a well-thought-out and liberal manifesto for the future of modern working women who favour career over family, Corbett's predictions can be surprisingly illiberal and un-forward-thinking too. The offspring of any illicit affairs are killed at birth, the men responsible are banished, and the women condemned to a life of drudgery. As well as taking a severely uncharitable attitude to the poor and the poorly, controlling the population in the future was still, over a hundred years after Malthus' warnings, a big question for the future. In Corbett's utopia this means that crippled and malformed babies are brutally disposed of at birth, and anyone daring to produce more than four children is treated as a felon.

Like Bellamy, Corbett could not ignore the shopping question, and her desires for the twenty-fifth century offer a far more female and practical solution than Bellamy's. Written just ten years after Bellamy's *Looking Backward*, Corbett imagined that under her future houses 'the basement consisted entirely of shops, which were connected by means of telephones with every suite in the block, and could, with the aid of electric lifts, supply anything ordered per telephone at a moment's notice.' Given today's progress and delivery services, the year 2472 seems like a reasonable proposition for the arrival of such a service. Corbett also takes a swipe at Bellamy's home-entertainment programme, calling such a thing a 'namby-pamby apology for social entertainment'. The visitor learns that 'everyone went in for this sort of spiritless amusement' when it became possible to hear a concert or a lecture without leaving one's home. In her hurry to foresee the antisocial couch-potato-like behaviour that has come to be associated with modern cocooning, she skipped over Bellamy's equally prophetic point – the democratization of technology.

The advantage of using the romantic and entertaining novel as opposed to a manifesto as a vehicle for future prediction was that the writers could be liberal, though it has to be said not always discreet, with their monkey traps. Corbett's desire to see life insurance abolished so no one could bump off their relatives to get rich quick is, one hopes, the result of the imagination rather than experience. However, where she did reveal herself was in her ideas for the future of the book industry. As a hack writer and novelist dependent upon the whims and ideas of her publisher, she was like Verne, concerned with the future of serious writers in the publishing industry. In New Amazonia she generously created state aid for 'capable industrious' authors, and progressive copyright laws that meant after a hundred years the state had all rights to the work – so 'no grasping publisher was allowed . . . to reap the profits of an author's brain toil'. Domestic drudgery was another bugbear of hers, and like Gilman she judiciously invented a superb and enviable domestic home service. In the future 'The Domestic Aid Society' does all the cooking, washing and sewing, carried out by the splendidly efficient domestic assistants who are trained by the state and occupy a 'very honourable position in our social economy'.

The only people who do not occupy an honourable position in the future appear to be the men. Hash-smoking Mr Fitz-Musicus, who has unwittingly landed in the future too, cannot wait to get out of the place: 'Upon my life, one gets no peace in this miserable place. Only yesterday I was asked in cold blood to select some way of earning my own livelihood. Me! Who never had even to dress myself without assistance . . . The women are such fools too . . . I have proposed to no less than six of them, and what do you think they all did? Nothing but laugh.'

The original Amazonians, as described in the fifth century by the historian Herodotus, were no less frightening. According to Greek legend they were a race of female warriors living in Scythia, north of the Black Sea, hostile not only to men, but also to men or women in positions of power traditionally held by men. The moniker was revived and adopted by nineteenth-century feminists in the struggle for the vote, became something of a cliché in the twentieth century, and is still used today as a symbol for tough, uncompromising have-it-all career women of the twenty-first century. Corbett lived to see women over thirty get the vote, but died in 1922, six years before women got equal voting rights. For all their faults and foibles, Corbett along with Verne, Gilman, Bellamy and even Marx were all pivotal in popularizing the belief of a bright and better future. Through the universality of their ideas they brought the dream of a better future for the first time to the masses. It was a dream that was not to last.

CHAPTER 3

IN NEXT WEEK TO-MORROW

With a kind of madness growing upon me, I flung myself into futurity.

The Time Traveller, *The Time Machine*, H. G. Wells

On 24 January 1902 H. G. Wells gave a speech entitled *The Discovery of the Future* at the Royal Institution in London. A pen-and-ink drawing he made of the event shows a distinctly unimpressed audience of snoozing elderly gentlemen and a few fawning ladies seated at the back. The speaker himself is leaning resignedly at the lectern as if to say, 'why isn't anyone taking me seriously?' Although he was a notoriously dreadful public speaker who spoke too fast, far from being sent to sleep the audience was captivated and the lecture was to prove a turning point in his career. From then on he was no longer just a popular fiction writer of books such as *The Time Machine* and *War of the Worlds*. He was a futurist in all but name.

Wells had always fancied himself as a kind of prophet. He believed that the future could be foretold, and at the Royal Institution he was Moses leading the way to the promised land of the future. We should not dwell, he said, on history and the past to try to look into the future. 'The man of science comes to believe,' said Wells, 'the events of the year A.D. 4000 are as fixed, settled and unchangeable as the events of the year 1600.' Furthermore, if you grasped the whole of the present, knew all its tendencies and laws, you would clearly see the future,' he wrote in *The New Review Time Machine* of 1895. We have, he said, modern science to thank that the 'veil between ourselves and things to come' can be raised. The idea that science will lead the way to the future was not entirely new. What was new, however, was his belief that prediction itself is a science.

Herbert George Wells' own future did not initially look very promising. Born in England in 1866 to a shopkeeper and a domestic servant, he was a sickly child who grew up under the permanent threat of poverty. When his parents separated he was sent out to earn his living, and after several miserable apprenticeships his saving grace was a scholarship to study biology under T. H. Huxley. Known as 'Darwin's Bulldog' for the ferocity of his defence of Darwin's theory of evolution, Huxley was an enigmatic scientist and thinker who made a deep and lasting impression on the young Wells. Wells proved to be not only a gifted and enthusiastic student, but also a born teacher, and his first published work was actually a biology textbook for schools printed in 1893. Just as one can hear the bitterness about his background scratching beneath the surface of his later work, his early vocation as a teacher never really left him either. It just increased in scale and purpose.

One of Wells' first great contributions to futurism was the 'invention' of the time machine in his novel of that name which was first published in 1895. Writing to a friend, he called the book 'the latest Delphic voice'. This was an essentially pessimistic book, coinciding not only with the impending arrival of a new century, but also with the fact that he had been diagnosed with a fatal illness. Led to believe that he did not have long to live, he fortuitously foresaw the collapse of civilization. Plunging boldly into the far future of the year 802,701, Wells' time traveller encounters a world divided into two races – the naïve Eloi in the Upperworld, and the Morlocks who live in the Underworld and eat the Eloi. Back from the future, the time traveller reports 'as I see it, the Upperworld man had drifted towards his feeble prettiness, and the Underworld to mere mechanical industry.' Not only does this imagery have distinct shades of the English 'upstairs and downstairs' class system that deeply affected his upbringing, but it also reflects the social Darwinism that was in the air of the time and that was to colour most of his visions and predictions.

Like Verne's first novel, *Five Weeks in a Balloon*, *The Time Machine* was not only a success, but gained Wells the reputation as a writer of 'scientific romance'. The two writers could not, however, have been more different, though they were often compared and seen as rivals. Verne, ever the frustrated futurist, naturally took a competitive interest in what Wells was writing. In an interview with an English journalist in 1903, Verne admitted that he had indeed read Wells and commented that he found his books not only very curious, but very English. Personally he did not believe that they could be compared as writers because Wells did not concern himself with scientific principles. Referring to Wells' book *First Men in the Moon* published in 1901 and illustrated with some of the first photos of the real moon, Verne claimed 'We do not proceed in the same manner . . . I make use of physics. He invents. I go to the moon in a cannon-ball, discharged from a cannon . . . He goes to Mars in an airship . . . *Ça c'est très joli.* But show me this metal. Let him produce it.' Wells did not, to put it mildly, like having his work compared to that of Verne, and always hotly denied any influence. In a telling letter to the editor of *Outlook* who asked Wells to write something about Verne, he said, 'I've let the time when I might have punished him decently go by.'

Wells' unexpected recovery from his collapsed kidney and diseased lung allowed him a little more optimism in life and in his writings, and certainly drove the prophetic purpose in his works that were to follow. Never the unbridled optimist, he did, however, indulge in a little utopianism, which while highly fashionable was at the time shifting from the generally opti- mistic outlook of the late-nineteenth century to the predomi- nantly pessimistic one that was to brand the genre in the early twentieth. At the time many intellectuals were rather sniffy about utopianism. Wells, however, believed in its potential as a serious signpost for the future. As the writer George Bernard Shaw once said, 'we turned our noses up at Utopias as cheap stuff until Wells stood up for them.' His first real utopia was *Anticipations*, published in 1902, in which with renewed mental and physical vigour, he foresees the New Republic, a new world-state for the year 2000. The full title of his book, *Anticipations of the Reaction of the Mechanical and Scientific Progress upon Human Life and Scientific Thought*, while distinctly less snappy, reveals not only what he was aiming at in this view of the future but what further separates him in spirit and intention from the likes of Verne and Plato. He was also very different from Joseph Conrad, whose book *Heart of Darkness* was published the same year as *Anticipations*. Writing to his friend, Conrad said of their fundamentally different outlooks, 'You don't care for humanity but think they are to be improved. I love humanity but know they are not.'

Whichever way you look at them, some of Wells' anticipations for the future are not only inhumane, but really rather hair-raising. 'It has become apparent,' he wrote, 'that whole masses of human population are, as a whole, inferior in their claim upon the future'. There is no place for the 'swarms of black and brown and dirty-white, and yellow people'. They cannot, he believes, in a Wellsian world state keep up with Europe's technological advances. While he does not propose outright genocide, he believed just 2 billion people was perfect for a planet like ours, and encourages a gradual decline in the population of the non-Europeans as well as the 'vicious, helpless and pauper masses'. Procreation should thus be discouraged between the 'feeble, ugly, inefficient' and those 'born of unrestrained lusts . . . multiplying through sheer incontinence and stupidity'. Poverty and population problems of pure Malthusian proportions were still at this time at the forefront of many concerns and proposals for the future. 'The great city cannot grow,' wrote Wells, 'except as a result of some quite morbid and transitory process – to be cured at last by famine and disorder.' Later, in *The Shape of Things to Come* from 1933, he looked towards a time when as a result of these controls, the world population would be kept to an ideal of 2 billion.

Ever the Darwinist biology teacher at heart, he preferred to look at the species rather than the individual, and characteristically talked of how the broad distinction between the upper and lower classes remains intact, 'as though it was a distinction residing in the nature of things'. Generally it was the grand scheme of things and change that interested him, more than dull domestic detail or dialogue in the future. In *Anticipations* he did, however, provide a few of the smaller and more humane details for life in the New Republic including 'the probable diffusion of great cities' to relieve population pressure, buses and trains that run on time, and the widening of pavements to protect people from the rain and sun. It was not only the rapid growth of cities that was a cause of inspiration but the development of the telephone and transmission technology in the early-twentieth century. Of telecommunication, Wells wrote, 'we may confidently expect to improve', so much so that, 'it would be possible now to send urgent messages at any hour of the day or night to any part of the world.' He also anticipated that 'the business man may then sit at home in his library and bargain, discuss, promise, hint, threaten, tell such lies as he dare not write, and in fact, do every thing that once demanded a personal encounter.' In *Anticipations* Wells gave a confident and not unconvincing picture of how the telephone would change communication. These ideas of global communication were extrapolated a few years later by Robert Sloss who, in 1910, predicted that in a hundred years we would all be walking around with wireless pocket phones: 'citizens of the wireless age will walk everywhere with their receiver, which will, despite its smallness, be a wonder of miniature mechanics. Concerts and commands, all art of enjoyments and the whole knowledge of mankind, will be immediately transmitted. Kings, diplomats, bankers, officials and directors, will make their business and give their signatures wherever they are, on the top of the Himalayas or on a beach . . .' (*Die Welt in 100 Jahren*).

Wells also foresaw widespread regionalization and specialization of newspapers, of which 'the difference in character and tone renders the advent of any Napoleonic master of the newspaper world . . . improbable'. Today's media tycoon Rupert Murdoch would be amused by Wells' prediction in *Anticipations* that daily papers 'will probably not contain fiction at all, and poetry only rarely, because no one but a partial imbecile wants these things in punctual daily doses'. Wells was rather more accurate when he foresaw the demand, though not the exact means, for twenty-four-hour news services: 'One will subscribe to a news agency which will wire all the stuff one cares to have so violently fresh, into a phonographic recorder perhaps, in some convenient corner. There the thing will be in every house, beside the barometer, to hear or ignore.'

Like most futurists, Wells had a few pet predictions, or 'monkey traps' that were slipped in subconsciously among the greater world changes for his personal pleasure and peace of mind. In his capacity as generous intellect and teacher, in 1931 he proposed the idea of a world encyclopaedia that would function as a kind of 'world brain' bringing together thousands of experts to produce an integrated picture of human knowledge that 'would keep the thought of the world in a perpetual lively interchange'. Not, one could say, unlike today's free, multi-lingual Internet encyclopaedia Wikipedia, written by volunteers around the world. In *World Brain* (1938) Wells claimed 'the encyclopaedia of the future may conceivably be prepared and kept by an endowed organization employing thousands of workers permanently . . . mediating between the original thinker, the scientific investigator, the statistician, the creative worker and the reporter of realities on the one hand and the general intelligence of the public on the other.'

The most transparently personal of his predictions was perhaps the anticipation of 'considerable relaxation of the institution of permanent monogamous marriage in the coming years'. Monogamy was, he said, 'sustained entirely by the inertia of custom, and by a number of sentimental and practical considerations'. Wells followed what has been euphemistically called an 'individualistic course of sexual conduct'. Indeed, Wells' biographer Andrea Lynn quipped, rather bluntly, in *Shadow Lovers* that the author of *The Time Machine* was something of a sex machine. Wells was notorious for his extra-marital affairs, shared a lover (the writer Martha Gellhorn) with the French futurist Bertrand de Jouvenel, and fathered at least two children with two lovers. Writing about his uncharacteristic restraint in not sleeping with one lady friend, Wells rationalized, 'I have learnt this much of life that a good thing expected is better than a thing realised.'

The same could be said of most of his visions of the future. *A Modern Utopia,* published in 1905, is a strange mixture of novel and essay (the teacher trait again). Here, the World State is 'the sole landowner of the earth', English the reigning language, and breeding controlled by the state. In Wells' future everybody has access to healthcare and reliable transport, and even home design is so efficient that 'the room has no corner to gather dirt, wall meets floor with a gentle curve, and the apartment could be swept out . . . by a mechanical sweeper'. Efficiency is also about control – and he foresaw a World Index of Population whereby everybody is recorded Big Brother-style on cards in a huge index outside Paris. Furthermore, 'the trend of modern thought,' he wrote, 'is entirely against private property in land or natural objects or products, and in Utopia these things will be the inalienable property of the World State.' This was two years after the Bolshevik revolution. Lenin, the leader of the Bolsheviks, believed that Marxist theory posed questions 'not in the sense of explaining the past but also in the sense of a bold forecast of the future and of equally bold practical action for its achievement'. By 1920, when Wells visited him at the Kremlin, Lenin had put words into action, but had also long been fascinated by the problem

of how to build a tunnel under the English Channel. In 1913
Lenin wrote

> and yet the richest, the most civilised and the freest countries in
> the world are now discussing, in fear and trepidation – by no
> means for the first time the 'difficult' question of whether a
> tunnel can be built under the English Channel . . . Profit from
> capital invested in such an enterprise would be absolutely
> certain. What then, is holding the matter up? Britain is afraid
> of – invasion! A tunnel, you see, would, 'if anything should
> happen', facilitate the invasion of Britain by enemy troops.
> That is why the British military authorities have, not for the
> first time, wrecked the plan to build the tunnel. The madness
> and blindness of the civilised nations makes astonishing read-
> ing. Needless to say, it would take only a few seconds with
> modern technical devices to bring traffic in the tunnel to a halt,
> and to wreck the tunnel completely.

Such is the opportunistic nature of futurism that should a
terrorist attack or accident occur in the tunnel, or maybe even
when generous profits arise, there will be a cry of 'Lenin
predicted it first!' However, when receiving his British gentleman visitor, Lenin had more pressing things on his mind. He
was impatient to know why the Western world did not rouse
itself and join in the world revolution. Wells replied that this
was because the middle class was not interested: it was far too
comfortably off.

Winston Churchill was also an admirer of Wells and a
sometime sparring partner. In his correspondence to Churchill
in 1905 Wells replied, 'I'm very glad you liked my utopia.
You'd find it quite lively enough if you went there.' Churchill
also had his own futurist aspirations and in 1932 published an
article entitled 50 Years Hence in Popular Mechanics maga-

zine. In it he welcomes the rapidity of change and progress, amusingly quoting one of Wells' characters, who says, 'This 'ere progress . . . It's wonderful 'ow it keeps going on.' This is the Mr Toad of Toad Hall 'here to-day, in next week to-morrow' syndrome that was prevalent in the early-twentieth century. Progress was regarded, as Verne had found out, as a double-edged sword for the future – both out of control but also completely necessary. There was also at this time a flush of interest in the potential future of atomic energy. Already in his 1913 novel, *The World Set Free*, Wells had predicted the future development of 'atomic bombs' and foresaw that they would be used in a war in the 1950s. 'It was a matter of common knowledge,' he wrote, 'that man could carry in a handbag an amount of latent energy sufficient to wreck half a city.' Wells got the idea from reading Frederick Soddy's *The Interpretation of Radium*, and combined it with his unease about how 'the world still . . . fooled around with the para-phernalia and pretensions of war'. Churchill was also con-vinced about the potential of these new discoveries and said, 'there is no question among scientists that this gigantic source of energy exists'. He also believed that once its potential was harnessed, 'geography and climate would obey our orders'.

In his article, Churchill explored all aspects of life in the future including 'synthetic food'. Recognizable as a man who liked his food, he predicted that '50 years hence we shall escape the absurdity of growing a whole chicken in order to eat the breast or wing by growing these parts separately under a suitable medium.' In 2005 scientists managed to grow at vast expense a vegetarian-friendly spam-like substance, but pre-dicted that cost-saving lab-raised steaks or chicken wings are still a long way off the menu. Churchill also wrote of 'wireless telephones and television', the result of which would be that the 'congregation of men in cities would become superfluous'.

He also predicted that within fifty years 'it will be possible to
carry out the entire cycle that leads to the birth of a child, in
artificial surroundings'. He was, like Wells, not just interested
in science, but in the science of prediction and believed looking
at science rather than using hindsight was the way in which
'we can predict with some assurance the inventions and
discoveries which will govern our future'. But like many
futurists he was, however, less able and confident of his ability
to predict 'what reactions these discoveries and their applications will produce upon the habits, the outlook and the spirit
of men'.

A year after Churchill's article appeared, Wells published his
third utopia, *The Shape of Things to Come*. It was a peculiarly
pessimistic 'Short History of the Future' looking back from the
twenty-second century. As is often the case the best predictions
were some of the less sensational ones, such as Wells' ideas
regarding ageing and the perception of youth. Wells foresaw
the possibility that in the near future, 'there may be a natural
death for most people in the future about the age of a hundred
or a little more'. On the strength of the progress medicine had
made since he was born, he predicted not only an increase in
life expectancy but a shift in the whole perception and possibilities surrounding ageing. 'There was a time when the man
or woman over forty felt something like a survivor; he was
"staying on" . . . relatively the world swarmed with youth . . .
But now youth is well in hand forever, and when we speak of a
man to-day, we really mean a different being . . . Bodily he is
sounder and fitter, almost completely free from disease; men-
tally he is clear and clean and educated to a pitch that still was
undreamt of two centuries ago.'

Among the more headline-grabbing things the book predicted was the likely outbreak of the Second World War and
its repercussions. In the novel, even the Great Air Dictator

presiding over his World Council at Basra (yes, that Basra in Iraq) cannot save the world from anarchy. Global unity as the solution to war was one of the great preoccupations of Wells, and in *The Open Conspiracy* written in 1928 he proposed 'systems of world control' to bring about lasting peace and liberty. Already in 1918 in a short spell in the Ministry for Propaganda he had anticipated the setting up of the League of Nations, only to be bitterly disappointed when it later failed to prevent the rise of fascism. Wells believed in the idea that 'there will have to be a last conflict to inaugurate the peace of mankind'. The question of which one it is to be is something Wells couldn't predict – on the eve of the First World War he had already published a famous paper inaccurately entitled 'The War that Will End War'.

As he got older, Wells got grumpier and increasingly irritated that no one was listening to him and his increasingly pessimistic prophecies. In 1939 he declared to a friend that his epitaph should be 'God damn you all; I told you so'. Ironically, the one time that he was taken seriously turned out to be more embarrassing than satisfying. When Orson Welles' dramatization of Wells' *War of the Worlds* was broadcast over the radio in 1938, panic broke out in New York. The play about an invasion from Mars was so realistically presented that people thought it had really happened. Wells was not amused, and refused all demands to rewrite the novel in order to calm people down. Despite this, as his ex-lover Martha Gellhorn put it, 'he was enormously frustrated that he wasn't able to get the attention of the world in order to save it from itself'. On one brief visit to him towards the end of his life, she found him in despair, pasting on his walls drawings of devils, which he had named Churchill and Stalin. Despite his failing health he was still writing and ranting prolifically for newspapers, and in November 1942 predicted that Hitler 'will never commit suicide – he hasn't the guts'. Wells himself died in 1946, the year after Hitler had indeed committed suicide. Like Verne, Wells was honoured with having a lunar crater named after him. This is located on the far side of the moon, and noted for the extremely battered state of its outer rim.

The beginning of the twentieth century was a fertile time for futurism. It was liberated by the fact there was not just the literary possibility of a physical time machine to take one to the future, but a renewed metaphysical one. The First World War had had paradoxical effects on futurism. On the one hand it was a devastating defeat for the sense of future and on the other it represented a great challenge for thinking about the future. 'The outbreak of war crossed my perspective of the future like a wall,' wrote Christopher Isherwood in *Prater Violet*, 'it marked the instant, total end of my imagined world.' For others, the war, the worldwide Depression of the 1930s and the threat of another world war focused the mind as this was just when society and politicians really needed to think ahead. As Wells' time traveller said while contemplating the exigencies of war and evolution, 'there is no intelligence where there is no change and no need of change.'

Change was the mantra of one of the oddest movements that ever came to be associated with futurism. Shortly after the turn of the twentieth century a group of intellectuals and artists got together and called themselves Futurists and their movement Futurism. This is the first recorded use of the term; although the name stuck, thankfully many of their radical and provocative ideas did not. Futurism was officially declared a movement by the Italian poet Filippo Tommaso Marinetti in his 1909 *Fondazione E Manifesto Del Futurismo*. Published in *Le Figaro*, it was an anarchic and pompous declaration that celebrated the beauty of speed, innovation, danger and aggression. Marinetti was a manipulative self-publicist whose self-proclaimed 'violently upsetting incendiary manifesto', soon had a faithful following of writers, artists and, less surprisingly, fascists.

Wells had argued in *The Discovery of the Future* for looking forward from the present rather than the past, but Marinetti actively wanted to eradicate the past by destroying museums, academies and libraries in order to create the future. Whereas Wells looked forward to a brighter future where man will 'reach out their hands amid the stars', a few years later, Marinetti wanted to 'hurl defiance' at them. And while Wells warned of the imminence and dangers of war, Marinetti welcomed and glorified militarism as a form of 'hygiene'. Not surprisingly, interest foundered in the Futurist movement after the First World War, and while there was a second flush of Futurism in the 1920s, by the 1930s Marinetti was reduced to writing a manifesto against pasta.

The Futurist Cookbook was a serious joke, detailing the soporific effects of pasta on the mind and the body. In it, Marinetti railed against inept housewives who were poisoning the nation with food that caused 'pessimism, nostalgic inactivity and neutralism'. In the future, he declared, the traditional pleasures of the gourmet must be swept away. No more spaghetti, no more knives and forks, and certainly no more after-dinner speeches (except one assumes those to be given by himself). Marinetti also pompously declared that, 'in the ideal Futuristic meal, a certain number of dishes will be passed beneath the nose of the diner in order to excite his curiosity.' One of the principal features of the new cuisine would be 'a rapid sequence of dishes no bigger than a mouthful'. Recommended for those in a hurry, but not for the hungry. For real basic bodily needs as opposed to aesthetic ones, Marinetti recommends 'scientific nourishment by means of pills and powders', which he calculated would lower the cost of living and eventually lead to a reduction in the working hours. 'Soon,' he prophesied, 'machines will constitute an obedient proletariat . . . at the service of men who are almost totally relieved of manual work.' While many still feared man becoming the slave of the machine, Marinetti was bounding ahead happily anticipating a reduced working week.

The ideas of the Futurists were dreamt up more for the sake of provocation than prediction, yet they foresaw not only the obsession for vitamin supplement pills, but the nouveau cuisine cult of the 1990s and the Slow Food appreciation movement that has gathered pace at the turn of the twenty-first century. As well as wanting to 'prepare men for future chemical foodstuffs', Marinetti believed that when food was consumed all five senses should partake. His bizarre but beloved 'Sunshine Soup', 'Divorced Eggs', 'Network in the Sky' pudding and 'Carnaleap' cocktail would certainly not look out of place on the menus of some trendy restaurants today.

Marinetti's contribution to futurism is considered marginal but entertaining, but that of the economic prodigy Nikolai Kondratieff is quite the opposite. In fact in 1914 while Marinetti was pontificating to the Futurists in St Petersburg, Kondratieff appears to have been blissfully unaware. With his head buried deep in his books at the university there, while the Russian Futurists were working on their manifesto entitled 'A Slap in the Face of Public Taste', Kondratieff was busily studying American, British and French wholesale prices and interest rates. Looking all the way back to the figures from the eighteenth century, he discovered that the peaks and troughs in economic activity occurred at regular intervals. From this he confidently concluded that Western capitalist economies have predictable long-term cycles of forty to sixty years of boom followed by depression – so-called Kondratieff waves.

His own life followed a remarkably similar pattern. Kondratieff rose to deputy minister of food at the age of twenty-five, and was later promoted to economic advisor to the Revolution. In the early 1920s he acquired an international reputation as a distinguished economist, exchanging ideas with foreign economic agencies, and lecturing in the United States and Britain. During this period he also worked on the first of the Soviet five-year plans. Although he approved of Josef Stalin's New Economic Policy, Kondratieff's personal standing started to wane when he spoke out boldly against the total collectivization of agriculture and warned against the disproportionate development of industry and agriculture. By 1930 Kondratieff was branded a 'kulak-professor' and a threat to the Stalinist regime. The evidence that there were predictable patterns of change and hence economic forces beyond his control was too much for Stalin. Not to be undermined by the forces of the future, Stalin had Kondratieff arrested, tried and sentenced to eight years in prison. In 1938 Kondratieff was summarily executed.

Kondratieff's ideas have survived to the present day, and trend analysts and researchers still look to his waves when looking at the lifespan and progress of innovation. This was largely thanks to a contemporary of his, the Austrian-American economist Joseph Schumpeter who saw the potential of this work and incorporated Kondratieff's waves into his popular business cycle model. For someone who developed a model of economic predictability, it is ironic that Schumpeter was himself such an unpredictable character. Like Kondratieff he was an economic genius, and from an early age he made no secret of his ambition to become 'a great lover, a great horseman and a great economist'.

Schumpeter's contribution to futurism lay wholly in his ability in economics, and he named the largest of the three business cycles in his model after Kondratieff. These Kondratieff Cycles are best visualized as a sequence of waves rising and falling. Each incoming wave rises up in the wake of the previous one, so that as each new raw material or technology gathers pace and acceptance, productivity peaks for a decade or two, and then wanes as a new driving force comes along. Historically this has been well documented. One such wave, driven by the steam engine and cotton, began with the early Industrial Revolution towards the end of the eighteenth century. By the mid-nineteenth century railways and steel were taking over as the driving forces of the new wave of commerce and innovation, and in the early-twentieth century a new wave led by advances in electricity and new chemical techniques took over. Retrospectively we can see also that the Kondratieff Cycle predicts the Great Depression of the 1930s and the new cycle of prosperity that came in the late 1950s, fuelled by developments in the automobile and oil industry. At last here was a solid theoretical model by a respected economist which could provide a sound basis for futurists' imaginings and predictions. Using this model many futurists show how today's computer, telecommunications and information-led economy is already past its peak, and that the next cycle of prosperity will be driven by the development of gene and bio-technology. This is predicted to peak at around 2030, followed by a wave of nano-engineering that will peak in the year 2090. In terms of business practice and application, the real practical value of the Kondratieff Cycles can be realized only if you can determine what will actually constitute the substance of the next wave. It cannot tell you what that will be, but if you have an inkling, it will help determine the temporal progression of that trend. This is, however, still a very controversial idea, and like

Stalin many economists deny the very existence or predictability of these cycles. In the 1980s the Technological Forecasting Group at the University of Dayton concluded its
research on it with the statement, 'the Kondratieff Wave
may be real, but the evidence for it is weaker than the evidence
against it. Hence the running joke: "economists have predicted
nine of the past five recessions".'

Like Kondratieff, Schumpeter was a victim of his own
success. In the 1930s he began work on a major opus predicting the end of capitalism. The Depression was, he maintained, a 'necessary cold douche' before the arrival of the next
Kondratieff wave, which would wash away old and outmoded
commercial practices, and make room for new innovation. So
far, so predictable. Only this time, he foresaw like Marx, that
capitalism would in the end become a victim of its own success,
and would give way to socialism. Schumpeter also courted
controversy between the wars with his belief that you could
actually create markets and trends, and this has since been one
of the crucial tenets of the debate surrounding the use or
indeed the purpose of futurists. Schumpeter claimed it was
actually the entrepreneurs rather than the consumer who were
the driving force of capitalism. Until the beginning of the
twentieth century it was assumed that the role of entrepreneurs
was secondary (if not entirely passive) as they were simply
fulfilling consumer wishes and demand with the available
resources. Schumpeter was one of the first to turn this idea
on its head, and look at it from the other perspective. Entrepreneurs, he argued, take the risks that promote growth.
His second, related and equally controversial, belief was that
most changes in commodities had been 'forced on the consumers'. At the time, Schumpeter's claim that consumers are
initially resistant but eventually succumb to 'the elaborate
pyrotechnics of advertising', was frankly, shocking. In terms

of consumerism, free will was perceived as flying out of the window followed closely by Pavlov's dog.

The proof of Schumpeter's ideas was then, as now, there if you wanted to find it. At the turn of the nineteenth century you needed to look no further than the example of Coca-Cola, which people were reluctant to buy because of the cocaine content (it was removed in 1905). Between 1890 and 1900, however, the company ran a huge nationwide advertising campaign in the USA that pushed up sales from 9,000 gallons to 400,000 gallons. What Schumpeter postulated, that trends and markets can be created, is still controversial – from one point of view it represents economic opportunity, and on the other, fear of manipulation. The public perception of the choice-less and gullible consumer was not popular then, and is certainly not popular today. Needless to say, one of the first questions that today's futurists are asked by business-people is usually 'can you make a trend?' closely followed by 'if so, can you give me one?' The answer, most modern futurists will agree, is certainly 'no' to the second question, and 'how much time do you have?' to the first.

Annoyingly, most futurists do not give simple answers. But nor do they ask simple questions. This was particularly true of the great twentieth-century writer Aldous Huxley. Huxley was just six years old when Wells made his landmark futurist speech and the grandson of Wells' charismatic mentor, T. H. Huxley. He also came from a distinguished line of writers and intellectuals from whom, as one biographer pointed out, 'nothing but the best would be tolerated'. With such a back-ground he had two choices: to sink into complete depression and obscurity, or to make his mark. Despite near-blindness and the devastating death of his mother when he was fourteen, Huxley went on to great things. Unable to use a microscope he gave up his ambition to become a doctor and turned to literature. Huxley read and wrote voraciously, aided by drops to dilate his pupils, a large magnifying glass and various therapies over the years. It was one of Bertrand Russell's running jokes that when Huxley was a student you could tell which volume of the *Encyclopaedia Britannica* he was reading by the number of subjects starting with a particular letter he inserted into his conversations. Huxley was an endearing character who, with his quiet charm and humour, managed to court controversy without the arrogance that is associated with his near contemporary Wells. Unlike Wells, Huxley did not see himself primarily as a prophet. He gained his reputation as a satirical writer, of 'house party' society novels, but is best remembered for his futurist novel *Brave New World*. Huxley had played around with the future in *Crome Yellow*, published in 1921, in which he explored the idea that 'an impersonal generation will take the place of Nature's hideous system. In vast state incubators, rows upon rows of gravid bottles will supply the world with the population it requires.' It was ostensibly a witty satire on English society, but it was also deeply infected by serious questions about the progress of science. Not only was it a dig at Wells' pre-war utopian optimism, but, rather cruelly, the chief architect of this Rational State, Mr Scogan with his beaked nose, dark eyes and thin high voice, bore an uncanny resemblance to Wells. Wells' own prophecies about selective breeding are also mirrored in Scogan's belief that 'human beings will be separated out into distinct species, not according to the colour of their eyes or the shape of their skulls, but according to the qualities of their mind and temperament.'

It was ten years before Huxley developed these themes into the fully blown dystopia, *Brave New World*. Published in 1932, when Hitler was on the brink of becoming Chancellor of

Germany, it was, in Huxley's own words, 'a novel about the future – on the horror of the Wellsian utopia and a revolt against it'. Not amused, Wells condemned the book as 'blasphemy against the science of religion', and Huxley 'a degenerate descendant of a noble grandfather'. *Brave New World* was classic pessimistic post-war prophecy, with the coming horrors of regimentation further illustrated by the setting of the novel in the year AF 632. The AF stands for After Ford, and the atheist in Huxley took obvious delight in the creation of the world of Our Ford. This was a sharp, undisguised dig at Henry Ford, the controversial American industrialist who had in effect invented the assembly-line and revolutionized factory production, and whose plant was, by 1914, turning out a complete chassis every 93 minutes. 'Fordism,' wrote Huxley, 'demands the cruellest mutilations of the human psyche . . . Rigorously practised for a few generations . . . will end by destroying the human race.' While in America, Huxley – it has been famously said – 'saw the future and hated it'.

In *Brave New World* Huxley used the image of the production line to great and terrifying effect in the creation of the human race. Six centuries after Ford, natural procreation and childbirth is obsolete, if not downright disgusting, and in the opening scene we are led by the Director through the Central London Hatchery, where 300 fertilizers are at work preparing fertilized eggs in test-tubes for x-ray treatment. This *in vitro* fertilization method is, he explains, 'the principle of mass production at last applied to biology' and 'a prodigious improvement . . . on nature'. The Director proudly shows the visiting students how 'on a very slowly moving band a rack-full of test-tubes was entering a large metal box . . .' The embryos that survive are sent off to the Social Predestination Room where they are conditioned using varying amounts of oxygen to become one of five grades of designer babies. These 'products' range in intelligence and ability from the top dog Alphas, through the Betas, Gammas and Deltas to the lowest, the semi-moronic Epsilons. This was his brutal but humorous answer not only to his own disabilities, but to the pressing question as to whether utopias would be feasible in the future. As he put it, 'no society provides openings for more than a limited number of superior people . . . If every individual is capable of playing the superior part, who will do the dirty work and obey?'

Huxley, like many futurists of his generation, stirred up deep fears – but also some promises – about the future that are still at the research stage of science, and are echoed today in the 'designer baby' and human cloning debate. *In vitro* fertiliz-ation, meanwhile, has become almost a standard procedure for infertility following the birth of the first test-tube baby in 1978. Some other good news in Huxley's *Brave New World* was that medical science has eliminated cancer, syphilis and typhoid along with all the boring and nasty debilitating effects of old age. In his last novel, *Island*, published one year before his death in 1963, he describes a time where 'Deep Freeze' and 'Artificial Insemination' have eliminated hereditary disease. One of the characters talks openly about improving the race: 'There's been some diabetes among my father's people, so they thought it best . . . to have both their children by AI.'

In the absence of suffering there is sex, but no romance nor monogamy. 'Everyone belongs to everyone else', and the state thoughtfully supplies free contraceptives to make sure there is no unwanted natural childbirth. One woman, Lenina, even carries the contraceptives like ammunition around her waist in a 'Malthusian belt'. Birth control as we know and rely on it today was still in its infancy in Huxley's time, but he would have been inspired by the pioneering work of one of his contemporaries, Margaret Sanger. She was a lifelong advocate of the use of birth control for the wellbeing of women and, in 1950, while in her eighties, she underwrote the research necessary to create the contraceptive pill. When sex gets boring in the Brave New World (not that it appears to), inhabitants can go to the 'feelies', a five-senses version of an IMAX movie experience, which has electrodes implanted in the armrests. And just to make sure everyone really *is* happy, they all take a euphoria drug ('delicious soma'), which has been compared favourably with Prozac. As one of the characters resignedly points out, it is a world in which 'there is no leisure from pleasure'.

In 1931, while Huxley was writing *Brave New World* he believed there were a good few generations to go before his prophecies would be realized. 'I was convinced that there was still plenty of time. The completely organised society, the scientific caste system, the abolition of free will by methodical conditioning, the servitude made acceptable by regular doses of chemically induced happiness, the orthodoxies drummed in by nightly courses of sleep-teaching – these things were coming all right, not in my time, not even in the time of my grand-children.' However, in 1958 he felt 'a good deal less optimistic . . . The prophecies made in 1931 are coming true much sooner than I thought they would. The nightmare of total organisation, which I had situated in the seventh century after Ford, has emerged from the safe, remote future and is now awaiting us, just around the next corner.'

If you treat Huxley's book as satire, it is very funny. If you treat it as a serious prediction of the future, it is deeply unfunny. As Bertrand Russell wrote, 'I am afraid that while Mr Huxley's prophecy is meant to be fantastic, it is all too likely to come true.' However, read as a kind of pick-and-mix for the future – ignoring the electric shocks in the Neo-Pavlovian Conditioning Rooms, the Nazi number and other unpleasant details – the book has something for everyone. Students of one American college in the 1950s found the idea of free sex and drugs in the future rather appealing and, according to Krishan Kumar, author of *Utopia & Anti-Utopia in Modern Times*, many contemporary feminists supported the attack on the 'stifling' monogamous family and responded positively to the idea of the abolition of parenthood. One radical feminist in the 1970s went so far as to say that women should support the development of *in vitro* fertilization as only by rejecting their role as mothers did they have any hope of gaining true equality with men.

Huxley had the great fortune – or misfortune – to see the seeds of his predictions growing during his lifetime. In a 1946 foreword to *Brave New World* he pointed to the evidence of the breakdown of the traditional family in the rising divorce rates in New York and predicted that in a few years from then, 'marriage licences will be sold like dog licences, good for a period of twelve months, with no law against changing dogs or keeping more than one animal at a time'. When he died, the sexual revolution was well under way, and the Kondratieff boom of the 1950s had brought widespread economic prosperity. From his home in America he had made a living writing feel-good film scripts for Hollywood and was fascinated by the benefits of 'totalitarian' mass consumerism and popular culture. The hallucinogenic drugs that he foresaw would allow you to 'take a holiday from reality', were readily available in the form of mescaline and LSD. Huxley's own legendary experiments with the drugs led to altogether different kinds of 'visions' than those about the future.

From the turn of the twentieth century to the end of the Second World War futurism was dominated not only by a growing mood of predictive pessimism but by three main writers. Like

Macbeth's three witches, members of this triumvirate were also adept at stirring up a hocus pocus of fears, hope and trouble with their pot of predictions. If Wells was the one gathering the nasty ingredients, and Huxley the one who mixed them up into a nasty satirical soup, then George Orwell was the one who wickedly kept the fire going under the cauldron long after it should have decently gone out. Optimism was not Orwell's strong point, and he neither dreamt of, nor foresaw, utopia. With Huxley's writing there was a deliberate ambiguity as to whether you are dealing with a utopia or a dystopia. The answer lies in your sense of humour or your degree of optimism or pessimism. With George Orwell's novel *Nineteen Eighty Four* (more commonly abbreviated to *1984*, and published in 1949), there is absolutely no doubt and there is no deliberate humour. This is a profound dystopia. 'If you want a picture of the future of humanity,' wrote Orwell, 'imagine a boot stamping on a human face – for ever.' The book was also the proverbial boot in the face of optimistic futurism, leaving a bruise long beyond 1984.

The 1940s were not a time for pussyfooting around politically or idealistically with the future. While he was writing the book, these were difficult years, and with difficult questions, and Orwell did not shy away from provocative answers. From early on, Orwell was always one to follow his convictions, from resigning from the Imperial Police in Burma because of the inherent racism, to fighting against fascism on the streets of Barcelona during the Spanish Civil War. One of his first political statements was to change his name from Eric Arthur Blair to his *nom de plume*, which he first officially used at the age of thirty with the publication of *Down and Out in Paris and London*. This was not simply a writer's whim but a deliberate attempt to disassociate himself from his family, who he memorably called 'landless gentry', and an attempt to reposition himself as a political and literary rebel. Young Eric (George) was always a bit of an outsider. Farmed out to a posh prep school in Sussex when the family returned from Bengal in 1911, he was soon stigmatized for his lack of money and remembered for his wealth of talent. Writing about his time at St Cyprian's, he reveals his memories sculpted by a deep feeling of worthlessness. 'I had no money, I was weak. I was unpopular. I had a chronic cough. I was cowardly. I smelt.' Things did not get much better at Eton. Acutely aware of the fact that he was only there as the result of winning a scholarship, he spent several more miserable years suffering the rigours and injustices of the British public-school system. As one of his fellow pupils later put it, he was 'a boy with a permanent chip on his shoulder'.

Much has been made of the influence of Orwell's school days on his ideas, especially when it comes to the sadomasochistic scenes. Biographer D. J. Taylor pointed out in *Orwell, The Life*, 'Eton left a profound impression on Orwell which, if anything, became more marked the further he moved away from it.' Similarly, Orwell tried to distance himself from his family upbringing that was dominated by an atmosphere of impoverished snobbery. Again, paradoxically, the more he tried, the nearer he got to it. Meanwhile, he took the only route he could away from his past – and became an anarchist. He later downgraded to simply 'socialist' in the 1930s and, contrary to popular belief, was never a communist. The decade was a time of great inspiration for Orwell. He went out to Spain to report on the Civil War, and ended up staying and fighting with the Republican militia on the fronts and in Barcelona, where today there is a small square named in his honour. As a result of the insidious in-fighting between the factions opposing Franco's fascism, Orwell was forced to flee for his life from the communists. Later, in 1945, during a brief career as a correspondent for the *Observer*, Orwell described a walk through the ruined cities of Germany and doubted 'the continuity of civilisation as a whole'.

It is not perhaps surprising then that his infamous book *1984*, which was written in 1948, can be read as a Cassandra-like warning of the menaces of both communism and fascism. In his imagined world of 1984, life is dominated by three rival superpowers. These three permanently warring police states consist of Oceania (England and America), Eurasia and Eastasia. The story is set in England, renamed Airstrip One, which has become a controlled world of propaganda and surveillance. The irony was not wasted on the Greenham Common protesters who in the 1980s were fighting to remove American military bases from England, nor more recently did it bypass the critics of Tony Blair's alliance with America during the Iraq war. The hero of the book, Winston Smith (named most probably after Churchill), rebels against the totalitarian world he lives in. He was, like Orwell, a writer, searching for truth and liberty in a seemingly hopeless situation. The all-watching all-powerful leader of Airstrip One is the legendary 'Big Brother', a Stalin look-alike with a fat black moustache and a memorable mania for greatness and control. What makes Orwell's vision of the future so insidious is that it is set in the recognizable urban topography of London. While Jules Verne set his books in the recognizable present in order not to frighten his audience, Orwell deliberately set it in a recognizable future for the very purpose of frightening his readers. Similarly, the technology that they both imagined was an extrapolation of the potential promise – or in Orwell's case the threat – of existing devices.

In Orwell's time, television had not reached anywhere near the household saturation levels of today, but it was certainly a growing and powerful phenomenon that he cleverly developed into an all-seeing all-knowing medium for the future. Similarly, spying and listening devices were a key weapon in the war against Germany, and the potential for using them to spy on the general population did not escape his notice nor his imagination. Along with the permanent threat that 'Big Brother is watching you' the inhabitants of 1984 are surveyed by police patrols skimming over the rooftops in helicopters in scenes worthy of reality TV cop shows. Worst of all are the 'Thought Police': 'It was conceivable that they watched everybody all the time . . . You had to live – did live . . . in the assumption that every sound you made was overheard, and, except in darkness, every movement was scrutinised.' Although Orwell clearly did not predict the use of night-vision cameras, which have since been used to appallingly voyeuristic effect in the TV reality show *Big Brother*, there is a knee-jerk reflex to paraphrase Orwell whenever such things as the installation of CCTV in public spaces are discussed.

More than any other books of this period, this is the one that has shaped the popular pessimistic imagination and language about the future. The term '1984' is not so much a date as a symbol, and phrases such as 'Big Brother', 'Thought Police', 'double think' (the acceptance of conflicting opinions or beliefs at the same time) and 'Newspeak' have, in a strange twist of futurity, embedded themselves in our language. One of Winston's colleagues at the Ministry of Truth says to him, 'Don't you see that the whole aim of Newspeak is to narrow the range of thought? In the end we shall make thought crime literally impossible, because there will be no words in which to express it.'

This was not prediction based directly on clear-cut political, economic or scientific theories or waves. It was, instead, a cruel and calculated form of futurism that exploited a common fear of the future and the fate of mankind. It was a sign of the times that this unequivocally pessimistic book with an unhappy ending became a bestseller. Some wondered that it ever got published. Even Orwell's trusted friend and official biographer Malcolm Muggeridge remarked of a proof copy that it was really 'rather repugnant', and did not bear any relation to 'anything that could happen'. Orwell himself always disingenuously denied he was writing a prediction, but in a note to his publisher at the end of 1948 admitted, 'What it is really meant to do is to discuss the implications of dividing the world up into "Zones of Influence".' One of his inspirations for the book was the Teheran conference, the first Allied summit meeting of the Second World War attended by Roosevelt, Churchill and Stalin. It was here that they discussed how Germany would be divided up between them once the Nazis were defeated.

After much wrangling and many rewrites interrupted by Orwell's illnesses, *1984* was published a year before his death. The book was a huge success, with the publisher claiming that, seen as an attack on socialism and communism, '*1984* is . . . worth a cool million votes to the Conservative Party'. Interestingly, as the real 1984 approached, the book was often alluded to by the Conservative Party in its campaign and played a nasty little role in the political discourse. On an election poster in 1979 the Conservatives asked, 'Where will you be in 1984 if Labour wins?' It worked. This was the year that Margaret Thatcher swept to power. According to writer Paul Chilton in a book called *Nineteen Eighty Four in 1984*, during another successful election campaign in 1983, a caller to BBC Radio 4 suggested to the Defence Secretary that American military bases were turning Great Britain into Airstrip One. The Defence Secretary's reply was worthy of Orwell's doublethink: 'I've read *1984* and we'd all agree . . . that relatively few of Orwell's forecasts have come true.' Even the failed catchy Conservative campaign slogan of 2005, 'Are you thinking what we're thinking?' had rather uncomfortable echoes of Big Brother speak.

Predictably, the book enjoyed a much-anticipated revival in the year 1984, and it was picked to pieces in the popular 'what Orwell got right and wrong' game. The usual suspects were the police helicopters, the spread of surveillance cameras and the control of the media and government over public thinking. In the rush to examine the prophetic details, what is often over-looked is how sharply magnified and modern his language and vision are compared to Wells. Orwell was born the year after Wells made his *Discovery of the Future* speech, and admitted to being an avid reader of Wells during his childhood. At the age of thirty-eight Orwell went so far as to say it was 'a sort of patricide for a person of my age to find fault with Wells'. Needless to say, he did find fault with Wells, particularly with an article in which Wells had predicted that Hitler's power was spent. In a piece in *Horizon* called *Wells, Hitler and the World State,* Orwell claimed that Wells' greatest achievement was his lower-middle-class novels of the 1930s, and that he had totally underestimated Hitler. 'The people who have shown the best understanding of Fascism,' wrote Orwell, 'are either those who have suffered under it or those who have a Fascist streak in themselves. A crude book like *The Iron Heel*, written nearly thirty years ago, is a truer prophecy of the future than either *Brave New World* or the *Shape of Things to Come.*' The ensuing exchange resulted in Wells writing a letter to Orwell and politely telling him to 'read my early works you shit'.

The Iron Heel by Jack London that Orwell refers to was an indigestible dystopia about the rise of a fascist tyranny in the United States that was published in 1908. While Orwell condemns Huxley's key work in the same breath as he does Wells', in *1984* he brutally takes the future one horrible stage further and makes the idea of the Malthusian belt look positively old fashioned. Winston has it explained to him that, 'in the future there will be no wives and no friends. Children will be taken from their mothers at birth, as one takes eggs from a hen. The sex instinct will be eradicated. Procreation will be an annual formality like the renewal of a ration card. We shall abolish the orgasm.'

Towards the end of his life when he was writing *1984* in failing health, Orwell was living as a single father on the barren and remote Hebridean Island of Jura. It was not only, reasoned Orwell, a healthy place for a small boy, but according to one of his old comrades, he prophesied a nuclear holocaust, and believed it to be safer there. Guests who made the long and difficult journey were often shocked by the austerity of the surroundings, the shabbiness of Barnhill, Orwell's house, and his unsuccessful attempt to grow vegetables in the unforgiving landscape. Those who expected scintillating and inspiring conversations sprinkled with a few poignant predictions with their host were also deeply disappointed. His biographer Taylor describes how the young writer David Holbrook found his entire visit 'an exercise in disillusionment', and Orwell 'hostile and grumpy'. Holbrook later admitted to having sneaked a look at the pages of the manuscript of *1984* and was not impressed. 'Pretty depressing stuff . . . these dismal sexual episodes . . . lacking in hope.' But although it did not bring hope it brought a heightened awareness, and that is Orwell's lasting legacy to futurism.

Orwell was one of the rare breed of writers in the history of futurism bold enough to put a definite see-by date to his visions. In and out of hospital with tuberculosis while he was finishing *1984*, he knew it was a date he would not live to see. The British journalist John Langdon-Davies, a contemporary of Orwell, did not have such luck. Unlike Orwell he did not pussyfoot around with satire or parody but made real hardcore political predictions, and lived to see the day. The day, that is, that they did not come true. His book, *A Short History of the Future,* included a list of hard facts and prophecies for the future that makes even the boldest of futurists look slightly impotent.

Like many of this generation Langdon-Davies flirted with Marxism in his youth, and spent several formative years in the early 1930s in America. When he returned to England he found a new generation of intellectuals that he dismissed as 'taking a delight in bitterness, and not wanting anyone, even themselves, to enjoy anything at all'. If this was a dig at the dystopian visions of the future that were popular at the time, it has to be said (with the benefit of hindsight), that his own predictions were not particularly optimistic either. And if it was fashionable to be pessimistic at the time, it was also necessary to be idealistic and, like Orwell, pack your bags and head out to the Spanish Civil War. (Huxley, meanwhile, stayed at home and ruminated on how his 'pacifist' friends were heading out to fight.)

A measure of the ideological incest and bickering that went on between the intellectuals and writers in Spain at the time is revealed in Langdon-Davies' review of Orwell's *Homage to Catalonia* in which he cynically quipped 'the road to Wigan Pier leads on to the POUM [the Spanish Workers' Party of Marxist Unification]'. Despite the fact that Langdon-Davies was a pacifist (he spent a short time in prison for being a conscientious objector during the First World War), in 1936 he was out there too, reporting for the *News Chronicle* from Barcelona. It was a city he described as 'struggling to establish a new order and ruthlessly liquidating the old'. Appropriate then that he wrote the introduction to his book *A Short History of the Future* here.

The aim of Langdon-Davies' extraordinary and long-forgotten book was to 'describe a future which seems logically most likely to happen', rather than the future he would prefer to see (no delicious monkey traps then). It was not a future that he would write if he was 'god', he says, but one that seems probable according to 'unalterable laws which all life obeys'. In his own words, Langdon-Davies predicted:

- there will be no war in Western Europe for the next five years (from 1935)
- democracy will be dead by 1950
- by AD 2000 every community will have adopted a planned birth rate and population will be kept at a fixed level by state-controlled contraception, abortion and sterilization
- England will have a population one-tenth of its present size
- large tracts of America will go back to the primeval wilderness
- by 1960 work will be limited to three hours a day
- by 1975 sexual feeling and marriage will have nothing to do with one another
- crime will be considered a disease after 1985 and will cease to exist by AD 2000
- by AD 4000 the race problems will all be solved. There will be one race . . . with a pale-coffee-coloured skin . . . That will be history's answer to *Mein Kampf*.

Interestingly, one of the points Langdon-Davies did get right was the one about changing attitudes to sex, marriage and birth. He saw that the opposition to anaesthetics in childbirth would have to change, but feared stupidity would prevent new scientific methods being used. Better still, he foresaw that 'the time is almost upon us when everyone above the age of sixteen will be aware of the whole science of contraception' (pointing out meanwhile that in 1935 it was illegal in America to sell contraceptives unless they were sold as prophylactics against disease). When it comes to sex outside of marriage, the three-times-married Langdon-Davies had strong views. In the future, marriage, he believed, 'will stand or fall on its own merits as an economic function. It will not be required to whitewash man's natural sexual desire.' He also uses the book to take a few direct swipes at the conceit of 'that dangerous speculator' Wells, who believed 'if the world listens to me, then all will be well'. Langdon-Davies may have been right when he predicted that 'the world will not listen to Mr Wells', but he missed the point that many of his own ideas (including those on marriage) are about as reassuring as those of Wells. Even his prediction of a reduced working day is less attractive than Marx's as it is marred by the prospect that 'most of the increasing leisure time will be taken for the next two or three generations by the state for its own purposes'.

Though he may not have approved of it, had Langdon-Davies been alive today he would have done well as a trend researcher. Already in 1935 he looked at the spurious marketing methods used for different sorts of soap and saw the potential for doing the same with water.

> If we bought water as we buy soap, we should be forced to choose between a dozen different kinds of water . . . Jones would pay eminent actresses, boxers and expatriated aristocrats to say that they can distinguish Jones' water from the others blindfolded. Smith would demand that we bought his water because 'it's filtered' . . . Robinson in desperation would hire men to start a whispering campaign that cholera bacilli had been found in his competitor's products; which would bring from them an indignant demand for 'truth in advertising'.

> A fabulous sum of money would be spent to show pictures of naked beauties in or near pools of Robinson's waters . . .

This, he pointed out, is 'a perfectly accurate picture of how we organize to buy and sell almost every other commodity except water'. If only he knew.

With what one can only hope was dry humour, Langdon-Davies even predicted that the obsession with the benefits of pure mountain water would go so far as to result in advertising campaigns with professors of literature who 'persuade us to read a six-inch shelf of the world's classics printed on rubber during our morning dip'. Luckily Langdon-Davies' claim to posterity does not lie with his predictions for how we live today, but in a more personal and humane act. Legend has it that while reporting from Santander for the *News Chronicle* in 1937, he came across a small child wandering alone through the streets. In the child's pocket was a note that read 'This is José. I am his father. When Santander falls I shall be shot. Whoever finds my son, I beg him to take care of him for my sake.' Deeply moved, Langdon-Davies took care of the child and went on during the Second World War to set up the 'Foster Parents Plan for War Children' (today known as Plan International). Not only was this a bid to help, but a reflection of Langdon-Davies' own uprooted, unhappy and fatherless childhood. He was born in Zululand, South Africa, and his Church of England minister father died when he was just three years old. At the age of seven he was, like Orwell, packed off to public school in England. Of his first day, he recalled sitting with some 400 boys in the school chapel, all of whom 'like myself, had come to be trained for a future about which certain guesses had been made'.

It would be an understatement to say that Langdon-Davies put his neck on the line with his own 'guesses'. While others hid behind the cover of utopia and fiction, he dared to write real unambiguous political predictions with specific dates. The fact that he lived until 1971 meant he had a good few years to face up to the brutal fact that broadly speaking he was completely and utterly wrong. Reading his book in a Western democracy in the twenty-first century, where the average working day has if anything increased, rather than shrunk, it is a quaint and perversely entertaining catalogue of prediction that tells us more about the fears and fantasies of the 1930s than it does about the facts of life in our time. But as he rightly pointed out, 'We cannot wash our hands of the future . . . We are now entering upon the phase of our history when the whole matter is likely to be decided.' It was just not to be the way he and his fellow futurists imagined.

CHAPTER 4

HERE LIVE LIONS

The only way to predict the future is to have power to shape the future.

Eric Hoffer, *The Passionate State of Mind* (1954)

Towards the end of the Second World War, the future was like a bride left waiting for her groom to return from the front. Utopias and romantic adventure stories that had for years been the imaginative staple of future thinking had eloped with fascism and Stalinism, and were henceforth considered highly unsuitable partners. Former suitors of optimism were flirting with pessimism, and even reliable 'grooms' like Wells had sunk into interminable and loudly voiced pessimism for the future. Writing in a revised version of *A Short History of the World* in 1946 he claimed, 'Since then [1940] a tremendous series of events has forced upon the intelligent observer the realisation that the human story has already come to an end and that

Homo sapiens, as he had been pleased to call himself, is in his present form played out.'

'The future' desperately needed a new lover or at least some decent admirers – not just a respectable replacement for utopias and unrequited idealism, but new followers, ways of thinking and applications that could boost its confidence and reputation. Naturally, as in all good fairy tales, just when it seemed that the ceremony would have to be called off, the future was to come into its own. For the first time in its history, futurism was championed as a discipline, a respectable academic calling and even a proper profession. In the decades after the war it faced the biggest challenge ever – preventing another world war. Futurism went beyond simple optimism or pessimism, utopia or dystopia, and was actively looked upon as a widespread, effective and sometimes dangerous tool for planning and 'forming' the future. The 1940s and 1950s saw the awakening of the future into a movement that aimed to bring together ideas from a wide range of disciplines. Magazines and organizations to do with futurism, started to sprout up, and attract the interest of people from fields as disparate as anthropology, architecture and psychoanalysis. But, as we shall see, it was most pressingly the military in the USA that was attracted to the new discipline. The use of the first atom bomb meant that the rules of the game for the future of war had changed dramatically, and it was painfully apparent – though not exactly welcomed – that new tools for thinking the unthinkable were urgently required.

By a curious turn of fate, the man who first coined and proposed a science of 'futurology' was a Jewish intellectual who had fled fascist Germany. Ossip Flechtheim was a mild-mannered man whose short, neck-less form was a permanent source of amusement to his students at Bates College, New

England, where he spent part of the wartime. Despite appearances, Flechtheim had a long tradition of sticking his neck out. As soon as was decently possible he abandoned his parents' religious faith, and followed the zeitgeist by joining the Communist Party. A life-long humanist, he soon became disillusioned with the dogmatism of the party, and after five years decided to renounce his membership. By then he had moved on to another more pressing cause – the support of the Nazi resistance party Neu Beginnen for which he was detained in 1935 at the age of twenty-five. By a stroke of luck, money or influence (or perhaps all three), he was released and managed to flee to Switzerland. From here he joined, in 1939, a growing number of exiled Jewish intellectuals in America, many of whom were to provide invaluable support and inspiration for Flechtheim's new 'cause'.

It was here in 1943 in America that Flechtheim first seriously argued that universities should teach a real science of the future, and that it should be called Futurology. The initial response was not, it had to be said, overwhelming, though he did proudly register murmurs of approval and interest from a clutch of intellectuals that included writers Aldous Huxley and Thomas Mann as well as an impressive list of philosophers, psychoanalysts and historians that he was rubbing shoulders with at the time. The fact that there were reservations about futurology was due largely to the fact that in 1943 more attention was turned to the 'present' in terms of the war, but also because there was a bit of a tussle about the naming and framing. First of all it was debatable in his circle and in his own mind as to whether it could truly be called a science. 'If we think of the term only in the original meaning of "exact science", Futurology will, no doubt, not qualify,' he wrote. But, Flechtheim got round this by defining science as 'a system of organized knowledge concerning the facts of a particular subject'. Having wriggled his way through that tricky but very important obstacle course, Flechtheim later faced an obscure objection from an English philosopher who said it was doomed to fail because the term, like the word sociology, combined both Latin and Greek word roots (the same misguided and pedantic argument was also once used about the word 'television'). The critic naturally had his own suggestion at the ready – that it should simply be called 'mellontologie' after the Greek word for future. But Flechtheim, a trained lawyer and political scientist, knew that if it was to catch on, it had to be both modern-sounding and a universally and instantly recognizable term.

By the end of the war, Flechtheim was itching to launch futurology properly. He had taken a critical look at the history of the discipline and came to the conclusion that 'since the "dawn of conscience"' the future has been both the sacred preserve of the genius and the happy hunting-ground of the charlatan'. High up on his list of charlatans was Nostradamus who, he bitterly noted, 'had recently become a best seller because of the alleged prophecies they contain about the frightful happenings of our day'. Flechtheim may well have belonged in the genius camp, but in terms of understanding the future saw himself as following a sort of third way which he outlined in a landmark article for an obscure American magazine in 1945. Modestly called 'Teaching the Future', the article set out for the first time his mission in all its glory. There was nothing modest about its objective, though perhaps the smaller-print subtitle 'A Contribution to the Intellectual and Moral Growth of the Participants' was a bit of a giveaway. In this article he argued that the change from 'prophecy with scientific pretensions' to 'prophetic science' was in fact long since under way. This was, he said, thanks to a long tradition of people like Marx, though in this case Flechtheim obviously took more account of effort and output as opposed to accuracy.

'Instead of consulting the stars', proposed Flechtheim, 'the "futurologist" of 1945 can get his clews from historians and sociologists, from philosophers and psychologists, from political scientists and economists. He can make intelligent use of a tremendous reservoir of knowledge'. Flechtheim is magnanimous in his suggestions of theories, ideas and books that prospective analysts of the future should study. He also wholeheartedly recommended the work of fellow humanist Langdon-Davies. Even by 1945, which was nearly ten years after its publication and still five years before he predicted democracy would be dead, it was pretty clear that *A Short History of the Future* was not going to be the prophetic political light that the author hoped it would be. Flechtheim, however, generously – if somewhat diplomatically – said, 'if critically used, it should prove helpful' in future studies. He was on the right train when he said that to really get an accurate picture of the future, it is important to scan ideas from a broad range of thinkers from every field and from every political persuasion, from socialists to conservatives, and 'even of fascists'. He also welcomed the perusal of both dystopias and utopias as well as other 'daring and fantastic' writings such as those by Wells and Huxley which he rightly believed 'may yield insights that are more revealing than the voluminous writings of learned system-builders'. Flechtheim believed that having battled one's way objectively through all these sources 'a productive mind should be capable of presenting a meaningful synopsis of the future'.

Flechtheim taught at several universities during his time in the USA and grumbled loudly about the fact that the educational system was satisfied to simply teach 'what was and what is'. As a Jew who after the war had returned to Germany to work as a lawyer with the US war crimes staff at the Nuremburg trials, he himself knew and understood more than most people about 'what was'. Significantly, it was after his return to the USA in 1947 that he started in earnest to propose teaching what 'could be'. In *Futurology – The New Science of Probability*, published in 1949, he started to set out the function, limits and parameters of the discipline, based on the belief that the future is *not* pre-defined as a linear continuation of present trends. Futurology should, he said, 'limit itself to actual prospective developments trying to establish the degree of their credibility or mathematical probability and be aware of the difference between a prognosis with a high degree of credibility and an accidentally accurate prophecy'. To illustrate this he contrasted two forecasts concerning the First and Second World Wars:

> Frederick Engels ingeniously combined decisive trends in inter-related systems when, a generation before the outbreak of the First World War he predicted prolonged two-front trench warfare and a stalemate in the West as well as a Russian defeat and revolution in the East. On the other hand, H. G. Wells, who in 1933 prophesied the outbreak of the Second World War with only a few months margin of error and quite correctly as an outgrowth of a German-Polish conflict about the Free City of Danzig, may have stepped beyond the limits of more or less reliable forecasting into the twilight of pure chance.

Among the other things that bothered Flechtheim was not just what he called the dominance over the years of the 'lunatic fringe', but the traditional reliance on statistics and data when thinking about the future. What he in effect proposed was a whole new language or philosophy that uses the 'hitherto forbidden future tense'.' The fact remains,' he wrote, 'that ours is not the choice between knowing and not knowing . . . our real and only choice lies between less knowledge and more knowledge.' He had a vision, and the optimistic hope, that just as weather forecasters can help prepare for what is to come, so can futurological predictions enable us to avoid historical, social and cultural catastrophes such as the one he narrowly escaped.

When it came to the forecasting of technological inventions and developments he was a little more sceptical as to the reliability and benefits, believing that 'sheer novelty may be imagined, but cannot be deduced from existing conditions or trends'. Writing on *Forecasting the Future* in 1952, Flechtheim took a wry look at those futurologists who, perhaps emboldened by his new science, were coming up with what he termed a veritable 'history of the pots and pans' of the future. By now, Flechtheim was clearly beginning to enjoy himself in his self-appointed position of the pope of futurism and was liberally quoting pearls of prediction that were increasingly popping up in the media and books. One of his favourites was that 'by 2000 people will wear weather-conditioning belts and lightweight or glass clothing all year round', or that 'the classroom of tomorrow will find children napping while learning subjects far more advanced than today's by means of the dormiphone, which pipes in knowledge to their subconscious'. More worrying, he believed, were those predictions that claimed that by 1960 'industry will be experimenting with automatic factories in which men push buttons and watch instrument dials while machines do the rest'. In later works Flechtheim entertained his readers by quoting lesser-known Russian futurists who in the 1960s were predicting that in the future we would live to be 300 years old and need only one hour's sleep a night.

Hard-core futurology as he would ideally have liked it to be was a bit of a slow starter, but things took off gradually in the 1960s with the arrival of academic courses, futurological publications (including his own called 'Futurum') and even a Futurological Society in Prague. As early as 1966, Flechtheim was looking proudly back and claiming 'since the 1940s systematic concern with the days to come has made tremendous progress . . . At a time when Futurology is on the point of developing into a well-organized, large-scale field encompassing the efforts of many excellent minds in numerous disciplines, the reader may find it interesting to view in retrospect an earlier period, when the art or science of prediction and prognosis was still hardly more than the hobby of a few daring minds.' By the 1970s this 'hobby' of his had become much more politically significant and influential and he envisaged futurology as a 'third power' or what we would today term as a 'third way', between capitalism and communism.

By the time he died in Berlin in 1998 on the eve of his eighty-ninth birthday, Flechtheim had been largely forgotten as the formal founder of futurology. An informal poll of top world futurists at the European Futurists Conference in Lucerne in 2005 revealed that many had never even heard of him. However, those attending the conference who teach future studies at universities and colleges around the world lit up at the sound of his name as if he was the long-lost groom returning at last from the front.

It is naturally no coincidence that many of the formative contributions to future thinking and to the new literature of the future that flourished after the war came from Austrian and German exiles. In the same year that Flechtheim brought out his first paper on futurology, fellow countryman Hermann Hesse published his famous fable for the future, *The Glass*

Bead Game. Hesse had by then also long since left his home-
land, having become a permanent resident of Switzerland in
1919, and in disgust demonstratively renounced his German
citizenship in 1923.

Hesse admitted that he had initially and unwisely welcomed
the Weimar Republic that was established after the First World
War, but he soon withdrew his support when he saw that its
fall was inevitable and that the German people were still
clinging to nationalism. As an outspoken and life-long pacifist,
he had to have his novel *Demian* published under a pseudonym when it first appeared in 1919. It was in this novel that he
first started to experiment with what we now recognize as the
key philosophical concerns of futurism: 'For us mankind was a
distant future toward which we were all on the way, whose
likeness no one knew, and whose laws were nowhere inscribed.' By 1920 he was, however, already seeing 'likenesses',
and forecasting political disaster for Germany. Writing to a
friend, he stated 'in Germany . . . the spiritual mood has
something anarchical but also religious and fanatical; it is a
mood of apocalypse and of a future thousand year Reich.'

By the time he published *The Glass Bead Game* in 1943,
Hesse was on the Nazi blacklist, and many of his worst fears
and predictions had come true. Set in the twenty-third century,
a time when recollections of the twentieth century were vague,
it was both an attempt to take an objective look at the severity
of what was going on, and an escape. The game itself is a
highly sophisticated and complicated one played by intellectuals in the kingdom of Castalia, where the beads on the
abacus symbolize all branches of knowledge. In order to fulfil
his lifelong ambition to be the Master of the Game, the hero
Joseph Knecht needs, not unlike Flechtheim's description of
the ultimate futurologist, to acquire complete knowledge of
aesthetics, scientific arts, maths, music, logic and philosophy.

As Knecht explains of his education, there was 'a tendency toward universality and toward a linking of science and the arts . . . and the highest symbol of this tendency was the Glass Bead Game'. Knecht, whose name means 'servant' or 'slave' in German, finally does become the all-knowing 'Magister Ludi', but gives up the job of honorary futurist when he finally sees the flaws in a life of perfection, order and, above all, intellectual smugness.

The novel, with all its parables and metaphors, was hailed as a *Meisterwerk* by writer Thomas Mann for the 'genuine way it is prophetic and sensitive to the future'. As well as bringing him the Nobel Prize for Literature in 1946, it was also, perhaps a little too enthusiastically, called 'the most imaginative and subtle parable in the entire history of futuristic fiction', by I. F. Clarke in *The Pattern of Expectation*. Hesse himself actually got quite fed up with people trying to dig out specific prophecies about how he saw life in the future, and wriggled out of any specific commitment by claiming that what it represents is 'not an ideal which can be held eternally valid, but rather a possible world which is, however, aware of its relativity'. This get-out clause is rather disingenuous as the same could be claimed of and by most of his literary predecessors.

In keeping with this faux-modesty, Hesse's vision of a future society is deliberately vague when it comes to women, and particularly when it comes to technology. However, there are some interesting moments where he appears – whether by accident or design – to have got on to something . When, for example, one of the leaders writes characters on a small, palm-sized tablet, 'immediately the same signs appeared in the ciphers of the Game, in hundred-fold magnification, upon the giant tablet on the rear partition of the hall'. Hesse criticized blind faith in technology, and was not interested in the details of predicting the applications of wireless hi-tech computer presentations *per se*, but instead preferred to see how such technology could be brought under control to enhance spiritual experience. Hence, when the text is projected, it is simultaneously, in Big Brother style, 'called out from the loudspeakers and broadcast out into the country and the world'.

Hesse did not broadcast himself as a futurist, but as an 'artist-prophet' who believed he could shape the future through espousing spiritual values. As writer Roger Norton explains in his book, *Herman Hesse's Futuristic Idealism*, Hesse 'believed man can mould his future to a degree, but only for the better if his actions proceed from inner awareness and a firm spiritual basis'. Since his death in 1962 Hesse has been largely remembered as a seer and a spiritual dreamer, but there is more than enough evidence to prove that he was essentially a futurist at heart, deeply concerned about what he called the 'dangerous distances' of the future.

In the 1940s and 1950s the 'dangerous distances' were not as far away as some might have liked, and there was increased and intense activity among a small group of people who were desperately trying to figure out just how dangerous, and just how far. One of these was the brilliant Hungarian-born mathematician John von Neumann who, even before the Second World War was over, was thinking about how a Third World War would be conducted. Like Hesse, von Neumann developed a game, but when it comes to strategic thinking about the political future of the world, it makes the Glass Bead Game look like tiddlywinks.

Von Neumann originally developed game theory in 1928 for use in economics when he was just twenty-five years old but it was quickly found to be applicable to everything from Cold War nuclear strategy to foreign policy and, in an emergency, even to his love life. The attraction for futurism is that in his 'game' your predictions about what another person might do will affect your own decision about what to do. It boils down to two deceptively simple outcomes : so-called zero-sum games and non-zero-sum games. In zero-sum games, one side's gain always results in the other's loss (such as in tennis – when one player wins a match, the other loses). But in non-zero-sum games the result can be either a win-win situation or a lose-lose one. In the former, both players collaborate to get a bad umpire changed; in the latter, both lose when the new umpire disqualifies them for collaborating. As David McAdams from MIT put it in 2005, 'game theory is really a frame of mind and once you have it, you see it everywhere.' Rather like futurism.

What game theory did in von Neumann's time was to deliver a new dimension to understanding uncertainty. Most significantly for futurism, it showed that the true source of uncertainty about the future lies with the intentions of others. As Peter L. Bernstein put it in his bestselling book on risk, 'Choosing the alternative that we judge will bring us the highest payoff tends to be the riskiest decision, because it may provoke the strongest defence from players who stand to lose if we have our way.' This means that, for example, any decision about future political or military strategy depends, or should depend, on what you predict the opposition or the enemy is going to do. Applications in business are a little trickier to nail down, as illustrated by a survey by *Fast Company* magazine in 2005 which found no one willing or able to find or admit to a concrete commercial example of its application. Interestingly (or perhaps thankfully), a strategy of optimization does not always bring the best results (just think of all those angry tennis fans in a lose-lose situation). The critical example that revealed game theory at its best, and some would say at its moral worst, was American Cold War strategic thinking, when there was no doubt in many minds that the only way to predict the future was to have power to shape the future.

The Cold War was also one of the biggest and riskiest examples of using game theory, as satirized by Stanley Kubrick's controversial 1964 film *Dr Strangelove, or How I Learned to Love the Bomb*. Much of the film takes place in the War Room, where an incompetent bunch of senior military officials and a menacing wheelchair-bound genius with a mid-European accent are advising the American president. It is a critical and delicate political situation. The military is on red alert as it is revealed that a lone unauthorized American bomber has broken through the Soviet defences. On the hot line the Soviet ambassador reveals that if the pilot releases a bomb, it will trigger their secret Doomsday machine, resulting in a nuclear Armageddon. The President's mysterious strategic advisor, Dr Strangelove, is faced with the ultimate lose-lose situation and cries out with a strangulated Hungarian accent, 'The whole point of having a Doomsday machine is lost if you keep it a secret. Why didn't you tell the world?' As von Neumann himself said, 'Real life consists of bluffing, of little tactics of deception, of asking yourself what is the other man going to think I mean to do. And that is what games are about in my theory.'

Von Neumann was, at least in part, the original Dr Strangelove. He was not quite as mad, manic, or menacing as Kubrick's caricature, but he did have a distinctive Hungarian accent, and at one point wielded an extraordinary amount of political power over the future of America. He had not only worked at Los Alamos on the first atomic bomb, but more significantly during the Cold War he very nearly convinced President Eisenhower that, following his principles of game theory, the only possible action was to strike first and drop the hydrogen bomb on the Russians before it was too late. Rather than the lose-lose situation envisaged by Kubrick (everyone dies), this would have resulted in a win-lose situation for the Americans (destruction of Russia, if it did not have a secret Doomsday machine), as opposed, say, to the win-win situation we have today (no Cold War).

His strategy towards women was also pretty direct, and a compulsive sex drive led him to apply game theory to his personal life. Writing to his second wife after being caught cheating, he tried to turn it into a win-win situation by begging, 'I hope you have forgiven my modest venture in double-crossing.' Apart from women, his other main weakness was for food, and his prodigious consumption of Viennese cakes and pastries brought him the moniker of the 'man who counted everything except calories'. Living with a gentleman genius may have had its advantages but clearly also its set-backs. As biographer Norman Macrae ruefully points out, he was 'excessively polite to everybody except ... two long suffering wives'.

In the 1950s, when von Neumann was dying of advanced bone cancer (very possibly the result of his work on the bomb), he was still regularly whisked off under top security to and from the White House from his hospital bed. His crippled body was confined to a wheelchair, but he still commanded, Dr Strangelove-style, the attention of President Eisenhower. When he died in 1957, he left an extraordinary legacy. Not only had he almost single-handedly brought about a Third World War (or even possibly the end of the world), but behind the scenes had played a key role in the future development of the computer. While at the Institute for Advanced Study at Princeton he assembled a large prototype computer in the boiler room. It was his early version of one of the first computers known as MANIAC (Mathematical Analyzer, Numerator, Integrator and Calculator). In this field von Neumann's expertise was much in demand. He was a frequent consultant on ENIAC, the first programmable general-purpose digital computer, and he had plenty to say on the future of computers. In his lecture series at Princeton he presented the way he foresaw it. Computer technology, he said, would eventually lead to the development of a 'theoretical brain'. A self-replicating programme would enable computers to 'evolve' and reproduce themselves, correcting mistakes of their previous generation, and eventually becoming more intelligent than simple analogue humans. According to legend, he also once advised the US government that the country would need exactly eighteen computers in the future.

The name and acronym MANIAC could well have been used for von Neumann himself. He was incapable of even sleeping or driving without trying to solve a mathematical sum or six. His wives complained he did sums while tucked up in bed, and he relished driving in traffic jams and rush hour because they present a problem: how can so many different vehicles get through the same space at different rates of speed? On the open road, with no challenges in the foreseeable future, his interest lapsed, and he was, according to one terrified travelling companion, apt to run into trees at 70 miles per hour. But while von Neumann was busy driving into inanimate objects, womanizing *and* working on the ultimate über-strategy for the political future of the world, the down-to-earth nuts and bolts of future war were being mapped out by another Budapest-born mathematical prodigy.

Theodore von Kármán was, by a strange coincidence, like von Neumann, a charismatic figure with an eye for the ladies and a talent for military strategy. Kármán grew up in an intellectual middle-class Jewish family, dominated by his for-

midable professor father who had been 'ennobled' by the
Austro-Hungarian Emperor for his work in education. Maurice von Kármán had not only reformed the country's second-
ary-school system, he had also founded MINTA, a 'nursery for
the elite', whose graduates have included several renowned
scientists, including von Neumann. Despite his preoccupation
with encouraging talent and experiential learning (such as
learning Latin from public statue engravings), Maurice actively dissuaded Theodore from showing off and pursuing his
prodigious mathematical talents. By the age of six he could
multiply five- and six-digit numbers in his head, but his father,
worried he would turn into a clown at the family's legendary
parties, guided him towards engineering which he hoped
would not encourage party tricks.

Ironically, it was for his work in engineering for which
Kármán was eventually to receive lashings of awe and attention, and gain him the accolade of the father of modern
aerospace and supersonic aviation and, to all intents and
purposes, that of futurist. For all his father's cajoling, what
really in the end inspired Kármán to pursue aeronautics full
time was something that happened while he was a student in
Paris in 1908. In a tired, happy and very possibly inebriated
state after an all-night student party, Kármán was persuaded
by a friend to forgo bed and instead watch a flight by the
French aviation pioneer Henri Farman. Not only was Farman's 2-kilometre flight successful, he had also unwittingly
inspired the young Kármán to concentrate his work on pushing forward the possibilities in aeronautical engineering.
Though not, naturally, to the detriment of his party-going.

After the First World War Kármán led the development of
the first helicopter, and by 1926 his reputation and talent had
taken him to America, where he soon became a leading figure
in a number of organizations and research institutes devoted to

aeronautics. As the political situation deteriorated in Germany Kármán spent less and less time in Europe and by 1936 had become an American citizen (one year before von Neumann). Soon his pioneering work on rocket-propelled missiles at the Guggenheim Aeronautical Laboratory of the California Institute of Technology (GALCIT) had him and his colleagues branded as 'The Suicide Club' after the extremely dangerous nature of their experiments. As well as getting into serious trouble for a misfired motor that sent a toxic cloud over five floors of the GALCIT building, his work brought him to the attention of the top military brass.

Kármán thus found himself, one bright and breezy September day in 1944, in a limousine at the end of the runway at New York's La Guardia airport, poised to become the most powerful military futurist of his time. Inside the car was the commanding General of the Army Air Forces, Hap Arnold, who had just ejected his chauffeur and aide. 'I am not interested in this war. We've won this war,' roared the general as soon as they were alone. 'What I am interested in is what will be the shape of the air war, of air power, in five years, or ten, or sixty-five.' It sounds suspiciously like something out of a cliché-packed B-movie – an all-powerful, cigar-chewing commander with an eccentric Eastern European rocket scientist, hell bent on winning the next war. Not quite Dr Strangelove, but almost. But in fact Arnold was not just concerned with the next war and 'avoiding future national peril' but believed that the future stability of America depended on staying ahead in aeronautical science, and that Kármán was the best man for the job.

It was, as Kármán's biographer Michael H. Gorn put it, a beautiful day to discuss the future, but Arnold was certainly not in the mood or of the inclination to indulge in any small talk about the weather and got straight to the point. 'Gather a group of practical scientists for all the new things,' he demanded, 'I want to know what the impact of jet propulsion is, of atomic energy, of electronics. Get a group . . . and make me a report.' Kármán was caught by surprise and barely had time to object, let alone think through the prospect. Having hastily agreed to the challenge, Kármán, with the power of the great God at Delphi, made his own demands. 'I can do this only under one condition; that nobody gives me orders – and I don't have to give orders to anybody else.' Arnold reassured Kármán that he was the only person he had to answer to, saying, 'I will be your only boss.' In fact it was to be the general himself who jovially – if not perhaps a touch ironically – always referred to Kármán as 'the Boss'.

This was the ultimate challenge for an aeronautical visionary like Kármán, and he lost no time in getting together a team of experts who became known unofficially as the 'Kármán Circus', and officially as the Army Air Forces Scientific Advisory Group. They took to the task like the best Delphic intelligence gatherers, and by December 1945, after countless meetings and a whiplash tour of European Allied and enemy research centres and experts, they were ready. The report, a mere thirty-four monographs in twelve volumes, was after some wrangling, entitled *Toward New Horizons* and landed like a live bomb on a delighted Arnold's desk. In *Where We Stand*, one of the two monographs which Kármán authored, he extrapolated from the 'fundamental realities' of post-war air power. Based on what he had seen in Germany, he predicted that aircraft would reach speeds beyond the velocity of sound, and believed 'we cannot hope to secure air superiority without entering the supersonic speed range'. He foresaw developments in 'pilotless' aircraft, in-flight refuelling to reach remote targets, and that enemy aircraft would be intercepted by target-seeking missiles. He also wrote about the potential use of guided missiles, and heat-seeking, radar-homing and television-guided missiles. There were two key potential developments the group predicted would change the face of air power and thus world political power. First, jet propulsion, which was making great strides thanks to new discoveries of heat-resistant materials; and second, atomic energy. The latter, once harnessed as energy, could lead to complete – and potentially worldwide – command of the skies, as the planes would have an unlimited flying range. When it came to atomic weapons, he hinted at von Neumann's game theory when he forewarned 'future methods of aerial warfare . . . call for a reconsideration of all present plans'.

Kármán had more than fulfilled the expectations of Arnold, who was 'enormously pleased' with the boss. The power to control the future was there written out before him, and *New Horizons* was a momentous achievement that set a new standard in long-range technological forecasting. Hailed as the *Magna Carta* of postwar airforce R&D, it laid the foundations and the impetus for US aircraft and rocket programmes for many years to come and spawned new scientific cooperation. Kármán clearly revelled in the celebrity and notoriety that he gained from the report and his subsequent work, and became a regular on the after-dinner-speech circuit. He was an excellent raconteur who compared his speeches to 'a lady's dress – short, interesting, and covering the essential points'. Even at the age of eighty he was still holding his audience, and making bold and optimistic political and military predictions for the future. At a press conference in May 1961, he wooed the assembled journalists with his belief that the 'missile gap' between the USSR and the USA would close within the next five years, that nuclear war was unlikely and that the next few years would see America's space efforts surpassing that of the Russians.

In February 1963, two months before he died, Kármán was presented with America's very first National Medal of Science by John F. Kennedy in the Rose Garden of the White House. Crippled by arthritis, Kármán was a bit wobbly on his feet, and Kennedy reached out to help him negotiate the stairs to the reception. 'Mr President,' quipped Kármán, waving him away, 'one does not need help going down, only going up.' A reference not only to his beloved pet topic, jet propulsion, but also perhaps to his optimistic view of the future.

It was the work and ideas of people like Kármán who provided ammunition for the imagination of a growing number of science-fiction writers in the 1950s. One of the undisputed greats was the Russian-born Issac Asimov, whose formative futurist years can be traced back to his parents' candy store where he greedily gobbled up the stories of the science-fiction magazines such as *Amazing Stories* that were on sale there. Later he revealed just how bad he thought some of them were. 'One only has to read the science fiction of the late 1930s to see how abysmally blind it was to what was about to happen . . . Story after story talks about robots; not one talks about computers.' Asimov went on to study chemistry at Columbia but was drawn back to his childhood fascination for science fiction and began writing it himself in 1950. From then on it seems Asimov never stopped writing, and by the time he died in 1992 he had written around 400 books, including everything from mysteries to popular science and even a book of limericks and a guide to the Bible. Asimov was more than a prolific writer – he was a self-confessed 'writing machine' who claimed that unlike other writers he actually enjoyed writing (others, he teased, just liked getting ideas and being published but were not so keen on the bit in the middle). By his own admission, his most enduring contributions to the science-fiction genre were *Three Laws of Robotics*, a complete set of ethics for robots, and the *Foundation* series.

These were also the books that contributed most to his reputation as a futurist, and later brought him to the attention of the World Future Society. Of all his ideas, perhaps most seductive for futurists is his fictional concept of 'psychohistory' from the *Foundation* series, the first of which was published in 1951. Developed in the Galactic Empire in the far future the science of psychohistory is 'that branch of mathematics which deals with the reactions of human conglomerates to fixed social and economic stimuli'. Using this, Hari Seddon can predict 1,500 years into the future in detail and even further in rough outline. Rather disappointingly, because it is a statistical science, it is noted that it 'cannot predict the future of a single man with any accuracy'. In politics, this is what sociologist Daniel Bell has dubbed 'Brzezinski's Law'. Brzezinski, an expert in communist affairs, was once baited on American TV for his lack of foresight about Khrushchev's downfall, and retorted, 'If Khrushchev could not predict his own downfall, how do you expect me to do it?'

Asimov's theory of psychohistory is in essence what Wells believed when he declared that 'the events of the year AD 400 are as fixed, settled and unchangeable as the events of the year 1600', but is also a theory about the rules and predictive nature of mass behaviour that is popular with trend watchers and predictors today. James Surowiecki's 2004 book *The Wisdom of Crowds*, subtitled *Why the Many are Smarter than the Few and How Collective Wisdom Shapes Business, Economies, Societies, and Nations*, has, for example, been called Asimov's science of mass behaviour but without the fiction.

Under the guise of fiction, Asimov asks in *Foundation* all those things futurists always wanted to know about the future but were too afraid to ask. 'Can the overall history of the human race be changed?' Yes, replies Seddon, but with great difficulty. The problem, he explains, is inertia. 'The psycho-historic trend of a planet of people contains a huge inertia. To be changed it must be met with something possessing a similar inertia. Either as many people must be concerned, or if the number of people be relatively small, enormous time for change must be allowed.' Some things, it seems, never change. *Foundation* begins somewhere in the 12,000th year of the Galactic Era where, despite 'gravitic repulsion' elevators and 25 million inhabited planets, people are still rummaging around in their pockets for coins to buy paper tickets, and queue patiently for taxis (albeit space ones).

Asimov was more imaginative when it came to the future of robots. His first robot story was about a robot nanny, and he is credited with introducing the term into the English language (it originally comes from the Czech word for forced labour). But what *was* original and also much copied, was Asimov's concept of a future code of conduct for robots that he formulated in 1941:

1. A robot must not injure a human being, or, through inaction, allow a human being to come to harm.
2. A robot must obey the orders given it by human beings unless they conflict with the First Law.
3. A robot must protect its own existence as long as such protection does not conflict with the First or Second Laws.

These were ethical questions that, in one form or another, could be said to have already begun with Mary Shelley's *Frankenstein* in 1816, and most importantly were to play a role in the debate around the development and ethics of artificial intelligence. As Michael White, who wrote an unauthorized biography of Asimov, says, 'Despite the fact that in the early 1940s the science of robotics was a purely fictional thing, he somehow knew that one day they would provide the foundation for a set of real laws.' These laws were not only played out in his collection of stories *I, Robot*, but also to great gratuitous effect in the 2004 screen version. For all their 'futuristic' leanings, Asimov's robot stories were often not so much prediction as humorous provocation, with characters such as Susan Calvin, a 'robopsychologist' who regards robots as companions, 'a cleaner better breed than we are', and even a robot who knows 'all about everything plus a bit on the side', but hates maths and is curiously addicted to trashy romantic space novels.

Alongside his science fiction, Asimov did in fact make some 'real' predictions, such as when in 1964 he said that one day people would realize the full extent of the dangers of passive smoking. He also accurately predicted the appearance and functions of the pocket calculator, but then, for some bizarre reason, published a book on the delights of the slide-rule, which was instantly made redundant by the appearance that very week of the first calculators in the shops! By 1979 he had digressed (albeit with brilliant scientific persuasion and integrity) into that staple of much futurist thinking, alarmism. His book *A Choice of Catastrophes* was a spectacular display of potential disasters facing the planet – scaled from First Class catastrophes such as the collapse of the stars and the end of humanity, to mere Fifth Class catastrophes that involve the destruction of civilization resulting from such things as a depletion of resources. These were, he insisted, not inevitables, nor predictions, but possibilities. Even likelihoods. Such as his forecast of 'a future in which busy career women could contribute egg cells to be fertilized and then implanted in surrogate mothers'. As the book moves deftly from spectacular cosmic disasters (not really worth worrying about, he concludes) to those that are 'more immediate and dangerous', he throws a crumb of hope into the futurist feast of gloom. Most of the catastrophes are, in fact, avoidable if, as he recommends, we free ourselves of our planetary chauvinism. If, he concludes, 'we can spread into space to lose our vulnerabilities. We will no longer be dependent on one planet or one star . . . It is that which is, and should be, our goal.'

Futurists come in all measures, and with all sorts of hang-ups. Asimov was, for instance, terrified of flying, so space flights were a kind of mental therapy. Strangely, he also enjoyed enclosed small spaces, and his idea of heaven on earth was to run a newspaper stand down in the depths of the New York subway. But none perhaps was quite so strange as Bernard Wolfe. A part-time hack writer of pornography, Wolfe gives a whole new perspective to the notion of hard-core futurism. Like Asimov he was born to Jewish immigrant parents, but he led an extraordinarily bohemian life, flitting opportunistically between the intellectual extremes of Trotskyism, Hollywood, pornography and Cybernetics. Wolfe 'vaguely remembers having spent some years at Yale', where he studied psychology and dabbled in Stalinism. Restless from an early age, he soon became disaffected with the Stalinists and took up with the more edgy Trotskyites who seemed to be where the future was at. After graduating Wolfe found that working for Trotskyite publications such as *The New International* and *The Militant* was good writing experience, but that it did not satisfy his thirst for being where the action was. Hence in January 1937 he arrived expectantly in Mexico to take up the extraordinary post of Trotsky's secretary and bodyguard. Wolfe's wanderlust and very possibly a personality clash got the better of him, and while this unique position was to last just a few months, it was to provide the juice for his best-known novel about Trotsky's assassination, *The Great Prince Died*.

Around 1939, almost ten years before he sat down to thrash out his first futurist novel, Wolfe found much-needed employment as a writer of pornography through a judicious meeting with Anaïs Nin and Henry Miller in Greenwich Village. It was while living in New York that he churned out over ten such novels in one year, proudly earning the very grand sum of a dollar a page. Wolfe's decision to shift to writing fiction came in 1946 following a period as a military correspondent for science magazines, though this presupposes that his erotic writing was actually based on experience rather than imagination (for juicy details see his *Memoirs of a Not Altogether Shy Pornographer*). Wolfe had ostensibly moved on from writing pornography, but reading his 1952 novel *Limbo '90* you feel he never left it completely. If ever there was such a thing as futurist-porn, then this is it. Set in the year 1990, it is a truly shocking and sick sado-masochistic tale of life in the future and was hailed as one of the first post-war antiwar novels. It is also one of the great forgotten futurist novels in which with great and terrifying effect Wolfe brings together – Magister Ludi style – everything he breathed in the rarefied restless air of this period, and everything he learned in psychiatry, pornography and new technology.

Essentially it is a book about pacifism, asking to what lengths society and governments could go in the future to prevent war. As the plot develops we meet the 'amps' – young men whose aggressive war-mongering instincts have been pacified by the voluntary amputation of their limbs and they proudly wear 'pros' (prosthetics). 'There is no pacifism without passivity,' boasts one of the nastier characters, 'disarmament can't amount to much, unless, well, a man is really disarmed ... through amputeeism you make man into a perfect pacifist.' In Wolfe's perverted logic and imagination, there is even a hierarchy among the amps – with the 'uni-' (with just one false limb) well below the 'tri-'. A case of the more the merrier, or maybe the more the milder.

It is, as one critic pointed out, worth reading for the 'gloriously awful puns alone', the play on the meaning of limb and limbo, and the bold and barely disguised literary homage to mavericks such as Rimbaud, the French poet who had long since forewarned of the 'age of assassins'. But most of all he had a futurist's knack for picking up on the groundswell of fear and hopes that lie unanswered and unresolved. Whether he offers the most attractive solution is another matter, but he gives a deep insight into the fear and fascination of the future of technology that pervaded the 1950s. Wolfe did not hide the fact that the idea of controlling the mind and body was heavily inspired by the work of Norbert Wiener. In 1948 Wiener coined the term cybernetics for 'the science of control and communication in the animal and the machine', and Wolfe appreciatively names one of the ships in the story the *SS Norbert Wiener*.

Faced not only with a gruesome vision of life as an amputee of both the mind and body, the reader also has to digest the prospect of war in this future. 'World War III, it's clear,' exclaims one figure, ' is the first real war we've ever had. The essence of warness. War brought for the first time from the realm of concept all the way into the realm of thumping fact. For it is the first homicidal chess game in which the full gaming board has been used and all the pawns thrown into action with perfect mathematical precision. It was bound to happen of course. Once men stopped manufacturing gods, they began to manufacture machines. Whence EMSIAC, the god-in-the-machine, the god-machine . . .' This is Wolfe let loose on the power of von Neumann's game theory, and EMSIAC is an

unhappy marriage of MANIAC and ENIAC, the first electronic computers that von Neumann worked on. At one point
in the novel, EMSIAC is missing its sparring partner-cum-
enemy (another computer), and goes out of control like the
unstoppable Doomsday machine in Dr Strangelove. 'We could
have predicted it,' rants a character in the novel, 'if we'd had
our eyes open, we would have seen it coming. EMSIAC is
simply the end development of something that's been threatening for a long time in human affairs, especially in modern
times . . . I'd call it the Steamroller . . . What the Steamroller
does to the human spirit is immeasurably worse than anything
shrapnel and atomic blast could possibly do to the human
flesh, and infinitely more lasting.' The rest of the plot involves
people trying to wrest back their dignity and control from the
computers, and ends with the timely words, 'What prognoses
this day?'

For October 1972, Wolfe indulged in some wishful thinking
and envisaged the destruction and disappearance of Los Alamos, home of the atomic bomb. But despite his wild predictions, he believed 'anyone who "paints a picture" of some
coming year is kidding – he's only fancying up something in
the present or past, not blue-printing the future . . . this book is
a bilious rib on 1950 – on what 1950 might have been like if it
had been allowed to fulfil itself, if it had gone on being 1950,
only more and more so, for four more decades.' Wolfe even
went so far in the afterword as to admit 'what 1990 will really
look like I haven't the slightest idea . . . I don't even know if
there is going to be a 1990.' For Wolfe himself there was not to
be a 1990. He died of a heart attack in 1985 at the age of
seventy, having lived life to the full. He was lovingly immortalized by his biographer Caroline Geduld as a short, loud,
cigar-chomping, Stalin look-alike. The public image of the
born raconteur and showman who enjoyed the high life with

his actress wife in their deluxe Beverly Hills house is somewhat at odds with his pessimistic and perverse vision of the future in *Limbo '90*. His real conviction, and the zeitgeist that he captured so well, was poetically zipped up in the afterword, where he wrote simply, 'on the spurious map of the future . . . I have to inscribe, as did the medieval cartographers over all the terrifying areas outside their ken: HERE LIVE LIONS.'

In the same year that *Limbo '90* shocked a vulnerable public, the doors of another lion's den were thrown open. This time the ringmaster was Robert Jungk, with his jauntily titled work *Tomorrow is Already Here,* which as well as being an oxymoron was about as far from being jaunty as it was from being optimistic. A grimly fascinating diary of his extensive research as a journalist in America, it first appeared in German in 1952, and quickly established itself along with its author as a cult classic of gloomsday future thinking. Tucked inside the book, the subtitle – *Scenes from a Man-Made World* – reveals his intentions, and like a tired tourist guide who has lost the ability to enjoy his travels, Jungk illustrates with each place he visits something (and in the end everything) that is wrong with America and the world.

Fear for the future prowls across each page as Jungk writes with eloquent amazement at all the technological innovations and changes being introduced into society, and the ways in which man will have to adapt to cope with them. His fear is that 'Americans do not care, as do thinkers in other countries, to philosophize about the future but rather to do something about it: to conquer it and, in so far as is humanly possible, control its direction and marching steps.' The book sweeps with a series of snapshots across the USA, from Hollywood which he titles 'Beauty on the Market', to 'The Weather Makers' in Denver, Colorado. Jungk was a determined and canny journalist and managed to inveigle his way into both ordinary and odd places, from factory canteens to Einstein's lecture room at Princeton and most impressively into Los Alamos, 'The Place Marked Secret'. Jungk reserves particular vehemence for Endicott, the quiet New York State town that is immortalized as the birthplace of computers.

In the chapter entitled 'Robots in the Office' Jungk laments that Endicott is the first place 'to produce mechanical brains in quantity and has thereby become the starting-point of a development which may well have consequences at least as far-reaching as the mass production of motor cars'. The man responsible for this transgression was, according to Jungk, the founder of IBM, Thomas J. Watson, who in 1937 had been awarded a medal by Hitler for the punchcard machines that the Nazi regime used for tabulating census data. After the outbreak of the war, Watson returned the medal, albeit a little too late for Jungk's taste. Perhaps not surprisingly, Jungk likens Watson's presence in the town to that of a dictator, noting that his portrait hangs 'in hundreds of rooms inside and outside the factory' embellished with his famous motto THINK that 'gleams over every door, leaps at you from every wall . . .' Jungk gleefully echoed Orwell's thought-police when he recorded the 'ready-made' answers given to visitors. ' "I AM THE MOST SATISFIED MANAGER," purrs an executive . . . "WE ARE THE HAPPIEST WORKERS", say, at the lightest tap, the freshly shaven gentlemen and pleasantly smiling girls.' When Jungk moves on to see how the mechanical brains (implying both the machines *and* the people making them) are used in government offices for census-taking and social insurance, he claims 'it gave me a still clearer presentiment of the office of the future'.

In fact, visiting Endicott did not stir up just Jungk's fear of the future, but fear from his past. Born in Berlin to a Jewish family in 1913, he was just nineteen years old when Hitler came to power. Arrested for anti-Nazi activities the day after the Reichstag fire, Jungk was soon released thanks to 'good fortune and good friends'. Stripped of German nationality and status he left for Paris to study at the Sorbonne, but just two years later had smuggled himself illegally back into the Reich to work for an underground press-service. His unrelenting anti-Nazi activities took him to Czechoslovakia, Paris, Switzerland and, eventually in 1947, to America, where he worked as a journalist until 1953.

During these six years Jungk did not lose his highly tuned instinct for sniffing out what he called 'the approach of tyranny on every tainted breeze'. One of the most extraordinary chapters which reveals the precarious nature of prediction is 'The Electronic Oracle' about the computer that saved the world (well, almost). In April 1951 Jungk wangled his way into the National Bureau of Standards in Washington. It was a day of political excitement and unrest. The papers were reporting that General Douglas MacArthur, 'a famous war hero', had been 'brusquely dismissed'. 'Do you know,' said Jungk's guide as they approached two low buildings, 'the decision to call off the General was fundamentally taken in these two sheds?' Jungk was perplexed as he had assumed the decision had come from President Truman. The buildings he was looking at housed the Standards Eastern Automatic Computer (SEAC), and as he explains, 'with the best will in the world I was unable to grasp any possible connection between this highly developed laboratory instrument and the political *affaire célèbre* of the day.'

By now Jungk was fairly un-shockable, but even he admitted that he was rather taken aback to learn that SEAC spoke the deciding word.

You see [it was explained to him], the General stood for a strategy which would have led our country on to the brink or even into the middle of a world war [MacArthur had asked Truman for permission to use nuclear weapons on China]. Here in Washington there were many adherents of the strong policy. The President might perhaps have had to bow before them in the end if SEAC had not delivered an objective judgement against which there was no reasonable argument. We ran calculations on the thinking machine for several days which we formerly would not have attempted to do at all because it would have taken years. We had to work out how American economy in all its sectors would react to a sudden entry into war at this moment. SEAC gave the answer in clear, unambiguous numbers . . . every strategic variant was figured out by SEAC down to its final consequence. And these computations were the strongest trump in the President's hand when he decided against the General and his policy.

This story about the so-called Oracle of Washington in 'The Little White House' was a portent of things to come and the growing fears surrounding who or what actually controls the future. It set Jungk on a road of discovery, and the more he looked into the part played by electronic brains in planning and prediction, the more he found. Until one day, Jungk had a kind of epiphany when he 'realized with astonishment that the *machine à gouverner* dreamed of by Utopians in past centuries had become a reality'. Despite the fact that it could be claimed that SEAC had in effect saved the world with its predictions, Jungk was still highly critical of the belief that an electronic brain could give credence to the idea that 'to govern is to foresee'. For if, as some believe, the only way to predict the future is to have power to shape the future, Jungk certainly did not want a computer (nor come to think of it, a game theorist) making the decisions.

Jungk did not just reserve his fears about the future for high-level politics and electronics, but also warns of the 'tragedy of skyscraper building'. In the chapter 'The Church and the Skyscraper' he recalls the story of a plane crashing though the fog into the New York Empire State building in July 1945 in which eleven people died. Jungk eerily describes the one and only witness, a Dictaphone machine which continued running and recorded the whole tragedy. 'It was a sound picture of the end of a world, the end of a creation as sublime as it was rash.' Rash too, he believed, were the things going on behind the doors of industrial firms which he accused of being in a position to 'make the future'. This he warned 'is particularly true in one connection: the conscious furtherance or curbing of new technical inventions'. One of the firms that came under his scrutiny was the chemical firm Du Pont. At the headquarters in Wilmington, Delaware, he paid a memorable visit to a development department where employees were working on everything from fibres to fuels. Here he got himself introduced to 'the Seventies', which he soon realized, referred not to the age of the gentlemen, but to the expected arrival date of products they were working on. One of the laboratories even had 'AD 2000' written on the door. As his eager guide explained, it was no joke. Inside the Experimental Station there were men seriously at work on what they termed 'educated guesses' based on careful observation and monitoring of trends in technical science and economy. He was shown 'tables with chemical formulae that resembled family trees. But instead of going back into the past they reached out into the future'. Mendeleyev, who had predicted the existence of several chemicals, would have been delighted, but Jungk was characteristically torn between wonder and suspicion as he was shown through an Aladdin's cave of blueprints for the future; from a lubricating oil that will not freeze ('we'll be able to produce it in 1965 at the latest'), fibres to weave shirts for hot climates, and a new building material that would emit light and make all lamps unnecessary. Most proudly, predicted one scientist for 2010, 'is the dream of mankind: synthetic nourishment, arrived at by imitation of the processes of nature'.

What frightened Jungk the most was the cavalier way that many of the people he had encountered up to now in his life, such as Hitler, were on intimate terms with tomorrow and the day after. As he remarked of the scientist at Du Pont (which he reminds us had begun with the production of gunpowder, and was now equipping the first hydrogen bomb factory), 'he was as sure of the future as the self-righteous are of the Kingdom of Heaven.' Jungk was not one to sit around and do nothing; he wanted not just to understand the future, but have the power to shape it. His first reaction was to join the anti-nuclear movement, and then in 1962 to invent and implement 'Future Workshops'. His motto was that the future belonged to everyone – not just the computers, politicians and scientists – and the workshops were aimed at empowering ordinary people who were, like him, 'not prepared to wait and see, or to grin and bear it'. Ever since he had failed in Switzerland to persuade the foreign correspondents about the Holocaust, he had 'looked for ways that people can fight back and can influence the course of events'.

With high hopes and a head full of idealism, Jungk went marching off back to Europe in search of ordinary people's visions of the future to develop what he termed 'human forecasting'. His first workshops were, he admitted in his book *Future Workshops,* a disappointing disaster. The participants were more interested in moaning and drinking coffee than pondering on the existential nature of things to come. He was particularly discouraged after a visit to a Viennese factory in the mid-1960s when he tried to motivate young factory and office workers to talk about their dreams for tomorrow's world. Most did not have a clue and, worse still, recalled Jungk, if they said anything at all, they simply parroted the government line. At the end of the first day, Jungk went home in a huff. The next day was not much better and when he finally snapped at them, they retorted, 'Why don't you tell us what future would be best for us? After all, you're the future researcher, it's your job, not ours.' It was, feared Jungk, the 'man in the street' syndrome (who famously does not know what he wants, and needs to be told). But soon Jungk's independent Institut für Zukunftsfragen (Institute for Questions on the Future) in Vienna, which in 1964 was one of the first of its kind, had developed new techniques and tricks. Even today, more than a decade after his death in 1994, his future workshop methods guide people to their solution for the future through the crucial phases of 'moaning', 'fantasy' and 'reality' and are particularly popular with grassroots organizations in Germany and Austria.

Jungk is probably one of the few people along with Ossip Flechtheim who in the 1950s would have been flattered and even deeply understood what it meant to be called a real futurologist. They both not only shared a similar and traumatic German-Jewish biography but were to provide much mutual support for the 'cause'. In Jungk's 1965 foreword to Flechtheim's *History and Futurology*, he congratulates his colleague on his progress with it, but laments that futurology is 'still awaiting official academic recognition'. Jungk and Flechtheim were both instrumental in getting futurology on its feet and democratizing it, but while the latter concerned himself more with the philosophy and politics of the future, Jungk focussed more on practical ideas such as workshops and the establishment of 'prognostic cells' that would be linked in a vast network into a kind of 'world brain'.

In his one (relatively) optimistic chapter in *Tomorrow is Already Here*, Jungk describes his visit to a famous prognostic cell, the Institute for Advanced Studies (IAS) in Princeton, New Jersey. In 'The Return of the Thinker' Jungk marvels at the presence of great figures like Einstein, who potters past him 'entirely in a dream of beautiful equations'. The IAS is not only unique for the calibre of its guests, but for the fact that it is strictly devoted to theoretical and intellectual enquiry and there are no laboratories or machines (hence von Neumann's 'practical' computer-building experiment had to be carried out covertly in the boiler room). As Jungk noted, 'nobody's work is prescribed, and the result of labor belongs to the person who had performed it. The reckoning he owes is to himself and his conscience.' This is just the kind of thing Jungk appreciated – especially the fact that the new head of the institute was Robert Oppenheimer, who had been a key figure in the construction of the first atomic bomb and then repented and decided to 'work for the preservation of the good things for which man lives'.

What, asked Jungk, was this thinking tank really working on? What, he wondered, was the big agenda? 'I suppose,' explained one member to him, 'on the real foundations of tomorrow. All that you've seen in America in the way of technical developments is not what is to come but what is already passing . . . New and true thoughts must be found for the practice of tomorrow. I hope that some of them may be developed by us here.' Jungk was still sceptical. 'So don't you think the future will be simply an intensification of this alarming present?' he asked. 'No,' replied the man, 'in spite of everything there is hope.'

CHAPTER 5

SURPRISE-FREE FUTURES

. . . they lived in a world in which you could talk about future in the plural – there'd be 'futures' you could choose from.

Hans Speier

In a line-up of candidates for a TV 'Would You Trust This Person With The Future?' competition, Herman Kahn might well have come last. One of the world's foremost military strategists and an expert on nuclear war, Kahn had a penchant for black humour and was tipped by many as the real inspiration for *Dr Strangelove*, the film on which he was a well-chosen advisor. And if that wouldn't have been enough to get him voted off in the first round, he predicted that by 2000 human hibernation would become a form of therapy, 'non-harmful' methods of 'overindulging' would be available (he weighed around 300 pounds), and that we would soon be able to programme our dreams.

Herman Kahn was not as crazy or frightening as he first sounds, and he was just as funny and could be twice as shocking. He was also one of the most influential futurists of his time. His direct approach accentuated the growing divide between literary and practical futurism that had begun after the Second World War. Kahn started his career as a futurist at the RAND Corporation, the non-profit think tank of the US Air Force that was set up in the mid-1940s by General Hap Arnold to gather a broad range of 'pictures of the future'. This hive of over 200 minds included not just scientists, but psychologists, economists, mathematicians, logicians, sociologists and even a lone astronomer. RAND was placed in Santa Monica, so the legend goes, to be as far away as possible from the meddling of politicians in Washington, although some veterans have hinted that the beach was rather nice too. Kahn in fact loved swimming, but the real reason he took up the post was that it gave him the opportunity to exercise his brain.

Kahn had majored in physics and worked as a mathematician for several companies, but financial hardship had driven him to the brink of taking up a lucrative but dull career in real estate. Kahn was, however, rescued at the eleventh hour by a fellow physicist who recommended him to RAND in 1947. At first people at the corporation could not work out if he really was a genius, or simply off the planet (or possibly both), but they snapped him up for the physics division anyway. By 1948 he was promoted to senior physicist, and had soon hopped on to the advisory board studying nuclear-powered airplanes. As Kahn recalled of the latter, it was the place he 'first came in contact with the philosophy which is willing to ask any question and tackle any problem'. RAND was also the place that he met Jane Heilner, a smart New Yorker whose job was to enter formulae on calculators and perform computations.

When she was assigned to work for Kahn, he helpfully showed her how to compute three equations simultaneously, and after just three days she demanded a transfer. As she later told Kahn's biographer Sharon Ghamari-Tabrizi, 'I didn't understand a word of what he was saying.' Kahn was never one to shy away from a challenge: not only did he persuade her to marry him but he got to work developing and applying von Neumann's Game Theory, scenario-thinking and systems analysis to war strategy. What was most extraordinary about Kahn is not just that he revelled in thinking about the unthinkable, but the manner in which he did so. Kahn was like a loose cannon at RAND, not just in terms of his rotund form and the manner in which he bounced gregariously from office to office grilling his colleagues, but in his thinking about the future.

There was no precedent for the Cold War situation, just plenty of great minds and ideas, and Kahn's key contribution was the development of the surprise-free future. In this technique, different possibilities (scenarios) for the future are set out according to varying causes and effects. As sociologist Hans Speier recalled in awe, at RAND they discussed the future in the plural, 'there'd be "futures" you could choose from'. The rationale behind scenario-thinking is that you predict all eventualities, leaving nothing (including potential surprises), to chance. The predictive advantage of this method has gone in and out of fashion but has continued to the present day to be successfully employed for more mundane things such as oil-platform development. At the time, however, it was a brand new shiny tool that cried out, along with Game Theory and systems analysis, to be used Dr Strangelove-style on nuclear strategy. By the late 1950s when it was abundantly clear the Soviets had the means to retaliate, Kahn developed one of his more controversial scenarios that involved a $10 million device called the 'Doomsday Machine'. As caricatured in Kubrick's film, the machine was designed to destroy all human life. The idea was that if sensors dotted around America sensed explosions of a certain amount and magnitude, they would send messages to a huge computer that would automatically trigger a nuclear retaliation. Simple but effective, this scenario satisfied Kahn's key requirements for a stable deterrent. It was, he wrote, 'frightening, inexorable, persuasive, cheap, non-accident prone'. The problems with this strategy are, of course, that it works only if the other side knows of its existence (hence Dr Strangelove's famous outburst), it does not permit human intervention and, as Kahn himself conceded, 'it kills too many people'.

These were the kind of scenarios that made government and military planners (in the USA and Russia) sit up and take notice of futurists. So too did some of their analogies. Bernard Brodie, who was part of the RAND team, made a memorable analogy between sex and the different scenarios. He compared, apparently in all seriousness, the so-called city-avoidance and withholding scenarios to coitus interruptus, and the all-out nuclear scenario to uninterrupted sex. Kahn loved this memo, and did not miss the opportunity to announce to high-ranking Strategic Air Command officers who were in favour of going the whole way, 'Gentleman, you don't have war plans, you have war-gasms.' As Fred Kaplan points out in *The Wizards of Armageddon*, 'Kahn's speciality was to express the RAND conventional wisdom in the most provocative and outrageous fashion imaginable.'

Inside RAND, Kahn got away with murder. Outside, he was accused of inciting murder. When his book *On Thermonuclear War* (*OTW*) was unleashed on to an already jittery public in 1960, one enraged reviewer wrote, 'this is a moral tract on mass murder: how to plan it, how to commit it, how to get away with it, how to justify it.' Moral judgments aside, it is a riveting read, through all the possible future scenarios for wars up to and including an Eighth World War. Dubbed by one critic as a modern-day Cassandra, Kahn wrote bluntly that unless there were more 'serious and sober thoughts on various facets of the strategic problem we are not going to reach the year 2000 – and maybe not even the year 1965 without a cataclysm of some sort'. He helpfully laid out projected numbers of casualties, predicted the percentage of defective births, costs of fallout shelters, extent of contamination, economic consequences, etc.

When it came to the touchy subject of the future of international relations he remarked in *OTW* that 'while the increasing "bourgeoisation" of large segments of Soviet society should improve their international manners, it will still be clear to all that however the next crisis is touched off, the Soviets do not have to back down because of fear of an attack by the United States – but we may'. Kahn could not resist a provocative dig at Russian manners, and was well aware that the book would be read by the Russians and taken into account by some senior Soviet military planners. Or put another more direct way, 'by 1961 . . . all of the important decision makers will realize the extreme importance of either cooperating seriously with or eliminating the opposition.'

Kahn also warned that one of the main problems in the future – after dealing with the Russians – would be when nuclear weapons got into the less responsible hands of small nations. Never one to worry about being politically correct, Kahn made the point that 'A Hottentot, an educated and technical Hottentot it is true . . . would be able to make bombs.' Back in 1947 one country had nuclear weapons, in 1960 it was four countries, but by 1973 it was, he feared, 'impossible to tell'. While none of this was massively reassuring, Kahn was a true optimist, albeit of a rather unusual kind, and dedicated the book in true futurist fashion 'to the goal of anticipating, avoiding and alleviating crises'. Describing one scenario that involved a large nuclear strike in the USA he wrote, 'Despite a widespread belief to the contrary, objective studies indicate that even though the amount of human tragedy would be greatly increased in the post-war world, the increase would not preclude normal and happy lives for the majority of survivors and their descendants.' In another incident he referred to the fact that '*only* two million people would die'. As Amitai Etzioni, founder of the communitarian movement, said of him in 1961, 'Kahn does for nuclear arms what free-love advocates did for sex: he speaks candidly of acts about which others whisper behind closed doors.'

Among the potential doom and destruction in OTW Kahn threw in a few comparatively jolly predictions. 'Futuristic computers will,' he wrote, 'in all likelihood, have multimillion word memories, fractional microsecond multiplication times, self-programming capabilities . . . able to read and write books. They really will begin to justify the notion of artificial brains.' More accurately, though a little prematurely, he predicted that by 1969 'mass transportation and communication will be much more available, but one form of communication – worldwide TV, through the use of satellites . . . will be making its impact felt'. He also envisaged for the 'late sixties or early seventies' the 'development of cheap, fast transportation by both air and sea'. The latter, he predicted, would be in the form of 'nuclear-powered submarines or turbojet-propelled hydrofoils'.

Kahn became something of a celebrity, and passionately defended his work on the speaker and media circuit. He was an ebullient and entertaining speaker, but even so he occasionally lost his temper. According to biographer Ghamari-Tabrizi, in one incident he snapped, 'It is possible, isn't it, that parents will learn to love two-headed children twice as much.' As Kahn said unapologetically of himself, 'I keep on thinking where other people stop.' His only concession to convention was to change from his usual casual attire whenever he talked about all-out war. A friend of his modestly recounted to Ghamari-Tabrizi, 'The only effect I ever had on Herman was when I told him, "I don't think you can talk about thermonuclear war unless you wear a tie."' The makeover made no difference whatsoever. He was still regarded as a monster by the public at large, who were busy building fallout shelters and instructing children at school what to do in the event of an attack; he was seen as a genius forecaster only by a few loyal fans. Although it was never made official, RAND was not happy either with the notoriety, and Kahn left discreetly in 1961 with two colleagues to set up his own research institute, the Hudson Institute in New York.

This institute was an independent future studies institute with the 'aim of stimulating and stretching the imagination'. Its mission, Kahn liked to tease, was for the first year to be a think tank for the Secretary of Defence, in their second year for the President, and by the fourth year for God. While Kahn's arrogance and ambition were often camouflaged by his humour, his reputation as a respected futurist was growing, and in 1967 together with Anthony Wiener he published *The Year 2000: A Framework for Speculation on the Next Thirty Three Years*. One of the key things they did in the book was to describe and defend the use of scenario-writing. While it was an increasingly popular method, it was still suffering from the curse of OTW. As Kahn wrote, 'one criticism is that only a "paranoid" personality . . . could conceive of the kind of crises, provocations, and aggressions, and plots that characterize many politico-military scenarios.'

Kahn – certainly not one to suffer from paranoia – defended this view with the argument that his responsibility as a futurist actually required him to be interested in the unpleasant. In the words of Kahn and Wiener, scenarios are not 'a predictive device', but 'attempts to describe in some detail a hypothetical sequence of events that could lead plausibly to the situation envisaged'.

One of his scenarios for nuclear war is, 'A Central European Outbreak Scenario'. It begins innocently enough with Step 1, unrest in East Germany or Berlin. By Step 17 we have a Soviet attack on Western Europe or a US attack to deter Soviets, and it ends abruptly at Step 21 with a large counterforce strike. According to Kahn the advantage with scenarios is that they 'call attention', 'force the analyst to deal with dynamics he might easily avoid treating' and create artificial 'case histories' that can make up for a paucity of actual historical examples or precedents. The authors stress that although plausibility is a great virtue in a scenario, you should not worry about limiting yourself to *the* most probable situations. Hence, in *The Year 2000*, we find more reassuring tables of 'A Relatively "Surprise-Free" Early Twenty-First Century' listing 'the rise of new great powers – perhaps Japan, China, a European Complex'. More unsettling is the list of 'Some Possible Causes of "Surprising" Changes in the Old Nations': famine, pestilence, revival of fascism, development of 'inexpensive' doomsday machines. As usual Kahn pushes the predictive boat out, and we are treated to ten far-out possibilities including: life expectancy of over 150 years (possibly even immortality), almost complete genetic control (but still homo sapiens), major modification of human species (no longer homo sapiens), and interstellar travel.

In the future we should, said Kahn, 'expect to go on being surprised'. And he himself of course continued to surprise. He also – unsurprisingly – continued to be criticized, although he did receive a wonderfully surprise-free criticism from Russian futurist Bestuzhev-Lada, who called *The Year 2000* 'the "last word" in bourgeois futurology'. Unlike many futurists, Kahn remained an unwavering optimist to the end of his life, and one of his last missions was redesigning the public-school curriculum 'to redress the imbalance of unrelenting negativism' about the future. But for many, the biggest surprise of all was that by the time he died in 1983, there had been no 'big surprise'.

The scenario methodology that Kahn developed was just one of the hot new tools for foresight that were being developed at RAND in the 1950s and which have become a staple of much futurist methodology. Other techniques, which were later also adopted for non-military use, were war gaming and the Delphi method. War gaming started off as pretty rudimentary simulation of war situations played out on boards with star shapes on cards representing enemy bomb bursts, though it later graduated to sophisticated computer-simulated games. The military role-playing sometimes went on not just for days, but weeks, and one game apparently lasted through the whole of summer 1955. This raised the question not only of whether gaming really was a practical and reliable forecasting technique, but also whether its magnetic appeal was just a case of toys for the boys. The general conclusion was that while it was a considerable drain on resources, manpower and money, it was a great deal more fun than sitting around reading abstract studies and dryly written books on the matter. War gaming became a cult, and was probably America's worst-kept secret in the late 1950s and early 1960s, but since there were no apparent applications outside of the military, it did not take off as a general forecasting tool. Only more recently has it been rediscovered and put to civilian use by consultancy firms such as Booz Allen Hamilton which specialize in strategic gaming. One recent example of the firm's work was the 'gaming' of the HIV/AIDS situation for the Indian government, though other more traditional clients include the US Department of Defence. Just as in a traditional war gaming situation, a control team sits separately to the client team, throws in 'external shocks' and monitors and assesses the results. From planning to playing, a 'game' nowadays typically takes between eight and twelve weeks and can cost around $500,000.

If war gaming represented the sweaty locker room of forecasting at RAND, the Delphi technique was the sedate library. Developed by RAND mathematician Olaf Helmer and scientist Norman Dalkey in the 1950s, it proved that if there are no scientific laws available (as is particularly the case with the social sciences), your best bet for predictive purposes is to ask and bring together expert opinion. Helmer's technique was just an attempt to produce a more systematic and reliable methodology for what Hap Arnold had ordered Kármán to do back in 1944. It was in effect a modern take on the original Greek oracle principle, but without the added delights of drugs and virgins. In lieu of these props at RAND, Helmer proposed rigorous polling techniques that were designed to ensure that experts' opinions did not fall foul of 'bandwagon' dynamics, and that they were collected and collated both independently and anonymously. The Delphi technique is essentially a form of virtual brainstorming of alternative futures; its real potential lies in the ability of the pollsters to fish out and form consensus from the feedback.

In 1964 Helmer demonstrated the Delphi technique to great effect in a report on long-term scientific forecasts. In 1970 it was shown that of the twenty-two events forecast to have a 50 per cent probability of happening by then, five did not occur (for instance, manned scientific orbital station), fifteen had happened (for instance, large-scale fertility control by oral contraceptive and lethal biological agents) and two were still uncertain (economically useful desalination of sea water and use of laser in space communications). Others, such as 'direct link from stores to bank to check credit and to record transactions' were deemed to exist but not pervasive enough to be significant. More predictions he yielded with the method were published in *Prospects of Technological Progress*. This 1967 paper, which appeared the year before Helmer left RAND to set up his own Institute for the Future, asserted 'with some confidence' that by the year 2000 'people will largely live in urban complexes, surrounded by numerous automata. In particular, there will be central data banks and libraries with fully automated access, a credit-card economy in which cash transactions will be virtually eliminated, highly sophisticated teaching machines will be in wide use, portable video telephones will facilitate communication among persons everywhere, and this process will be further enhanced by the availability of automated translation from one language to another.' If that seems a bit hit and miss, there was also the assertion that 'men will almost certainly have landed on Mars'. Although even today this still seems a bit far fetched, it was at the time a popular prediction, along with being able to control the weather, which was reported as being not quite so certain, but still very probable. Listed as much less probable but still in with a good chance of making it by 2000 were fully automated highway transportation, control of hereditary defects, and a permanent base on Mars. But as former space engineer Theodore J. Gordon said of the technique, 'Delphi studies do not produce "truth" about the future; they yield, even under the best of circumstances, only consensus opinion about what might be. If the participants are experts, perhaps their opinion represents a possible future which deserves consideration in planning.'

The 1960s were the honeymoon period for futurism. This was not just the result of the reaction to the military and psychological pressures of the Cold War, and increasing concerns about planet earth and its growing population, but thanks to the leaps, bounds and promises of technology. Of particular significance was Gordon E. Moore's prediction in 1965 that the number of components (transistors and resistors) that could be placed on a silicon chip would continue to double every year or so for the foreseeable future (this is today known as 'Moore's law' and still holds true). Hand in hand with accelerated computer power went the belief in statistics as a reliable predictive tool. Logistical curves, trend extrapolation, relevance tree techniques and systems analysis were the buzzwords among the new journals, organizations, conferences, courses, books, magazines and institutes that sprang up to deal with all possible futures. By the late 1960s there was an embarrassment of organizations throughout America and Europe whose titles involved permutations of the word future, such as The World Future Society, the Institute for the Future, Futuribles, Futuriblerne, Futurum and other such similar-sounding bodies.

One of the effects of all this activity was that fields hitherto fixed in the present or to the past began to look to the future. If, as E. H. Carr once said, historians should have the future in their bones, then good futurists should have history in their bones. A prime example is anthropology, which was very much glued to the past and to the 'now' until the American anthropologist Margaret Mead championed 'anticipatory anthropology'. This is a form of anthropological prediction that looks beyond the 'ethnographic present' to what is possible, probable and preferable for a society in the mid-term future (typically five to twenty-five years). When it comes to change, anthropology has a reputation for sentimentality, yet Mead believed that change was not only inevitable but not always for the worst. Interestingly, most of her anticipatory anthropological writings are from the late 1960s and early 1970s, when she was getting towards the end of her career and her life (she died in 1978). Significantly, she was the only woman to be included in Alvin Toffler's 1972 book *The Futurists*, a landmark collection of writings from the best future thinkers of the time. Summarizing the extract from Mead's *Culture and Commitment* Toffler writes, 'the famed anthropologist argues that we have shifted from a culture that is "post figurative" (one in which the young learn from the old) to one that is "cofigurative" (one in which both children and adults learn chiefly from their peers). She appealed for a "prefigurative" culture in which, as the future explodes into the present, the old learn from the young.'

Mead was a natural-born futurist who, despite being apparently unaware of the uses of the scenario method, was very obviously making great strides in outlining possible social and ethnographic futures. Already back in 1943 she was writing: 'It is possible to imagine – at a not too far distant date – complete control of her own fertility in the hands of a woman', and foresaw changing attitudes to the traditional family. By the 1950s she was demanding – independently of Ossip Flechtheim – that universities introduce a Chair of the Future. Later, looking back disappointed, she said, 'I had envisaged a group of people who were as responsible about the next decade, the next quarter century, the next fifty years, as say a Medievalist would be about the whole of what we know about the Middle Ages, that is, someone who would be responsible for fitting it together as well as he or she could.'

Mead continued to do the best she could as an 'unofficial' futurist. In response to the Cold War, she examined among other things the psychology of war-less man, pointing out in 1962 that in the absence of war there will be 'an increase in other kinds of organized violence', pointing with great prescience to the 'sharply mounting number of small dangerous acts of anarchy – terrorist bombings and bombs hidden in civilian planes'. On a more optimistic note she later unequivocally welcomed the man on the moon as 'this new exploration – this work at the edge of human knowledge' which she believed 'is what will keep us human'.

Thanks to Mead, anthropologists were starting to take more notice of the future; more importantly, the futurist community had started to take notice of people like Mead. As Toffler pointed out, 'Her voice, crossing generational and academic lines, has been influential in preparing the soil for the futurists.' Even in her seventies, she was still active, advocating lifelong learning and the usefulness of anthropology in designing new urban centres, and shaping what she called our 'open-ended' future. Unlike some of her more old-fashioned colleagues, she did not shy away from the pleasures and promises of new technology, significantly insisting that 'there can be no science of the future without the use of the computer'. In her forthright manner she surprised everyone, not only by blowing away the image of the fusty old anthropologist shuffling around with a clipboard in a mud hut, but by declaring with a cheeky metaphor that the greatest contribution anthropology can make to the science of the future is 'to keep men's imaginations open, as they tend to let the predictable hardware coerce the form of the software'.

*   *   *

It is tempting to apply Mead's observation to France's most famous futurist, Bertrand de Jouvenel. For not only can the first part of her observation be irreproachably applied to his contribution to the science of the future, but the remainder to his love life. Bertrand was the son of Baron Henry de Jouvenel, one of the most influential and charismatic political journalists in Paris. When Bertrand was just three years old, his parents separated and after taking various scandalous lovers, Henry shocked French society even more by taking up with the author Colette, who had just left her aristocratic lesbian lover. Colette and Henry married in 1912, but it was not until the spring of 1920 that Bertrand was finally allowed to meet his infamous stepmother. At sixteen, he was still shy, but was showing all the signs of having inherited his father's good looks and charm. Within a year he had become Colette's lover, and would remain until he was twenty-one, becoming the source of much gossip and speculation. As Colette's biographer Judith Thurman remarked to a family friend, 'I could understand Colette's attraction for Bertrand, but what, I asked bluntly, did a beautiful boy of sixteen see in a fat and domineering woman of fifty however charming she might be?'

The answer lay not just in her powerful seductive charms, or revenge on his inattentive, domineering father, but also his thirst for knowledge and experience outside the conservative confines of Parisian society. Writing late in his life de Jouvenel recalled, 'the pleasures she gave me were all those which open a window on the world, which I owe entirely to her.' Another woman who opened a window on the world for him was Martha Gellhorn, the famous war correspondent and some-time lover of H. G .Wells, whom he met in the early 1930s. Martha was instantly attracted to this handsome young 'playboy . . . scholar and thinker', and according to some accounts they were briefly married in 1933. By now de

Jouvenel had built up not just a reputation as a Don Juan, but as a prolific political writer who had moved out of his dominant father's shadow and begun to develop his own distinctive ideas on society.

De Jouvenel's interest in politics and the future began in his youth when he accompanied his diplomat father to the peace conferences after the First World War, but it was later fuelled by the works of H. G. Wells, of which he read everything he could. Writing admiringly to Wells after meeting him, and almost certainly before he found out they shared Martha Gellhorn, he said, 'your books . . . light up the long winding road we have to travel toward the distant goal of civilisation.' For de Jouvenel, Wells' works were not merely fiction, but 'an ensemble of speculations on possible futures'. However, de Jouvenel still had a lot to learn before the launch of his future think tank in the 1960s. He travelled through America and Britain during the 1930s and like Orwell observed, at close hand, poverty, the soup kitchens and the plight of the homeless. Following a shameful and much-regretted flirtation with the unemployment policies of the Nazis during the Second World War, de Jouvenel became engaged in the problems of authoritarian governments that were gripping Asia and Africa in the 1950s.

It was, however, the Ford Foundation that gave de Jouvenel his first big break in futurism in 1960 when it financed a project called Futuribles. This was a think tank of experts who got together to speculate and write essays about the future of society and politics in the spirit of the sixteenth-century Spanish Jesuit theologian Luis de Molina, who first coined the term 'futurible' to fuse the ideas of future and possibility. As de Jouvenel explained, 'the purpose is to generate a habit, the habit of forward-looking.' Less reassuringly, but rather charmingly, he took pains to explain: 'Our authors . . . certainly do not pretend to any knowledge of the future, which would be foolish, but neither do they pretend that they have no opinion about it, which would be evasive.' Furthermore, he admitted to his critics that, yes, their purpose was essentially unscholarly, and no, it was not scientific, but in the great tradition of French philosophizing, it took them into the realm of 'possibles'. It was this period in which de Jouvenel was inspired to put to paper his ground rules and philosophical parameters for thinking about the future.

The result was a handbook, *The Art of Conjecture*, published in French in 1964. In it he distinguished between the possible (what we know) and the desirables (what we wish for), and pointed out that 'Man is fortunate when the desirable and the probable coincide! The case is often otherwise, and thus we find ourselves trying to bend the course of events in a way which will bring the probable closer to the desirable. And this is the real reason we study the future.' There was no prediction *per se* in the book, but lots of philosophical ruminating on defining the future and the fact that knowledge of the future is a contradiction in terms. For de Jouvenel there was no one future, but a fan of possibilities to be unfolded. How too, he philosophized, can we even begin to define the future if it is 'pre-existent – something existing before it appears'. At the time his book was considered a groundbreaking contribution to futurism, but today it has been rendered more or less redundant. As Edward Cornish tactfully wrote in his book *Futuring*, 'De Jouvenel put into words much that might be viewed today as fairly obvious but whose importance had not been recognized clearly in the past.'

When funding from the Ford Foundation ran out, de Jouvenel had the prescience to keep the catchy name Futuribles, and in 1967 set up his own research institute in Paris with his wife, Hélène. For a while he enjoyed considerable success and a reputation as a suave political philosopher, travelling the world to give speeches and advice. By the time of his death in 1987 he had rather fallen off the futurological radar, and it was left to his son Hughes to run the institute. Today Futuribles still publishes journals on a wide range of themes using a Delphi-like network of some 350 correspondents to identify 'possible' global trends and Hughes is working, as his father before him, to emerge from the paternal shadow as a thinker in his own right. As well as setting a high standard for his son in terms of women and work, Bertrand de Jouvenel's legacy was that he believed that we should try to forget about prophesy *per se*, and simply take time to imagine what makes a good day for an ordinary man. Writing in *The Art of Conjecture* he poetically recommended, 'Take this man when he wakes up; follow him through to the time of sleep. Plot as it were, the sequence of his pleasurable and unpleasurable impressions, and now imagine what a "good day" should be. Picturing this "good day" is the first step into a modern utopia; then you will have to seek the conditions, which can bring about this good day.' As his French biographer Jean Mabire liked to say, Bertrand de Jouvenel was always in advance of the times, or behind the times, but never quite came to grips with reality.

Along with Kahn and Wiener's *The Year 2000* and the opening of de Jouvenel's Futuribles institute, 1967 was filled with a flurry of important futurist activity. One of the biggest projects of the year was the publication of *Toward the Year 2000* by the Commission on the Year 2000 that had been founded by the American Academy of Arts and Sciences two years previously. Putting this tome together was an act of Delphic proportions that pulled together a broad range of opinion and thought from lawyers, to psychologists and even zoologists. For the general public, the editor, sociologist Daniel

Bell, whipped up the contributions into readable chunks, but what made it completely different from previous future studies, he claimed, is that it was oriented to specific social-policy purposes, and that the methodology gave 'the promises of providing a more reliable foundation for realistic alternatives and choices, if not for exact prediction'.

No book of prediction at the time would have been complete without a contribution from Herman Kahn. As well as a provocative chapter on 'the Next Thirty Three Years' (taken from his book *The Year 2000*), Kahn provided much-needed levity in what otherwise may well have been interminably dull and depressing working sessions. Bell shrewdly included the dialogue and the jokes from these sessions in the book, and they give a rare insight into what happens when you put a flock of futurists (and egos) in a confined space. First, the participants ignore each other's ideas, and move swiftly and magnanimously on to their own. Second, they resort to politically incorrect jokes when things start to get a bit gloomy. Kahn, the *rapporteur* for his group, set the standard with his comment about the problems of protectionism in the communist Eastern Bloc: 'A Rumanian tells me that both a Rumanian and a Hungarian will sell his grandmother to the devil, but only a Rumanian will deliver.' He also warned more seriously, 'if in the past we have tended to overrate the Russian's power, recklessness, and intensity, in the future we may underrate it.' Or, as Eugene V. Rostow more cautiously put it to the commission, 'it is not fantastic to imagine the Eastern European countries, and even Russia, becoming part of Europe again.' Even the chairman of the Political Science Department at MIT, Ithiel de Sola Pool, was carried away in this hothouse of visions, to wrongly predict that this would happen 'around 1980'. As Daniel Bell reminds us, it is very difficult to make predictions about single critical events.

The mission of the commission was not to restrict predictions to hardcore facts and politics, and surprisingly one of the most insightful soft-fact visions came from Kahn. He suggested that when talking about the future, we should lay out descriptions of styles and quality of life, an idea which resonates remarkably well in our individualistic society today. People in the future would, he said, if they are not completely achievement-orientated, define themselves via their hobbies as opposed to work. 'When you ask a European what he does, instead of saying he is a clerk, he is likely to say, "I'm a motor driver", or . . . "I'm a mountain climber".' He also predicted that by 2000 'Europeans' hours of work may be decreased to thirty or thirty-five hours a week, with two or three months of vacation a year.'

Among the rich patchwork of contributions was that of Ernst Mayr, a professor of zoology, who readily admitted he felt a little out of place in the project. What, he sighed gloomily, is thirty-three years to a biologist? 'Biological man will not be different in any appreciable way from what he is today.' Mayr was more challenged when it came to suggesting what we could do to make a better world. This included the worthy 'elimination of disorders due to single genes', and the rather more dubious 'behaviour control technology'. Of the latter he said, 'one can safely predict that techniques for controlling behaviour and modifying personality will grow more effectively by the year 2000.' Implants in the brain controlled via microtransmitters and receivers would be used for the handling of delinquents and criminals, so that 'ongoing action could be rewarded, punished or prevented'.

The promises of technology took on even more Orwellian proportions in Harry Kalven's prediction for the commission that 'by 2000 it will be possible to place a man under constant surveillance without his ever becoming aware of it'. Kalven, a professor of law, focussed sharply on the problems of privacy, making the astute prediction that 'the privacy of the famous, the great, and the important may yield to the notion that it is in the public interest to have every last detail of their lives and correspondence fully in the press and public record. Henceforth the great will live, so to speak, in the public domain'. As well as being alert to the potential of the media-celebrity symbiosis, he foresaw 'fantasy invasions of privacy as a form of public amusement'. At the time, the big shock was shows such as 'Candid Camera', which he marked out as being 'a special threat for life in the year 2000'.

Another insightful contribution came from John Pierce, executive director of research and communication at Bell telephone laboratories, who revealed 'the Bell System is engaged in a determined effort to introduce person-to-person television or picturephone service on a large scale, to see if there is a real public demand for it.' As well as seeing 'the possibility of greatly improved mobile telephony – car telephones and even pocket telephones', Pierce was, like many at the time, seduced by the promise of automated services replacing people. He envisaged a world where 'the telephone can reply to queries in spoken words . . . In the future we may be able to query, from a distance, any number of information sources about weather, hotels, stores, sports, theatres, or other matters and receive specific voice replies.' He did, however, forewarn that the device 'will only be able to respond to only simple unambiguous questions'. Although he did not foresee the boom in manned call centres that took over this function, the results, some might argue, were much the same.

What characterized this age most of all was a sense, as Pierce put it, that at the beginning of the next century, science and technology would 'provide an environment as different from the present as the pre-telephone world'. One of the rather bizarre obsessions at the time along with regional weather control (due for a comeback soon), was automated learning. The idea that you could pop into a booth, hook yourself up to a computer, and hey presto, learn Latin, was not just an obsession of lazy people but some of the great minds of the time. In *Toward the Year 2000* a professor of psychology called George A. Miller described such a system in a classroom of semi-isolated booths linked up to a central computer and equipped with headphones, a keyboard, a screen and a photo-sensitive 'light gun'. Pierce underestimated the need for social interaction and teamwork in the learning process, but did much better in picking up on the growing talk of the potential for an 'on-line intellectual community with shared data base'. It was with caution that he said 'with just a little foresight in the development of these systems, they could turn out to be one of the greatest educational innovations since the invention of printing'.

As a highly respected social scientist, professor and author with a beady eye on the future, Bell was much in demand for forewords and stamps of approval. He did not shy away from putting his neck on the line, as illustrated not only by his legendary declaration at his bar mitzvah that he did not believe in God (to which the rabbi huffily replied 'do you think God cares?'), but by the fact that he wrote the introduction to *The Next 500 Years*. Written by economist Burnham Putnam Beckwith, and subtitled *Scientific Predictions of Major Social Trends,* the book appeared in the same year and with the same enthusiastic spirit as the commission's report, but could not have been more different. In his introduction Bell described the author as a respectable social scientist and the book as 'a rare act of intellectual courage'. Looking back (albeit only after forty rather than 500 years) at what Beckwith wrote in 1967,

Bell's remark was clearly not an overstatement but a warning. For not only was the book often utterly wrong, but also very shocking.

Beckwith approached unfashionable subjects such as eugenics without the cover of fiction, and surgical gloves off. 'The most important of all social trends during the next millennium,' he wrote, 'will be the introduction, extension, and constant improvement of compulsory eugenic measures . . . bringing the average for all men up to at least the level of the best 1 percent in 1960.' The 'ideal means' of doing this, was he claimed, 'large scale artificial insemination . . . Coercion will first be applied to couples with the least fit husbands. By 2300 most husbands will be sterilized before marriage, and couples will rely on artificial insemination.' The good news was that by the year 2500 this practice would be rendered redundant as people would be intelligent enough (an estimated 90 per cent would be geniuses), and that the process would not interfere with a normal and enjoyable sex life! If after all this you actually still wanted to make a baby in 2100, he or she would be tattooed at birth with a serial number enabling lifetime control and collection of information such as how many cigarettes he or she smoked and how many cups of coffee he or she consumed. And by 2200 everyone over twelve years of age will be subjected every year to a lie-detector test to find out if they have committed any crimes. If Orwell's Big Brother would be satisfied with the latter, then Woody Allen would be overjoyed with the idea that 'by 2200 psychiatric examinations will be required of all persons in the world at least once a year', and that by 2500 'the average normal adult will then consult his psychiatrist more often than his dentist'.

Social scientists, admitted Beckwith, cannot predict all trends, but some, such as the spread of birth control, the advance of feminism and the rise of meritocracy and growth of monopolies are as easy as 'predicting the arrival of the milkman'. This belief relies on simple linear extrapolation of existing trends, but it does not make room for fast-moving innovation and surprise. The failure of this kind of linear thinking, and the reason it went out of favour with many futurists, is well illustrated by his idea that 'by 2100 most new book editions and magazines will be produced on slides'. The existing photographic method of recording information was a seemingly safer bet compared to digitalization that was, by comparison, in its infancy. Similarly, his prediction that 'long before 2500 most sea mammals – seals, walruses, porpoises, whales – will have been domesticated', and would be a chief source of meat was a reflection of fears of overpopulation and factors such as the quadrupling of commercial catfish farming in America in the 1960s.

Like many writers, he also used his book as a platform not just for the good of the world, but to grind his personal axe. It is quite hard to guess which is Beckwith's monkey trap, but a good contender is his thoughts on the publishing industry. Like Jules Verne a century previously, he too was worried about the future of his livelihood. 'By 2100 most non-fiction authors will be salaried experts who will be well paid whether or not any particular manuscript is accepted and published. For them writing will become a secure profession, rather than a sideline or a series of personal speculations.' Purely from the point of view of a social scientist and without any gratuitous speculation on Beckwith's private life, it is fascinating to read his thoughts on friendship and family life in the future. 'To promote wise friendship and marriage, all governments will eventually establish special agencies. These agencies will design suitable cultural, medical, psychiatric and other tests.' Here he was right about the arrival of partnership agencies, but wrong about the means being public as opposed to private. This was partly a reflection of his belief in nationalization, also apparent in his vision that most land in non-communist countries will be nationalized before 2100: 'Britain will be among the first, and the United States one of the last . . . to nationalize land.'

Reading books like this is a stark reminder why so many futurists cop out and hide behind a veil of fiction or satire, or write under a pseudonym. As Bell diplomatically pointed out, it was a courageous book, which in its conclusion describes a grimly fascinating view of typical American family life in the year 2500 based upon his observation and extrapolation of existing trends and behaviour. 'Both children will live in public boarding schools . . . Adults will spend two to ten hours a week in formal education . . . Comprehensive simplification and tranquilization of urban life . . . will help to reduce mental illness.' The results, claimed Beckwith, will be utopian, but then, as he points out, 'a medieval European peasant would look upon a modern American town as utopian'.

Struggling somewhere at the bottom of the pile of the attention-grabbing futurist voices in the 1960s were the architects and city planners, left to figure out how to transform social visions of the future into a working urban reality. On the one hand there was the artist Salvador Dali, proclaiming unhelpfully that the future of architecture would be 'soft and hairy', and at the other extreme, the architect Buckminster Fuller presenting hard, smooth geodesic domes as the solution to mankind's problems. Fuller was arguably one of the few modern architects along with Le Corbusier to really warrant the added extra title of futurist. For he not only developed new structures for living in but also the philosophical manifesto to accompany it. In addition, he gave his readers and interviewers a frank insight into the workings of an unusual and inventive mind.

The impressive 250-foot-diameter and 200-foot-high geodesic dome that he built for the US pavilion at the 1967 World Fair in Montreal was Fuller's blueprint for living in the future. Domed living was, he believed, the alternative to doomed living. Such structures would enable us to not only reduce energy losses in winter heating or summer cooling, 'domed cites are going to be essential to the occupation of the Arctic and the Antarctic . . . will be used in desert areas . . . gradually the success of new domed cities in remote places will bring about their use in covering old cities particularly where antiquities are to be protected.' In his 1969 book *Utopia or Oblivion, Prospects for Humanity* he also foresaw that 'by 1975 it would be possible to air-deliver geodesic domes able to cover small cities'.

In the book Fuller acknowledged that Malthus' predictions of overpopulation were wrong, but he still believed that in order not to deplete the surface of the earth, we would one day live on 'cloud nines', 'sky-floating geodesic spheres . . . designed to float at preferred altitudes of thousands of feet'. These prefabricated 'clouds' could house many thousands of passengers and, better still, in a few decades hence, 'passengers could come and go from cloud to cloud, or cloud to ground, as the clouds float around the earth or are anchored to mountaintops'. As well as reflecting the contemporary concerns about the environment, Fuller's pet predictions were closely linked to the idea of mobility. Along with 'floating tetrahedronal cities, air-deliverable skyscrapers, submarine islands . . . flyable dwelling machines', he had a vision of skyscraper-size aeroplanes that 'may be economically occupiable and economically flyable from here to there with passengers living aboard as on cruise ships. It may be that human beings will begin to live in completely mobile ways on sky ships and sea ships . . . Man will come to occupy mobile habitats which may at will be anchored habitats and live independently of day and night and season schedules.'

What is most extraordinary about Fuller's vision is not that it stretched well beyond the Easyjet and Easycruise imagination of today, but that it came from an American born at the end of the nineteenth century to parents who believed manned flight would never be possible. Born in 1895, Fuller was cross-eyed, abnormally far-sighted and could apparently see only large patterns. At the age of four he was given glasses to correct his sight, but his imagination, it appears, never really recovered. Even in kindergarten, while others were off playing with cuddly toys, Fuller was busy constructing an octet truss out of dried peas and toothpicks. As further befits the image of maverick futurist, Fuller was expelled twice while at Harvard. He then joined the US Navy, where he learnt the fundamentals of engineering that were to be of key importance to his future inventions.

The first of Fuller's futurist inventions was the Dymaxion House that was part of his moral drive to develop proper housing for the people using mass production. Patented in 1928, it was a hexagonal structure that aimed to obtain maximum human advantage from minimum use of technology. It was naturally air-deliverable. The term Dymaxion came from 'DYnamic plus MAXimum tensION' and was a method he applied not only to houses but also to bathroom and vehicle design. In 1934 Fuller's Dymaxion car, which looked like a squat three-wheeled submarine, hit the headlines when Mrs Eleanor Roosevelt went for a spin in one. H. G. Wells was equally impressed by it on a visit to the USA and subsequently used some of the Dymaxion concepts in the film of *The Shape of Things to Come*.

If the Dymaxion principle was applicable to transport and housing, it also succinctly summed up just how a happily married visionary like Fuller worked. As he revealed to interviewer Anwar Dil in the book *Humans in Universe*, 'Every time I am about to make a discovery and am developing a high sensitivity of thinking, along comes, to me, an exceptionally charming female with whom I find myself tending to fall in love. Only when I have successfully restrained myself from falling further and have applied myself exclusively to the discovery or inventing, only then do the critically-relevant conceptions occur which secure my comprehension of the significance of the discovering and/or inventing and what my responsibilities are in making the discovery and inventions effectively available to humanity.'

As well as being noted for his honesty, Fuller, who lived to 1983, was essentially an optimist. When *Utopia or Oblivion* was published it was popular to moan like Jungk against automation, but Fuller was meanwhile proclaiming that 'the comprehensive introduction of automation everywhere around the earth will free man from being an automaton and will generate so fast a mastery and multiplication of energy wealth by humanity that we will be able to support all of humanity in ever greater physical and economic success anywhere around his little space ship *Earth*'. Understatement was never his style, as Albert Einstein discovered back in 1935 when the typescript of Fuller's book *Nine Chains to the Moon* was submitted to him for scientific verification. In the chapter entitled $E=mc^2$ = *Mrs Murphy's Horse Power*, Fuller attempted to depict world behaviours based on the 'assumption that humanity would be behaving in accord with the philosophy of Einstein'. Einstein was apparently impressed with this unforeseen 'practical application' of his theory and gave his approval to the book. Reviewing the book in the *New York*

Saturday Review in 1938, fellow cutting-edge architect Frank Lloyd Wright was moved to write 'Buckminster Fuller – you are the most sensible man in New York, truly sensitive. Nature gave you antennae, long-range finders you have learned to use. I find almost all your prognosticating nearly right – much of it dead right, and I love you for the way you prognosticate.' Fuller also had the honour of being included, along with such futurist luminaries as Bell, Kahn, Flechtheim and de Jouvenel, in Alvin Toffler's *The Futurists*. Not only did Toffler introduce him as the 'world's youngest old futurist' but pointedly let him have the last word in the book, which said: 'If you are going to be wise . . . you are going to have to look at things in these big ways.'

Another cult figure on the fringes of the 'official' futurist movement who was well known for looking at things in 'big ways' was Marshall McLuhan. McLuhan is best remembered for his book *The Medium is the Massage*, which appeared in that busy futurist year, 1967. It should of course have been called *The Medium is the Message*, the aphorism for which McLuhan is best remembered. But owing to an error at the printers, it appeared as 'massage', though it did not really matter as it was fortuitously taken as referring to 'Mass Age', which was fine by McLuhan, and got the book even more publicity.

McLuhan was a reluctant optimist and did not believe that machines would homogenize the human race. Writing in 1964 he said, 'Panic about automation as a threat of uniformity on a world scale is the projection into the future of mechanical standardization and specialism, which are now past.' Although he saw himself, as did Fuller, as a philosopher, McLuhan was also a communications theorist and 'educator', whose work is best summed up by Mark Federman, who wrote: 'To understand McLuhan you must read McLuhan, but to read McLuhan, you must first understand McLuhan.' It is true to say that while McLuhan is not a straightforward read, his message – and verbal *massage* – is disarmingly simple. His two central observations which conferred his cult status in the 1960s and 1970s were his belief that the television, computers and other electronic disseminators of information were shaping our styles of thinking and thought (i.e. the medium is the message), and that they would ultimately create a global village in which we will interact 'like villagers in an earlier time'. Furthermore, 'the circuited city of the future will . . . be an information megalopolis'. Writing in *Understanding Media* in 1964 in his characteristic prophetic tone, McLuhan observed: 'Men are suddenly nomadic gatherers of knowledge, nomadic as never before, informed as never before – but also involved in the total social process as never before, since with electricity we extend our central nervous system globally, instantly interrelating every human experience.' This was written just five years before the launch of ARPANET, the communication system developed to link US government and academic computer laboratories, and the forerunner of the Internet. Even more poignant today, some say, was his view that 'electric circuitry is Orientalizing the West. The contained, the distinct, the separate – our Western legacy – are being replaced by the flowing, the unified, the fused.' Whether he was referring specifically to forthcoming spiritualism, the current rise of the economic power of the East, or even both, is characteristically ambiguous and part of the guru image that he cultivated so well.

Futurism had at last arrived. It was edgy, it was exciting and it was even fashionable. Research institutes and think tanks were springing up everywhere, and it was the point at which business started to take serious notice of the potential of these peculiar people for their own purposes. As the *New York Times Magazine* reported in April 1967, there was even a trend for businesses to retain science-fiction writers 'for much the same reason that medieval monarchs used to like having a court astrologer about'. As it took off, so naturally did doubts about such practices, and the magazine voiced worries that it would induce 'moral simple-mindedness'. The 'leap into the future', it complained, 'is too often a bolt away from the stubborn, the grubby, the unfathomable and the infuriating complexities of the present into a sort of carefree playland in which the shorter week appears to promise more water skiing (but not more alcoholism) and a helicopter is pictured on every suburban rooftop (rather than in more Vietnams).'

Although they had been unceremoniously muscled out of the limelight by the arrival of 'real' futurists, science-fiction writers were still there avidly and vividly grappling with the big themes of overpopulation, technological determinism and uncontrollable shifts in 1960s society. One of the most revered and even feared science-fiction writers and forecasters was Stanislaw Lem. Compared to McLuhan, Lem was literally in another universe when it came to the potential of technological progress and communication. Two years before McLuhan published *The Medium is the Massage*, Lem on the other side of the planet in Poland brought out *Cyberiada* (published in English as *The Cyberiad* in 1974). Subtitled *Fables for the Cybernetic Age*, it was a collection of satirical short stories about the exploits of two intelligent robots that address the questions and consequences of artificial intelligence or AI as it is now known.

The book appeared just one year after scientist Marvin Minsky co-founded the Artificial Intelligence Laboratory at MIT and boldly predicted that one day computers would be powerful enough to simulate human intelligence. 'The human brain,' Minsky famously said, 'is a computer that just happens to be made out of meat.' He also famously warned that 'once computers get control, we might never get it back . . . if we're lucky, they might decide to keep us on as pets.' Lem was also a bit of a drama queen when it came to pushing the boundaries of prediction, and in the tale of *Trurl's Electronic Bard* a robot challenges another to construct a machine that could write a poem about a haircut. The only small technical hitch was that 'in order to program a poetry machine, one would first have to repeat the entire Universe from the beginning – or at least a good piece of it.' Undaunted, Trurl sets to work with his machine that could 'in one five-billionth of a second . . . simulate one hundred septillion events at forty octillion different locations simultaneously'. The machine flies seamlessly past the dawn of time and the ice age and then with the help of auxiliary units whizzes through to civilization whereupon he has to hose down the machine to stop it overheating. Wry warnings of the potential pitfalls of artificially simulating evolution were spelled out in a surreal scene where a fly gets into the works, and 'after going from fish to amphibian to reptile to mammal, something odd took place among the primates and instead of great apes, he came out with grey drapes'. More characteristic absurdity and musings on the dangers and limits of technology can be found in the tale of *How the World Was Saved*, where Trurl puts together a machine that can create anything starting with the letter 'n', from negligées to narcotics, noodles and even negatives. Trurl asks it to produce 'natrium' and the machine says it cannot because it has never heard of it. It is only sodium in Latin grumbles Trurl, and the machine replies indignantly, 'Look old boy, if I could do everything starting with *n* in every possible language, I'd be a Machine That Could Do Everything in the

Whole Alphabet, since any item you care to mention undoubt-edly starts with n in one foreign language or another. It's not that easy. I can't go beyond what you programmed.' Even more poetically the robot protagonists at one point can be found herding stars together to create a cosmic billboard. Lem dismissed this as 'pure fairy tale' but there are surely a few adventurous advertising sign companies out there who are busy working out how to fill up all that empty space up there.

Lem had a peculiar sense of humour even as a child. As he himself pointed out, 'Norbert Wiener begins his autobiogra-phy with the words "I was a child prodigy". What I would have to say is "I was a monster".' He also reveals rather pompously that he could write by the age of four, 'but had nothing of great importance to communicate by that means'. His first letter he recalls, was a 'terse account' to his father of how he had pooed through a hole in a cabin floor while on holiday with his mother. Despite this delightful revelation, Lem defied expectations, and heavily encouraged by his father went on to study medicine albeit 'half-heartedly'. Lem's studies were interrupted by the German occupation, during which he worked as a mechanic and welder. When he was finally able in 1946 to return to studying medicine, he judiciously did not complete his exams for fear of being drafted for life into the Polish army, a fate that had befallen all of his friends.

Lem started writing in his spare time while a research assistant in a scientific institution, and bitterly recounts how his early works were 'tortured' by publishers because they were considered ideologically improper, and how reviewers marked him out as counterrevolutionary and decadent. This was the trait that he had already shown at the age of four, but the strength of his writing, as I. F. Clarke pointed out, was that 'like Wells, he had a scientific education and his thinking follows a strict didactical line which is comparable to the clear-cut Wellsian ideology of social evolutionism'. It was this dogged determinism that characterized not just his work but also his love life. In 1950 he met and fell in love with Barbara Lesniak, a medical doctor, who 'after two or three years of siege', finally accepted his proposal of marriage.

Meanwhile, Lem in his determined manner had also laid siege to his writing. Following government reform in 1956 things became a bit easier politically and he wrote a series of successful (but no less subversive) science-fiction novels, including one of his best known, *Solaris* in 1961. It wasn't until 1964 that he published his greatest and arguably his most accurate work of prediction, *Summa Technologiae*. The book has been called 'a landmark work of futurology' and was Lem's 'General Theory of Everything' as he modestly liked to call it. A philosophical treatise on everything from Norbert Wiener's concept of cybernetics to biological engineering, AI and phantomology (which we now call virtual reality, VR), it also took a sharp look at evolution. Lem for once did not hide behind what he called the *licentia poetica* of science fiction that renders people pleasurably unaccountable for their predictions, but attempted real futurological prognosis. 'Can one,' he asked, 'create a synthetic reality which, like a face-mask, will cover all of a person's senses, to the point where he will not be able to tell that he has been separated from the real world . . . ?' When the book appeared in Poland, it was 'scrupulously overlooked' and 'sank without trace', aided by a damming criticism of Lem's predictive competence by a certain Mr Kolakowski, whom Lem never forgave. Even thirty years later, Lem was raging that Kolakowski had not retracted his words, despite that fact that 'so much of what I wrote there has in the meantime come true'. Just look, Lem challenged him, at the abundance of literature on cyberspace, virtual reality, and 'price catalogues which offer a rich sampling of the apparatuses which I had once imagined . . . with names like Eye-Phone and Data-Glove'.

Summa Technologiae was, indeed, in many ways an extraordinary book, which Lem in his essay *Thirty Years Later* was more than happy to remind us in great detail. 'By phantomatics I designated a method by means of which a person can be linked up via his entire sensorium to the computer (which I refer to as the machine or, simply, the phantomat). The computer inputs into the sensory organs, such as the eyes, ears, dermis, and others, stimuli which perfectly imitate the stimuli which normally are supplied continuously by the world, that is, the ordinary environment. At the same time the computer is feedback-linked, which means that it is functionally dependent on the perceptory activity of the phantomatized person. In this way it creates an unshakable conviction in the subject of this procedure that he is in a place where he certainly is not, that he is really experiencing what is in fact only an illusion, that he is behaving in ways in which he normally never does.'

Although the ghostly term phantomology never caught on, he had foreseen the methodology of VR in more technological detail than anyone previously. The psychological benefits (and even needs) of such virtual experiences had, it should be remembered, been beautifully sketched out by Francis Bacon over 300 years previously. But what is perhaps most extraordinary is that Lem, who was securely tucked away in Poland, claimed he was blissfully unaware of all the futurological and technological happenings outside of his isolated country and that he arrived at his predictions independently. When he wrote *Summa Technologiae* he had no idea, he boasts, that Ossip Flechtheim had worked out a concept for futurology already back in 1943, or even about the pioneering computer work of Kahn and his collaborators at the Rand Corporation and the Hudson Institute in the 1960s.

Lem must have been at least partly aware of the burgeoning futurist community, conferences and organizations, because he ruthlessly satirized them in his 1971 book *The Futurological Congress*. Written as the memoirs of Ijon Tichy, 'the year is 2098 . . . with 69 billion inhabitants legally registered and approx another 26 billion in hiding. The average annual temp has fallen four degrees. In 15 or 20 years there will be glaciers here.' In the bizarre story, futurists from all over the world have come together in a hundred-storey Hilton in Costa Rica to discuss the population explosion. But as the main protagonist points out, 'since the number of futurologists grows in proportion to the increase in magnitude of all humanity, their meetings are marked by crowds and confusion.' The first confusion Mr Tichy experiences is when 'two stunning girls in topless togas, their bosoms tattooed with forget-me-nots and snowflakes, came over and handed me a glossy folder.' He then wanders into a room where the banquet 'was arranged in the unmistakeable shape of genitalia'. Tichy sadly accepts that he has strayed into the wrong hall, and heads off to hear about an imminent world famine facing humanity and the warning of impending cannibalism from a Swiss futurist. At one point the hotel bar is seized and destroyed by demonstrators and the conference collapses further into chaos when the water supply is contaminated with a hallucinogen, causing the unsuspecting participants to dream about being in the future.

In this surreal future 'natural birds no longer exist', there are 'defrostees' and we live in a 'psychemized' society in which major violations are 'mindjacking (mental abduction)' and 'gene larceny (sperm bank robbery, particularly when the sperm is pedigreed)'. The grim consequences and wicked potential of VR are also laid out by Lem in a scene in which

'A certain Mrs Bonnicker, desiring to dispose of her husband, a man inordinately fond of safaris, presented him on his birthday with a ticket to the Congo and a big-game-hunting permit. Mr Bonnicker spent the next several months having the most incredible jungle adventures, unaware that the whole time he was lying in a chicken coop up in the attic, under heavy psychemization. If it hadn't been for the firemen who discovered Mr Bonnicker in the course of putting out a two-alarmer on the roof, he would surely have died of malnutrition, which *nota bene* he assumed was only natural, since the hallucination at that point had him wandering aimlessly through the desert'.

Evil applications of VR were also well predicted in *Summa*, though Lem admits he overlooked any application of a sexual nature. As he rather prudishly put it, 'my main focus did not extend to haremic computerization, nor any other of its licentious forms'. He did, however, predict in 1991 that in terms of VR 'the erotically orientated industry will prove more profitable than one administering space walks'. He also admitted that he originally overestimated the potential of AI. 'Thirty years ago I could not see as well as I can today the colossal obstacles on the road to humanlike artificial intelligence.' Not only did Lem readily admit his mistakes but, also less popularly, those of others. Legendary for his outbursts against what he believed was largely non-scientific science fiction, he had his honorary membership of the Science Fiction Writers of America revoked in 1973.

Brutal though he was in his condemnations, as I. F. Clarke forgivingly says, 'When he attacks the specious arguments of "the apologist for the culture-shaping, anticipative, predictive and mythopoeic role of SF", his castigations are not envious but loving. He has the highest ideals for a form of fiction that is rarely serious enough for his ambitious conception of the illuminating and interpretational duties of a science-based literature.'

Until he died in 2006, Lem lived modestly and reclusively in his native Poland, and took great and obvious pleasure in refusing to be coaxed out for absurd sums of money for predictions, appearances, conferences and TV interviews. To date, 27 million copies of his books have been printed and translated into forty-one languages – something that even he could not have predicted when back in the 1950s he lived in a small flat with mould on the walls and had to commute to see his wife because they couldn't afford to live together. Towards the end of his life he turned his back on science-fiction writing and returned to what he called 'real' future forecasting. This, despite his bitter experience that 'a precursor who appears a year or two before a big wave wins fame and fortune. Whoever makes an entry thirty years before it, though, is at best forgotten, and at worst derided. My fate was the latter.'

CHAPTER 6

FAST FORWARD

The one fact about the future of which we can be certain is that it will be utterly fantastic.

Arthur C. Clarke

When President Kennedy announced on 25 May 1961 that the USA would put a man on the moon before the decade was out, it was not so much a prediction as a promise. The space race had already begun in earnest when the Russians launched Sputnik I in 1957, and Khrushchev crowed 'Let the capitalist countries catch up.' And despite the belief by some Americans that their country would lose the race because 'their Germans are better than our Germans', Kennedy was determined to fast track America into the future. 'No single project in this period,' he said, 'will be more impressive to mankind, or more important for the long range exploration of space.' But if he never doubted that America would achieve this goal, nor did most futurists. The only difference was that on 20 July, 1969, when Armstrong put his left foot on the moon, many futurists had long since imagined another, even more fantastic, future.

For writer and futurist Sir Arthur C. Clarke, the moon landing was old hat. He had already been there and back again countless times in his mind, and was way off in the future on another predictive planet envisioning space tourism and extra-terrestrial colonies. In a characteristically bold epilogue to the astronauts' account, *First on the Moon*, he was already fast-tracking space tourism. 'Let us not overlook the use of space for recreation,' he wrote. 'This, after all, will be the greatest industry of the centuries that lie ahead.' This was not just momentary light-headedness: back in 1953, Clarke had written an enthusiastic article for *Holiday* magazine in which he de-scribed in great detail a space hotel with gymnasiums, swim-ming pools and even specially curved billiard tables to take into account the radial gravity field. Even the administrator of NASA, Thomas Paine, was swept along in the post-landing euphoria to announce that the first space passengers would be visiting the moon by the 1980s. But as Peter Ryan remarked in *The Invasion of the Moon* published just two weeks after the event, 'What the fare will be remains an interesting question – at present the return ticket for three comes to $350 million. Yet one day a trip to the moon may be the only way for some of us living today to see our grandchildren. Some enterprising Amer-ican airlines have already started their waiting lists.' Ryan also predicted that 'ordinary healthy citizens will be able to make the journey in the same comfort that they enjoy in jet liners.' Perhaps it isn't so surprising then that airline entrepreneur Sir Richard Branson is already selling places on a waiting list for the Virgin Galactic spaceship which will take you for a quick day trip outside the atmosphere in 2008 for a mere $200,000. Meanwhile, space tourism confines itself to millionaires who, after two years of training and a generous payment (an estimated $20 million), can accompany the Russians to the International Space Station.

It appears to be both a hazard and a privilege of the job that futurists will at some point in their career indulge in predictions about life and travel in space. But as Clarke warned in 1970, 'Anything written about the moon at the beginning of the 1970s will probably look silly in the 1980s, and hilarious in the 1990s.' Not, he implied because we would overestimate the potential, but because we would underestimate it. Our predictions would, he teased, be of particular amusement to the 'increasingly numerous inhabitants of our first extra-terrestrial colony'. Clarke has been forgiven for many an intergalactic indiscretion, because unlike other futurists he did actually get a few things very right, but also because he has, over the years, openly and un-sheepishly admitted to those things which he did not.

Clarke was from the same remarkable generation that brought us Asimov and Lem, but they were in many ways light years apart. Clarke was brought up on a farm in Somerset, England, where he voraciously read second–hand American science-fiction magazines that had made their way from children across the Atlantic as ships' ballast. More ballast for the brain came from his engineer uncle, who gave him electrical components to fiddle with, resulting in early rocket-to-the-moon fantasies and experiments. Inventive from an early age, Clarke also impressed his school friends with a home-made telescope, a map of the moon that he had drawn himself and his budding storytelling skills. Despite the fact that he could not afford to go straight on to university and was waylaid by a relatively dull job as a civil servant, Clarke's imaginative talent was not to be wasted or repressed for long. In 1941 he joined the Royal Air Force and became a radar technician working on the early warning defence system that contributed to its success in the Battle of Britain.

During his time in the RAF he published not only his first science-fiction stories but also some of his most influential non-fiction. In 1945 Clarke wrote a detailed, illustrated, four-page article for *Wireless World* entitled 'Extra-Terrestrial Relays, Can Rocket Stations Give World-Wide Radio Coverage'. In it he predicted – and proposed – the idea of communications satellites in geosynchronous orbit above the earth that would be able to send radio and television signals over the entire surface of the planet. 'A true broadcast service,' he wrote, 'giving constant field strength at all times over the whole globe would be invaluable, not to say indispensable, in a world society.' At the time even expert readers raised a sceptical eyebrow at this idea, even though as Clarke was busy pointing out 'everything envisaged here is a logical extension of developments in the last ten years', including his proposition that they could be easily and efficiently powered by solar energy. Twelve years later, when the Russians launched the first artificial satellite Sputnik I, not only had they thrown down the proverbial space glove but brought Clarke's idea one step nearer to reality. Not to be outdone, the Americans got to work and in 1962 the Telstar I satellite was the first to transmit telephone conversations and live television signals across the Atlantic. By 1969 Intelsat satellites were in place in the three positions and at the height foreseen by Clarke, and beamed not only live coverage of the moon landing across the world but expert commentary from Clarke himself from the 'global broadcast booth'.

Clarke received the grand sum of £15 for his 1945 article, and was still joking on the sixtieth anniversary of its publication that he really should have patented the idea. But while Clarke permits himself 'the modest cough of the minor poet' for the accuracy of his prediction, he also readily admits to his failures closer to earth. In a series of articles for *Playboy* magazine in the early 1960s, Clarke wrote enthusiastically about the coming revolutions in transport that he believed would change the very pattern of human society. The future of transport, was, he predicted, with Ground Effect Machines (GEMs) that hover a few inches from the ground supporting themselves by downward blasts of air. 'Because they have no physical contact with the surface beneath them, GEMs can travel with equal ease over ice, snow, sand, ploughed fields, swamps, molten lava – you name it, and the GEM can cross it.' He not only wrote great potential advertising slogans for the mini-hovercrafts, but envisaged whole motorways for 'aircars' in the early twenty-first century with road signs warning 'NO WHEELED VEHICLES ON THIS HIGHWAY'. Because of their unique ability to get about, he foresaw that 'breakdown vans of the future are going to receive SOS calls from families stranded in some very odd places'. This is in fact just what happened to Clarke himself. He moved to Sri Lanka in 1956 and during his initial enthusiasm for GEMs imported a four-seater 'Hover Hawk' in which to get around. He soon realized to his dismay that it was difficult to control and didn't dare take it out on the roads. Instead, he ventured out to sea, where the spray obscured visibility. His last outing in it was to a superb sandy beach, where a pile of brushwood ripped open the rubber skirt and deflated both the ego and the machine.

The driving force of personal practicality was also behind his 1962 predictions about the future of communication. Living in Sri Lanka, and not keen on travelling, it was clearly in his interest that, 'as communications improve, so the need for transportation will decrease'. Furthermore, from his 'tech-nopolis' in Colombo today he can look back to the time when he foresaw 'the business of the future may be run by executives who are scarcely ever in each other's presence'. He also dreamt that no one need ever be lost or lonely again, envisaging 'a simple position and direction finding device', and a 'personal transceiver, so small and compact that every man carries one with no more inconvenience than a wristwatch'. While his predictions of GPS systems and mobile phones in 1962 were not entirely groundbreaking, he admitted in 1999 that he never could have imagined the potential of the fax machine or the personal computer.

Clarke's endearing honesty and often humorous approach to prediction is also revealed in his legendary 'Three Laws', the first of which (with tongue in cheek), he updated for political correctness in the 1999 edition of *Profiles of the Future*:

1) When a distinguished but elderly scientist states that something is possible, (s)he is almost certainly right. When (s)he states that something is impossible, (s)he is very probably wrong.
2) The only way of discovering the limits of the possible is to venture a little way past them into the impossible.
3) Any sufficiently advanced technology is indistinguishable from magic.

By the early 1960s Clarke had established a modest reputation as a writer of science fiction and technological things to come. But what really catapulted Clarke into the limelight was his collaboration with Stanley Kubrick on the cult science-fiction film *2001*, which was based on his short story *The Sentinel*. Legend has it that they decided to make the film about intelligent life on other worlds (among other complex things) after a night at a bar when they spotted a UFO in the moonlit sky above New York. The UFO turned out to be a satellite, and the film, which appeared in 1968, brought Clarke the dubious honour of being the only futurist (to date) who can boast an Oscar nomination. While planning the film, Kubrick, who was known for his thoroughness, commissioned a Delphi-style opinion-finding mission. A group of twenty-one leading scientists and futurists that included Mead and Asimov were interviewed on their thoughts for the future of mankind. Most appeared to support Kubrick's belief in the possibility of benign extra-terrestrial life, and he planned to open the film with a selection of their musings. Above all Kubrick wanted to set the scene by showing it was a carefully considered and legitimate intellectual and scientific question rather than just part of the trend for paranoid B-rated science-fiction fantasies about little green men. Unfortunately, by the time Kubrick had finished the main film, it was so long that the 'real' future part had to be abandoned. A book of the original 1966 transcripts edited by Kubrick's assistant Tony Frewin reveals some of the popular predictions of the time, such as the one by Professor John Good who said mysteriously that extraterrestrial life will contact us when they feel the time is right, but that computers will one day be intelligent enough to repair their own neuroses. 'I think the moment that machines will become, as it were, an oracle, that they will decide to speak to give us advice, will be within a few years of the construction of the first ultra-intelligent machine.' In 2004 he still stood by his belief that computers can have a personality of their own (like HAL in the film).

Although it deviously and deliberately raised more questions than it answered, 2001 gave Clarke career's a lift-off. After this it seemed he could do no wrong, and Clarke wrote not just one sequel, 2010, but 2061, and also even more ambitiously 3001 The Final Odyssey, in which people are living in space colonies, but sadly still do not appear to have invented a decent improvement on the toothbrush. From the beginning of the fourth millennium, one of Clarke's characters in 3001 plays the popular futurist mind-game 'jumpers' (as in jumping into another time), and asks if 'the people of 2001 . . . would not feel as utterly overwhelmed in our age 3001 as someone from 1001 would have felt in theirs. Many of our technological achievements they would have anticipated; indeed they would have expected satellite cities, and colonies on the Moon and planets. They might even have been disappointed, because we are not yet immortal, and have sent probes only to the nearest stars . . .'

Clarke's status is such that he does not have a mere lunar crater named after him like Verne and Wells, but much more appropriately, like Asimov, a whole own asteroid. But Clarke himself would like to be remembered not simply as an asteroid, or the man who predicted satellites, but someone who foresaw something much more ambitious and magical – the space elevator, which he describes to great and vertigo-inducing effect in several of his books. The idea was, he willingly admits, invented by a Russian engineer who back in 1960 proposed the building of a habitable ring around the world linked to the earth by towers at the equator. In an article for *The Times* in 2005, Clarke claimed that rockets have 'as much future in space as dog sleds in serious Antarctic exploration'. The cheapest method to get to space will instead be via cables linking satellites to the ground 22,300 miles (35,780 km) below. When he first described this method in his novel *The Fountains of Paradise* in 1978, there was no material on earth deemed strong enough (apart from diamond, which appears to have been rejected on grounds of cost rather than aesthetics). The subsequent discovery of a third form of carbon, C60, or Buckminsterfullerene (so named because of the shape), means that building a space elevator is now a 'completely viable engineering proposition'. If, that is, 'the strongest material that could ever exist' can ever be mass-produced. Clarke even predicts that it will eventually be cheaper to make a round trip rather than a one-way journey to space, because of the energy generated on the return journey.

The question as to who might actually want to buy a one-way ticket up this stairway to the heavens is left tantalizingly open by Clarke. As for what you might do when you are up there is apparently less difficult to foresee – you get into a giant sling that shoots you off to your preferred destination in the solar system. You would, he concedes, probably still need a rocket or two to get back to earth, though that is only until slings and elevators are built on other planets. If this ever happens, he warns (sounding amusingly like a potential Easy-space airline promoter), 'the chief expense of space travel would be for catering and in-flight movies.' Space elevators are not so much a question of 'if', says Clarke, but 'when'. And the answer he says, has always been 'about 50 years after everyone has stopped laughing', although in 2005 he half-jokingly said, 'Maybe I should now revise it to 25 years.' As Clarke says, better to be a naïve optimist than a naïve pessimist.

The dream of populating the moon and other galaxies in the late 1960s and early 1970s was not just about a triumph of technology over terrain, but also a response to the Cold War situation, and growing pessimism about the state of spaceship earth and its burgeoning population. It was no coincidence that as Clarke was optimistically escalating civilization up on to other planets and satellites, there was a growing sense of Malthusian gloom and doom down below. One year before the moon landing, the Club of Rome was founded by a group of business leaders to address what they believed were more pressing forms of escalation – that demands on the earth's resources were fast-forwarding us to our limits. To put their urgent concerns about the state of socio-economic trends to the test, they commissioned four young scientists at MIT to investigate the future of the world using system theory and pioneering new computer modelling techniques. Using the World3 computer model the team produced twelve scenarios of possible world development to the year 2100. Their predictions were published under the title *Limits to Growth* in 1972; the title, like Cassandra, has ever since become a byword for pessimistic thinking about the future of the planet.

This was the beginning of big-time environmentalism, and the authors were an ostensibly diverse group that included Dana Meadows, a self-appointed 'unceasing optimist', Jorgen Randers, 'the cynic', and Dennis Meadows, the ideological piggy in the middle. Nevertheless, they had a unified message. 'If,' they concluded, 'present growth trends in world population, industrialisation, pollution, food production, and resource depletion continue unchanged, the limits to growth on this planet will be reached sometime within the next 100 years. The most probable result will be a rather sudden and uncontrolled decline in both population and industrial capacity.' The collapse of world order could, suggested the authors, be prevented by a 'Copernican revolution of the mind'. This, they believed, should entail nothing less than a re-evaluation of the belief in endless growth and a revocation of wastefulness. Also recommended were zero population growth, a levelling-off of industrial production, increased control of pollution and a shift away from consumer goods to a service-oriented economy. The report was instantly dubbed 'Malthus with a computer' and was as explosive as it was divisive. Interestingly, many of the critics of *Limits to Growth* mirrored Marx's opinion on Malthus' book on population, which he described as 'nothing but a sensational pamphlet'. But for others at the time, *Limits to Growth*, just a thin paperback by an unknown Washington publisher, took on the role of true eco-bible for the future and as a ghastly and serious warning that was to be ignored at our peril.

Herman Kahn and his staff at the Hudson Institute were among the first to voice their objections to the findings of *Limits to Growth*, which so enraged Kahn that he devoted much of the last ten years of his life to disproving its thesis. His reply to the book was that 'with current and near current technology, we can support 15 billion people in the world at twenty thousand dollars per capita for a millennium.' And that, he added in his inimitable firm style, 'seems to be a very conservative statement'. The MIT study thought, by comparison, that 3.9 billion was comfortably below the planet's carrying capacity, but 6 billion (as of the year 2000) certainly was not. Kahn did not, like the authors of *Limits to Growth*, expect the path to the future to be smooth. In fact, he conceded that it will be full of 'wiggles and reversals in the basic trends'. But essentially he was an optimist and did not believe he was in danger of repeating Malthus' pivotal failure to predict progress. Kahn's answer to *Limits to Growth* was *The Next 200 Years*, published with two colleagues in 1976. In it they argued that human reason would win and that resources were not a limit to economic growth as anyway there was still the rest of the solar system and all those resources to colonize. Interestingly, one of Kahn's main concerns was that a fashion for doomsday thinking could actually produce a self-fulfilling prophecy; i.e. if you preach resistance to economic growth it will lead to the kind of problems you were trying to prevent in the first place. Alongside this warning he happily predicted that '200 years from now, we expect, almost everywhere humans will be numerous, rich and in control of the forces of nature.'

More objections came from other serious quarters, including the Science Policy Research Unit of the University of Sussex in England. In their 1973 response, *Models of Doom*, the authors, a group of thirteen essayists, declared that they are critical of *Limits to Growth* 'not because they want to score points, but because they wish to clarify complex issues'. The group was, on the one hand, in agreement about the urgency of some of the issues raised by the book, but, on the other, critically examined the methodology and the data and assumptions about resources that were fed into the model. One of the main things the Sussex group objected to was what it called 'computer fetishism' or, more brutally put, the 'garbage in, garbage out' trap. It was far too polite and professional to say that the data MIT put in to the model was garbage, calling it instead 'Malthus in, Malthus out', and quoted Meadows' own admission that 'only about 0.1% of the data on the variables required to construct a satisfactory world model is now available'. Another complaint was that the method used by MIT was an attempt to 'substitute mathematics for knowledge and computation for understanding'. But as so many futurists have discovered to their peril, there is no definite knowledge about the future.

It was in a strange way a great compliment to the power and integrity of the authors' work that *Limits to Growth* was taken seriously enough to be rebuffed by such renowned institutes and futurists. Even the Organization for Economic Co-operation and Development (OECD) in Paris sat up and took notice, publishing its reply in 1979. This was the cumulative effort of three years' work from 1976, and was titled *Facing the Future , Mastering the Probable and Managing the Unpredictable*. Less modestly, it has recently been called by the

OECD 'one of the best future studies in the 20th century', as it predicted a 'possible second oil shock', 'the likelihood of declining growth' and the 'likelihood of rising unemployment rates' in OECD countries. On the other hand, the OECD sheepishly admits that it missed the fall of the Soviet Union as the possibility was not actually built into the scenario equations. In direct answer to the concerns in *Limits to Growth*, the OECD predicted that 'world food demand in the year 2000 will not be pressing against physical limits'. It also believed, unlike the doomsayers, that broadly speaking there were still numerous energy resources and economic options to be tapped.

Extraordinarily, the OECD publication was, according to one internal source, 'almost discarded, rejected, not largely publicised'. This was, he regrets, largely because of the fact it was against the opinion of some of the most important and influential member countries and mainstream staff at the time (i.e. the chief economist of the OECD didn't actually agree with the results).

Twenty years after it was first published, *Limits to Growth* was upgraded to *Beyond the Limits*, because by then the authors had decided that no one had listened to their early warnings and 'humanity had already overshot the limits of Earth's support capacity'. Then, in 2004, *The Thirty Year Update* was published and it not only reiterated and reheated the original warnings but used the popping of the dotcom bubble around the turn of the millennium as an illustration of 'global overshoot and collapse'. In all three books the authors stress that their work is not prediction, and claim that until the third book they were in fact generally optimistic. The difficult nature of the debate around *Limits to Growth* is a typical and apposite example of the pitfalls and problems of prediction in environmental issues (and characteristic of the heated debate around global warming today). On the one hand, the authors claim it is *not* a forecast, and that they are '*not* predicting that a particular future will take place'. But on the other, they warn that if we don't change our course of action, it will. As science fiction writer Ray Bradbury once quipped, 'I don't try to predict the future – I try to prevent it.'

The early 1970s saw a growing number of organizations and academic institutes established to deal with future planning and to provide ideas and research for government bodies. Unlike Kahn's brazen approach, most of these worked quietly, diligently and unspectacularly on less controversial issues such as city planning, natural resources and demographics. In 1973 the World Future Studies Federation was founded in Rome to promote future education and research, and by 1974 there were already some 200 courses in future studies scattered throughout North American colleges and universities, and one bona fide graduate degree programme in futures at the University of Houston. A course entitled 'The History of the Future' given by Warren Wagar at the State University of New York in Binghamton was proving to be a hot tip, although he initially suspected that students enrolled for the course because they thought it would be an easy ride. In the first year, he had a hundred eager students, which rose quickly to 450. As an overwhelmed and flattered Wagar recalled, it 'had become a monster', albeit a pleasant one. By 1975 the World Future Society was boasting that it had held the largest gathering of futurists ever. Of the 2,800 attendees, not all could really claim to be bona fide futurists (there were a few attendant groupies and voyeurs), but all were part of a growing bandwagon pointing in the direction of the future.

This 'fast-forward' spirit of the 1970s was summed up by one of the few female futurists, Eleonora Barbieri Masini, who said, 'The faster the pace of change the further forward we have to look.' Masini studied under Jungk and de Jouvenel but was also deeply influenced by Gaston Berger who, in true French philosophical style, said of thinking about the future that the faster the car the further the headlights have to shine in order to avoid pitfalls. As professor of Future Studies in Rome she is warmly greeted as a guest of honour at conferences today as the (only) European Grande Dame of futurism. Masini does not employ shock tactics, nor has she been seduced by the glare of the stage lights that attract some of her more prominent colleagues to such events. Instead, she makes speeches about her role in realizing Flechtheim's dream of a proper academic discipline, proudly sends her multi-national students back to their countries of origin with hopes for a better future, and preaches the simple message that: 'only by learning to look ahead and by learning to conceptualize and understand the future . . . can we think optimistically about the future'.

While government, academic and public interest were growing in the 1970s, there was also a belief that futurism could be of direct, hands-on use to down-to-earth, everyday business. One of the first to prove this was the American Peter Drucker, whose imperial middle name 'Ferdinand' reveals something of his Austrian roots. He was born in Vienna, but by the 1970s had been in America for over forty years, and had a long history of successful consultancy and writing behind him. He also had a lot ahead of him – in 2004 at the age of ninety-five, he published his thirty-sixth book and was showing no signs of retiring completely.

When he died in 2005 he was remembered as the man who is credited with teaching big business and management how to plan for the future. This is somewhat ironic since as a child

Drucker was deemed totally un-teachable. At school he loved to write, but his handwriting was illegible and his two Viennese teachers despaired of him. In an entertaining autobiography written in 1979, he recalled how they 'failed to teach me what both they and I knew I needed to learn'. He was brought up in a family of intellectuals: he proudly claimed that his mother was one of only 351 people who in 1900 bought a copy of the first edition of Freud's *Die Traumdeutung* (*The Interpretation of Dreams*). The intellectual cosiness of Vienna was such that as a child Drucker met Freud on several occasions. In *Adventures of a Bystander* he recalls how when just eight or nine years old, he shook hands with Freud and his father congratulated him with the words, 'You have just met the most important man in Austria, and perhaps in Europe.' Significantly, what impressed young Drucker was not the great man himself or his controversial ideas, but that someone could be even more important than the great Emperor of Austria.

Not long after this, in 1918, the last of the Habsburg emperors abdicated, and a 'Republic of German Austria' was proclaimed. As was the custom in Vienna, Republic Day was celebrated on the 11th of November every year, and it was on this day in 1923 that Drucker, a week short of his fourteenth birthday, decided to leave Vienna forever. As an old family friend said of him, Drucker always showed a 'willingness to go it alone', and the sight of socialist workers rallying and marching together from all over the city left him feeling peculiarly like a bystander rather than a participant. In 1927, which was as soon as was decently possible, Drucker left Austria, and continued his education in England. By the early 1930s he was in Germany working as a reporter for a newspaper and writing a biography of a Jewish philosopher, when a Nazi commissar of Frankfurt was announced and he realized that it was time to go. On the night he started packing in 1933 there was, he recalled, a knock at his door. When he realized who it was, Drucker wasn't sure whether or not to be relieved. It was Reinhold Hensch, a colleague of his from the newspaper from which he had just resigned, dressed in full stormtrooper uniform. Hensch, who was to become one of the most wanted Nazi war criminals (known as 'The Monster'), begged Drucker not to leave. Then, according to Drucker, Hensch begged him to look after his Jewish ex-girlfriend, and then broke down and revealed how scared he was of the 'madmen' in the Nazi party. That long, terrible night, before Drucker managed to catch a train out of the country, he had a dream of what was to be his first major book. *The End of Economic Man*, subtitled *A Study of the New Totalitarianism*, was published in 1939, and analysed the 'demons' that led to the emergence of a fascist dictator. When Winston Churchill reviewed the book for *The Times* he praised Drucker for being 'one of those writers to whom almost anything can be forgiven because he not only has a mind of his own, but has the gift of starting other minds along a stimulating line of thought.'

Drucker arrived in America in 1937 and turned to writing not about the past but the future, 'assuming that Hitler would ultimately be defeated'. In 1942 he published *The Future of Industrial Man,* which caught the eye of General Motors for its examination of the changing role of big business in society. Drucker was subsequently given his first consultancy job – the task of looking closely at the workings of the company from the point of view of a political and social scientist (General Motors had no illusions that he actually knew anything about the car industry). Ultimately, his observations and recommendations that were published in 1946 as *Concept of a Corporation* were to be responsible for the 'worldwide vogue for decentralization'. The book became the corporate bible at Ford, which, in Drucker's words, 'had been going downhill for thirty years'. His recommendations were for many companies way ahead of their time, but, it has been estimated that 80 per cent of the 500 biggest US companies in the 1980s subsequently decentralized following his advice.

Not only was Drucker instrumental in foreseeing and promoting the benefits of outsourcing and decentralization, he was one of the first to write extensively about that which we today call the 'knowledge society'. In *The Age of Discontinuity* he foresaw the growth of the industries 'which produce and distribute ideas and information rather than goods'. The demand for knowledge workers would grow, he predicted, but he also reassured his readers that it would not automatically lead to a disappearance of work, nor would it eliminate skills. The title of the book referred to his belief that while most industrial technology was merely a continuation, extension and modification of the inventions and technologies of the fifty years before the First World War, change or discontinuity was going to be a key characteristic of the years to come. In this book, published in the year of the moon landing, Drucker foresaw not only the take-off of new technology and a knowledge-based industry but also a shift from an international economy to a world economy: he presciently called this movement the Global Shopping Centre, and predicted that it would represent a triumph of economy over government.

Drucker never flattered himself that he was a futurist (there are enough others to do that for him), and preferred to use the term 'social ecologist', whose job he said is explicitly to improve the functioning of society. And for all his accreditations, his imagination only failed him, wrote one critic, when it came to book titles: they are not the most inspired titles (e.g. *Managing for the Future, Managing in a Time of Great Change*). However, the books continue to be widely inspirational and he strove to maintain his original thread that 'performing responsible management is the alternative to tyranny and our only protection against it'. Drucker's self-confessed 'monomaniac' single-mindedness, a trait he also acknowledged and valued in such friends as Buckminster Fuller and Marshall McLuhan, won him many awards but also a few enemies. He tried, in exemplary futurist fashion, to push forward the workings of civilization, and to improve the functioning of business and thus society. But in doing so he sometimes lost a few fans, such as the time when he proposed that in compensation schemes, senior management should not be compensated more than twenty times the lowest-paid employees.

Drucker once wrote that 'nothing is as powerless as a prophet whose time has come. He becomes a priest and vision turns into a ritual. Or he becomes a celebrity who appears on the Late-Late show or in the society column. The prophet whose time has come no longer shocks; he entertains.' While Drucker ostensibly set out to teach and to coach rather than to entertain or shock, there were others who were not so reticent. In 1970, just one year after Drucker's tentatively titled *Age of Discontinuity* appeared, Alvin Toffler published *Future Shock*, the first futurist bestseller (after Nostradamus). A journalist by training, and a futurist at heart, Toffler knew how to gauge, glorify and ride the wave of change and fear. Like Drucker, he was responding to what he sensed were deep seismic shifts in the socio-economic landscape and the incumbent fears and hopes that the moon landing had stirred in the collective consciousness. The title of Toffler's book was not simply headline-grabbing, it symbolized the subtle shift at this time from the future as a passive adjunct or mere adjective to the feeling that it was a force in its own right.

Toffler's book was billed a bit like a B-grade sci-fi movie, as if the imminent arrival of the future was on a par with aliens landing from outer space. 'Future Shock is the disease of change,' screeched one garish orange cover, 'Its symptoms are already here.' The ultimate in modern futurist hypochondria, it has sold over 6 million copies worldwide.

Toffler was, he declared in his doctor-like role, chiefly concerned with alleviating what he dramatically described as 'the dizzying disorientation brought on by the premature arrival of the future'. He believed that change was happening so quickly that people were not only in danger of being overwhelmed by the future but were basically unequipped to adapt to it. For Toffler, it was as if a fast-forward button was being pushed on people's lives. The idea for the book went back to an article he wrote in 1965 for *Horizon* entitled 'The Future as a Way of Life' in which he first coined the term 'Future Shock' and urged more futurist research. One of the people to notice the potential in the article was Arthur C. Clarke, who wrote to Toffler and suggested he get in touch with Olaf Helmer and his colleagues at the RAND Corporation. Toffler travelled to California to meet them and was impressed not only by their Delphi methodology but particularly with the 'Futures Game' they had developed. This was a real board game, recalls Toffler, that 'illustrated a key futurist precept; that the occurrence of an "event" in one field raises or lowers the probabilities of events in many other fields.' Soon Toffler was advising the group on its planned independent think tank, and revelling in the spirit of camaraderie of the 'incipient futurist community'.

Toffler's formative futurist years were spent studying English at New York University, where he met his future wife, Heidi Farrell. They were both part of the trendy, bohemian post-war Greenwich Village arts scene but by the time they graduated in 1949 America was still in recession and they had to take jobs not only well below their qualifications but had to lie to potential employers about them. Alvin worked for five years as a welder and a forklift driver, and Heidi made light bulbs at General Electric, where she recalls in remarkable good humour how she was paid *not* to think. As Toffler recalled, 'the factory was the symbol of the entire industrial era and, to a boy raised in a semi-comfortable lower-middle-class home, after four years of Plato and T. S. Eliot, or art history and abstract social theory, the world it represented was as exotic as Tashkent or Tierra del Fuego.' Alvin longed to be a writer, and eventually found his way on to a trade union newspaper and by 1959 was associate editor of *Fortune* Magazine and writing for many other publications including *Playboy*.

Following their 'graduate course in reality' on the assembly lines of grim midwest factories, Alvin and Heidi had a heartfelt concern about the effects of accelerating social and technological change. *Future Shock* was not only the result of their combined efforts, talents and experiences but also several years of research. For the book Alvin interviewed everyone from scientists to hippies, and businessmen to philosophers. He wanted to know just how people perceived the changes that were happening around them, and how society was (or was not) coping. The now-legendary term 'Future Shock' came to him while interviewing a psychologist friend about culture shock. 'It occurred to me,' he recalled, 'that you could be plunged into an alien culture in your own society if an alien future arrived more rapidly than you were prepared for.' The end result was indeed shocking to the readers. It was hailed as a 'disturbing and challenging book' for not only was the 'disease' apparently already widespread but also potentially deeply damaging to society's economic, social and personal health.

As Toffler reminds us, diagnosis precedes cure; hence, the

main thrust of the book is an examination of the symptoms and a gory glimpse into how the disease might develop if not checked. In a chapter called *The Experience Makers*, Toffler makes full use of his carefully honed headline grabbing skills, with '*SERVING WENCHES IN THE SKY*'. These were apparently ladies on special themed flights who were trained to meet the every wish of TWA passengers between major American cities. He also warned that BOAC 'recently pointed a wavering finger at the future when it announced a plan to provide unmarried male passengers with "scientifically chosen blind dates in London".' Although this idea was called off following Parliamentary criticism (it was, after all, a respectable government-owned airline), as Toffler tactfully put it, 'nevertheless we can anticipate further colourful attempts to paint a psychic coating on many consumer fields.' When he looked at the burgeoning experience industries (such as Club Meds, 'body awareness' seminars or alternative group therapy) he saw the coming boom was not the result of just a desire to learn something but the need for the experience of learning itself. 'All these,' he remarked, 'provide only the palest clue as to the nature of the experience industry of the future and the great psychological corporations, or psych-corps that will dominate it.' If the original experiential industry was prostitution, he argued, then tomorrow will bring bigger and better 'experience makers'. He fantasized that perhaps one day ladies at the hairdresser's would not only have their hair dried by a mechanical bowl, but 'by directing electronic waves to her brain, it may, quite literally, tickle her fancy'. Be it via computers, pleasure probes, super Disneylands or 'experiential gambling' for shareholders, Toffler believed they would 'form a basic – if not the basic – sector of the economy' of the future. Occasionally, however, his old student left-wing reflexes popped up amidst these fantasies, and he later said in the chapter, 'the poverty-stricken masses of the world may not stand idly by as the world's favoured few traverse the path towards psychological self-indulgence.'

What also interested Toffler were the effects of living in a world that runs like 'a fast-breaking story' on the family and human relationships. If it is true, he said, that the family represented the 'giant shock absorber' of society, then it was in for some shocks of its own. Could it be, he wondered, that society is moving towards a system that Margaret Mead described, in which 'parenthood would be limited to a smaller number of families whose principal functions would be child-rearing'? The rest of us with jobs to do and busy working wives (such as his Heidi) would be 'free to function – for the first time in history – as individuals'. He even envisaged advertisements for professional parents aimed at young married couples: 'Why let parenthood tie you down? Let us raise your infant into a responsible successful adult.' The bio-parents (biological parents) would, he imagined, be allowed telephone contact and visiting rights. Not in essence so very different from Plato's fantasy of farming off the children shortly after birth to be educated communally.

In stark contrast to his own love life, Toffler foresaw the arrival of the so-called serial marriage. A pattern of temporary unions is he believes, 'the natural, the inevitable outgrowth of a social order in which automobiles are rented, dolls traded in, and dresses discarded after one-time use. It is the main stream marriage pattern of tomorrow.' He also foresaw trial marriages, gay parenting, post-retirement child-rearing, polygamy (for both sexes) and the rather worryingly titled 'geriatric group marriages'. The last of these does not allude to subversive sexual preferences but to a genteel 'group marriage of elderly people drawn together in a common search for companionship and assistance'. While his radar for changing patterns and structures of family was clearly turned on, what he did not so readily consider is whether in the future people will even want an institution called marriage or a formal contract to seal a relationship.

Toffler looked too at the deep structural changes taking place in business. In fact, his ideas were not so dramatically different from those of Peter Drucker, but he used more juicy journalistic skills to shock people into facing up to an inevitable shift from a diet of certainty to a smorgasbord of change. One of the key structural changes Toffler foresaw was the breakdown of traditional hierarchical structures and roles within firms into what he named 'ad-hocracy'. This he described as 'the fast-moving, information-rich, kinetic organisation of the future, filled with transient cells and extremely mobile individuals'. Such workers have evolved from the traditional 'organization man' tied to a company for life, into 'associative man', who lives in a state of temporariness and change with his employer. For Toffler this was not just a welcome liberation from the drudgery of the industrial age, but a prescription for stress and other symptoms of future shock.

When he was writing the book in the late 1960s, Toffler was concerned that much of what had been written about the future had a 'harsh metallic sound'. This was the sound of science fiction and bright technological optimism that was sweeping the USA and drowning out what he believed were the voices and concerns of everyday life. But like any good doctor, Toffler was not interested in just his patients, but also in what his fellow colleagues were diagnosing. In 1972 he published *The Futurists*, in which he gathered together the opinions of a wide range of people who he, by now a card-carrying futurist, considered to be at the cutting edge of the field. Of the twenty-three contributions, just one, he regretted, was from a woman (Mead), and the rest were mainly white males with an average

age of between fifty and fifty-five. This, as he said in the introduction, was a reflection of the futurist movement as it was then, rather than how he thought it ought to be.

By the time of Toffler's next key book, he too was a prime example of this strange species. With his wife Heidi still very much at his side, he published *The Third Wave*, and while at the time she did not make it on to the cover, she is widely recognized today as co-author and co-futurist. Published ten years after *Future Shock*, it was a no less sensational update of 'the roaring current of change. A current so powerful today that it overturns institutions, shifts our values and shrivels our roots.' Borrowing bluntly from Kondratieff, he said that the first wave of change corresponded to the agricultural revolution, the second to the industrial revolution, and the third is currently crashing over us in the form of post-industrialism. In his signature sensationalist style, Toffler wrote, 'this new civilization, as it challenges the old, will topple bureaucracies, reduce the role of the nation-state, and give rise to semiautonomous economies in a postimperialist world.'

Again, it was an all-consuming (and as some have quipped all-assuming) book that predicted everything from the electronic cottage to so-called prosuming (customized manufacturing) and the de-massifying of the media (e.g. more individualized/specialized publications). Toffler had a knack for coining and picking up on terms and trends that encapsulated both fears and hopes for the future, and also for getting himself noticed. *The New York Times*, recalled Heidi, 'blasted us and said that the idea of people working at home was ridiculous'. Much to the Tofflers' delight, in 1994 the paper published an article identifying this new trend, 'as if they had always known that this was the case!' Less successful was Toffler's prediction that 'a key ingredient of office work – paper – will be substantially (though not wholly) replaced'.

While fully comprehensible at the time, it was, however, completely wrong, and a trap that many consultants until quite recently fell face first into as the computer began to make inroads to office culture. Another area where his assumptions were completely off course was his prediction that 'the child of tomorrow is likely to grow up in a society far less child-centred than our own'. What he did not take into account is the fact that the fewer children we have the more we seem to invest in them emotionally and financially. Furthermore, his belief that in the future more families would work together and that children would be reared in 'electronic-cottage families' was in part a projection of his own experiences (his children often appeared in the acknowledgements as co-workers on his books).

For all their faults and failures, the Tofflers' books were the racy thrillers of futurist literature and helped boost membership of organizations such as the World Future Society. Established in 1966, the society had an estimated 50,000 members in the 1970s, and despite competition with other societies today still has around 25,000. As well as propelling futurism into the popular public arena the Tofflers played a role in popularizing the field within the realm of politics. Such was the mood of the times that even Senator Edward Kennedy had apparently pledged to create a 'Department of Futures' if he were to become president of the USA. Later, even the deeply conservative Republican government was so curious to find out more about this peculiar and somewhat magical breed of people who called themselves futurists that in 1985 President Ronald Reagan and his new Chief of Staff Donald Regan invited eight of them to a cosy lunch at the White House. What was most memorable about the lunch, recalled Heidi and Alvin, was not the high-powered intellectual discussions about the future of America and the world, but the fact they could hardly squeeze a word in edgeways between all the talking egos. According to Heidi, Regan complained 'Aaah, you futurists, you all think we're going to run around cutting each other's hair and flipping each other's hamburgers. It's going to be a service society, and America's not going to be a great manufacturing nation any more.' She recalls vividly how everyone was talking but nobody was actually listening or answering the accusation. 'I couldn't stand it anymore,' she confessed in an interview with Mary Eisenhart of the *Micro-Times*, and when one of the talking male egos paused long enough to take a breath she launched into a carefully worded answer about the fact that she believed more automation would actually bring increased productivity. As she acknowledged of her heroic attempt, 'I think I might as well have spoken to the wall.'

One Republican who was more impressed with what the Tofflers had to say is Newt Gingrich, former Speaker of the US House of Representatives, who has gushingly proclaimed *The Third Wave* 'one of the great seminal works of our time.' He has been an ardent fan since the 1970s and was so taken with the work that he taught a course based on the book and outed himself as a 'conservative futurist'. According to a proud Toffler, Gingrich also 'called upon Congress to judge every piece of legislation according to whether it accelerates or slows the transition from a Second Wave or industrial society to a "Third Wave industrial society".' Riding their own wave of popularity, the Tofflers published *Powershift* in 1990, which was deemed to be yet another dramatic wake-up call to the world. 'This is a book about power at the edge of the twenty-first century,' claimed Toffler breathlessly. 'It deals with violence, wealth and knowledge and the roles they play in our lives.' Not one to pussyfoot about, he warned us straight away that 'this is the dawn of the Powershift Era. We live at a moment when the entire structure of power that held the world together is now disintegrating.' This he observed everywhere and on every scale, 'in the office, in the supermarket . . . in our churches, hospitals, schools and homes . . . Campuses are stirring from Berkeley to Rome and Taipei, preparing to explode. Ethnic and racial clashes are multiplying.'

War and Anti-War, published just three years later, was not much more reassuring, warning dramatically of future warriors and insect-sized attack robots. It opens *and* closes with the same chilling quote from Trotsky, 'you may not be interested in war, but war is interested in you', and doesn't deviate much from this tone in between. He even tried his hand at a little Kahn-esque humour with a chapter entitled 'The Genie Unleashed'. The chapter opens bluntly: 'On a bright spring morning recently eight of us met to decide whether or not to drop a nuclear bomb on North Korea.' Two North Korean nuclear bombs had, he explained, exploded over South Korea, and 'at our worktable a sharp-tongued blond women pushed for retaliation in kind . . . a cherubic stripe-shirted nuclear researcher from a leading think tank pushed for non-nuclear options . . .' Toffler used this example of a typical war-gaming exercise to full dramatic effect. Later, he even took a swipe at bungled International Atomic Energy Agency (IAEA) inspections in Iraq in 1990 (the bomb-making programme was subsequently found not to be 'at zero' in 1993), and called the IAEA 'no more than a gnat on the hide of a radioactive rhinoceros'. He also gloomily quoted nuclear strategist Thomas Schelling, who warned 'we will not be able to regulate nuclear weapons around the world in 1999 any better than we can control the Saturday-night special, heroin or pornography today.' Following these Cassandra-like proclamations Toffler sketched what he called a preventative strategy for peace, but after some 250 pages of being seduced by war, anti-war comes rather surprisingly as a bit of an anti-climax. But such are the time-old pitfalls and challenges of futurism – if you want to woo your readers with breathtaking finely honed and honeyed pessimism, can you then expect them to be equally won over to the lure of optimism?

Although he doesn't make so many appearances or grab headlines today, Toffler is still one of the most highly revered and respected futurists around. As an 'icon of futurology', in 1991 he commanded, according to one European speakers' agency, around $50,000 per speech to a guaranteed packed and eager audience. Heidi, who finally appeared as bona fide co-author on *War and Anti-War*, usually accompanied him to such events and joined in the much-anticipated question-and-answer sessions that followed. It was then, according to one bemused bystander, that the show really started – with the famously symbiotic futurist couple fighting openly on stage, shouting 'don't be ridiculous' at each other. Their public performances were said to be rather like their visions for the future: dramatic, shocking, and in the end, rather disturbing.

CHAPTER 7

JAM TOMORROW . . .

It's a poor sort of memory that only works backwards . . .
The Queen, *Through the Looking Glass*

On a dreary bit of motorway as you reach the Viennese city limits there was, in 2005, a small cheery welcoming sign by the side of the road that said 'Mega + Trend = Vienna'. Austria's capital is certainly not mega by today's urban standards and as a trendsetter it was hot about a century ago. But, to those in the know, it was a discreet homage to one of its recently acquired residents, the American John Naisbitt.

Naisbitt was to futurism in the 1980s what Toffler was in the 1970s. But while Toffler frightened us about the future with his warnings, Naisbitt calmed and coached people with a handful of 'new directions', the so-called megatrends that he depicted as transforming rather than disrupting our lives. He defined a megatrend as a large, over-arching direction that shapes our lives for a decade or more, and these included the now well-known and documented shift from an industrial society to an information society, from centralization to decentralization, and from a national economy to a world economy. He also predicted big shifts in society from hierarchies to networking, from institutional help to self-help, and from representative democracy to participatory democracy. While much of this was not brand-spanking new, Naisbitt, like Toffler, had a talent for taking a bird's-eye view on what was happening and putting it coherently together, coining talisman-like phrases such as 'we are drowning in information but starved for knowledge', and bringing the idea of the future to a wider audience. *Megatrends*, published in 1982, not only established the word 'megatrend' as common futurist currency, but Naisbitt as a much-sought-after futurist.

With his reassuring, bear-like appearance (attributable to Viking/Scottish ancestry), warm manner and determined optimism, Naisbitt is a man you would really like to trust with the future. But Naisbitt does not like to be called a futurist, not only because he complains there are too many unqualified people lurking under that banner, but more modestly because he sees himself merely as 'a spectator of the future'. From his penthouse, where he lives with his Austrian wife, overlooking the rooftops of Vienna, Naisbitt explains how from a young age he always dreamt of seeing the bigger picture. Born in 1929, he grew up on a sugar-beet farm in a tight-knit community of Mormons in Glenwood, southern Utah. His deeply devout Mormon grandfather had three wives, 'but only two of them at the same time', reassures Naisbitt, and he has a couple of hundred first cousins whose names he couldn't recall even if he wanted to. Glenwood was geographically and culturally a cul-de-sac, but one of his strongest memories is of seeing the broad backs of his big farmer uncles gathering around the radio to listen to President Roosevelt's fireside chats which aimed to boost morale during the Great Depression. This was the tantalizing voice of the outside world, and Naisbitt was determined to get out and find out about it as quickly as he conceivably could. His first escape route was at seventeen, when he joined the Marine Corps. While in the Marines he finally travelled away from home for the first time in his life and – more importantly – read his very first book. Today, Naisbitt still recalls the title – appropriately a book called *Lust for Life* about the painter Vincent Van Gogh. After that there was no stopping him, and he voraciously read anything and everything that came his way. By the time he was nineteen, he knew for sure that he had to get out of Utah for good, and also gave up three things that up to then had played an important part in his life – tenor sax, golf and religion. Leaving the Mormon faith caused such a huge scandal in the family that it wasn't until nearly sixty years later that he returned to the place of his birth. When Naisbitt left the insulated community of Glenwood he knew nothing about the world outside. When he went back in 2005, as one of the world's most famous writers about the future, it was with the same sense of curiosity, wonder and determination that marked his leaving and has defined his work ever since.

The writer Bruce Sterling once remarked that good futuristic forecasts are 'like detective work, based on three factors: means, motive and opportunity'. While Naisbitt clearly had the motive, the real means and the opportunity came later. In fact he can remember the very day when he started thinking in terms of 'the future' in the wider sense. Naisbitt had studied political science and worked his way up through the ranks of the White House to special assistant to President Johnson. It was the early 1960s, a time of pressure for new civil rights acts and a war against poverty, and he was given the daunting task of judging what the impact of various policies would be on America. 'I though that was a pretty compelling assignment,' says Naisbitt. The only problem, he explains, was that 'in this huge decentralized country, I couldn't even really say what was going on then, let alone what might go on as a result of the policies.' It was only a few years later while working for IBM that he found the key to tackling such monumental tasks. While he was standing at a Chicago newspaper kiosk, a paper from Seattle caught his eye, and he had an epiphany. 'I suddenly realized,' he says, 'that if I read all these local newspapers simultaneously every day, I would get a pretty good idea of what was going on in the country.' It was, like Darwin's Malthus moment, such a profound realization that Naisbitt left his job to set up the Urban Research Company. From then on, every morning 160 newspapers landed with a thud on his desk, and before long he had a staff of around fifty people to help scan, snip and analyse them.

While Naisbitt's was the first company to apply this method commercially, the media-scanning method of collating information has long been a staple of futurist work and is still one of the basic research techniques used in much trend research today. But the key, as all good futurists and researchers will tell you, is essentially to ask the right questions – to know what clues you are looking for, and then naturally how to interpret the 'evidence'. The key to the success of the Delphic oracle, behind the show and clever marketing strategy, was effective information-gathering and analysis, and it is well documented that Jules Verne got some of his best ideas and inspiration while flicking through the newspapers in cafes or reading the periodicals in his local library. During the Second World War this method was known simply and unglamorously as 'content analysis'. Despite censorship on the real figures and situation, by scanning the German newspapers for stories about factory openings/closings, local casualty listings and even train arrivals and delays, intelligence experts could pick up valuable telltale signs and areas of strain on the people and the economy. As Arthur Miller once wrote, 'A good newspaper is a nation talking to itself.'

The secret to the success of this system, explained Naisbitt in *Megatrends*, is that the newspaper is a closed system with limited space. 'In this forced-choice situation, societies add new preoccupations and forget old ones. In keeping track of the ones that are added and the ones that are given up, we are in a sense measuring the changing share of the market that competing societal concerns command.' What in effect happens is 'the collective news hole . . . becomes a mechanical representation of society sorting out its priorities.' Simply put, in the end it all comes down to column inches. For example, as the concern about the environment increased in the early 1970s, news on civil rights decreased on a visible line-by-line basis. This bottom-up method also tracked how concerns about racial discrimination were squeezed out by increasing amounts of reporting on sexism in the 1970s, both of which then yielded their columns to concerns about ageism.

This method is not without its critics, and many snigger readily at the idea of highly regarded and expensive futurists flicking through newspapers for a living (though, to be honest, they tend to leave the dirty work to the lowly researchers). One of the main criticisms is of journalistic and proprietary bias, i.e. how to filter out lobbying, political pressure and publishers' own hidden agendas from the results. Naisbitt defends these charges by claiming that his methodology is 'free from the effects of biased reporting because it is only the event or behaviour that we are interested in'. For many years Naisbitt's Urban Research Company successfully sold such carefully digested information in the form of trend reports and seminars to companies such as General Motors, Merrill Lynch and AT&T under the motto 'The most reliable way to anticipate the future is by understanding the present'. When he began with the reports it was a time, he recalls, of acute urban unease and unrest, with cities burning, race riots and deep concerns about the growing numbers of underprivileged. Local governments were one of the main subscribers to Naisbitt's *Urban Crisis Monitor*, as it gave them valuable insights and information on how other parts of the country were dealing with such crucial political and social issues.

Naisbitt's reputation and interest in his work was beginning to grow, and in the early 1980s he published *Megatrends*, which set out his methodology and many futurist mantras that you still hear repeated reverentially today: 'Trends are bottom-up, fads top-down' or 'Trends, like horses, are easier to ride in the direction they are already going'. The book represented a big breakthrough in wide-reaching business and commercial futurism that had begun with Drucker and gained momentum with Toffler. In fact, *Megatrends* did for Naisbitt what *Future Shock* did for Toffler, and together they paved the way for a new form and forum for more popular futurism that was not hidden sheepishly behind a guise of science fiction or fantasy. Coincidentally, Naisbitt like Toffler also attributes much of his success to the work and support of his (second) wife, and had to fight many a battle with his publishers to get her name on the cover (ironic that the publishers resisted while he was busy measuring column inches given over to sexism). Patricia Aburdene eventually appeared as co-author and co-futurist on *Megatrends 2000*, published in 1990. Riding on the success of the mega-trend formula, and with millennium fever thick in the air, it set out ten hot new trends for the 1990s including the 'Age of Biology', the 'Triumph of the Individual' and 'The Decade of Women in Leadership'. Again, it was essentially an optimistic book, which took a swipe at the doomsayers like Paul Ehrlich, who, as Naisbitt remarks, 'surfaces every couple of years or so to warn of the end of the world, apparently unembarrassed that earlier predictions are now viewed as hysteria'.

Books on trends and prediction were by now big business, and a target for people like Australian academic futurist Richard Slaughter, who, in *Futures* 1993, accused Naisbitt of providing a 'right-wing, up-beat view of a future that never happened (at least not yet)'. There has never been a cosy community of futurists who rush altruistically to each other's defence, and it is not so difficult to predict that there never will be. When Naisbitt was once asked at a big conference in São Paulo why he and Toffler never quote each other, he said in a grave ironic manner – and after a long, pregnant pause – 'because we are competitors'. Naisbitt was joking, because in his characteristically generous spirit, he believes there is room enough for all of them in the business. The real reason they never ever appear together is not that they don't respect each other's views, but for the simple fact that no one can afford them both at the same time.

When Naisbitt's book *Megatrends Asia* appeared in 1996 and was hailed as the 'Mother of all megatrend books', there was some nasty snickering from other, perhaps less successful, futurist writers as to what on earth he was thinking of. Naisbitt's book pointed the futurist finger to a coming Asian domination of world market, a stagnating Japan and a rising China, and suggested that instead of trying simply to just open branch offices, Western companies should create new markets and ideas there. As he remarked at the time, 'Most people in the West don't have the faintest idea what's going on in Asia,' and the book was aimed at those who 'have this nagging sense they ought to know something'. Schadenfreude soon turned to frustration when it turned out to be yet another mega bestseller – particularly in the Far East, where he now has superstar status – and there was subsequently an undignified scramble among many others to bring out their own books predicting what the big changes happening there could mean for the future. As Naisbitt stressed at the time, the economic growth in Asia is 'the most important thing going on in the world, not just for Asia'.

Naisbitt and Aburdene were also among the first to spot the potential in the 'what do/will women want?' gap in the futurist market. *Megatrends for Women*, published in 1992, was addressed amusingly, 'only to women – and to men who come into contact with them'. While male readers were clearly encouraged to buy it, if only for educational and not business reasons, some may well have been frightened off by the chapters boldly entitled 'The Menopause Megatrend', 'The Goddess Awakening', or even 'To Hell with Sexism'. The book predicted among other things that a woman would be president of the USA by 2004 (there have since been two female Secretaries of State) and that a wave of female baby-boomers facing the menopause would transform society and healthcare. Even closer to home they predicted that there would be an increase in so-called collaborative couples, 'working together for themselves'.

Naisbitt has been called the 'great noticer', with the modern-day equivalent of Leonardo's 'knowing how to see'. But one thing he insists – if he is going to be thrown into the futurist camp – is that it has never been his aim or his job to create the future, or to predict it. Instead, he believes it is to educate people to notice things and to encourage optimism for the future. 'Cynicism and pessimism are mindsets that cannot contribute to much good,' he told one interviewer. 'My mindset is: The history of civilisation shows that things get better.

Just look at how well we live today.' Naisbitt does not claim to have personally made things better, but with sales of over 14 million books worldwide he has clearly inspired a lot of people to do so. How he has done this is told in his latest book *Mind Set!*, in which he shows how to set your mind to see the future. As a way of thinking, futurism is in this respect perhaps not so dissimilar to game theory. If you once have it, you see it everywhere.

Despite all the fame, fortune and even glamour that appears to come with the job, even the most optimistic and successful of modern futurists moan that it can sometimes be a depressing, thankless and much misunderstood task. 'You get much more press and attention if you simply predict the end of the world for a hundred years after you assume you will be dead,' says one irritated European futurist. It is also a common complaint among futurists that history is usually assumed to be right, the far future is where the excitement (and fame) is, and today is, well simply, 'now'. The modern-day futurists' dilemma was curiously well summed up by the author of *Alice in Wonderland*, Lewis Carroll. Carroll, surely a closet futurist, endowed the Queen in *Through the Looking Glass* with great insights on the paradoxes of predicting the future. 'The rule is,' she declares pompously to Alice, 'jam tomorrow and jam yesterday – but never jam to-day.' The Queen also boasts, in true futurist fashion, that her memory works both ways. 'It's a poor sort of memory that only works backwards,' she declares. And when Alice dares to ask her what sort of things she remembers best, the Queen answers casually, 'Oh, things that happened the week after next.' But the downside to living backwards, as the Queen points out, and a futurist or two will readily tell you, is that it 'always makes one a little giddy at first'.

*   *   *

The *real* queen of futurism is the American trend-guru Faith Popcorn, whose work marks the beginning of a new era in commercial futurism. Even her surname, which was invented because her boss at an advertising agency couldn't pronounce her real name (Plotkin), is a smart marketing ploy. Why anyone would want to be named after a lightweight cinema snack is questionable (it's even in her passport) – but the name has stuck to the teeth of futurism like a stubborn toffee coating. At over $50,000 a pop for a speech, she is one of the highest paid future consultants on the market today, with companies such as American Express, Procter & Gamble and the soup company Campbell's paying for her ability to 'think backwards', and to tell them what the 'jam' of tomorrow will be. While many futurists will happily hedge the question as to whether they predict and even create trends so companies can profit from them, Popcorn and her company BrainReserve don't even need to be asked. Even the opening statement on her website makes the mother-of-all futurist promises to potential clients: 'own the future'. In her book *The Popcorn Report* she offers a simple, upbeat guide to doing just that, explaining, declaring – even promising – that you can profit from trends, and that the practical application goes simply like this: 'From a trend prediction . . . To a trend production . . . to a trend product'.

Published in 1991, *The Popcorn Report* caused a sensation, and she was quickly crowned (rather unenviably) as 'The Nostradamus of Marketing'. The book boasted boldly to be about the future of everything, 'Your company, Your world, Your life', set out her working methods, listed her company's clients, and gave the rundown on ten hot major new trends no self-respecting business should or could ignore. 'America is a consumer culture,' she shouted, 'and when we change what we buy – and how we buy it – we'll change who we are.' This marked a distinct departure from Naisbitt and Toffler's political and socio-economic approach to creating a better future to one that implied that you could create a better future with better products. Since she set up her marketing consulting firm BrainReserve in 1974, Popcorn has sold her predictions with a brand of optimism, enthusiasm and evangelical conviction that is hard to ignore. Sometimes it is as if she is trying her hardest to create a self-fulfilling prophecy, such as when she predicted the 1990s would be the age when people rise up against the prevailing pessimism – there would be a 'socioquake' starting probably in 1992 when 'you'll feel the mood rise . . . conviction will replace caution . . . Companies will have to realize that you don't sell only what you make. You sell who you are.' In 1991 she wrote 'For the last ten years, we've been telling our clients about this socioquake that's on the verge of happening. And now, as the signs of the shift begin to appear, it's the strangest feeling – almost like a sense of *déjà vu*.'

One of the biggest trends she is credited with accurately predicting is 'cocooning', a term that has made it into common parlance and also several dictionaries. As a noun, cocooning is now officially defined by the Random House Dictionary as 'the practice of spending leisure time at home, especially watching television or using a VCR'. Popcorn herself was infinitely more dramatic, describing it as the 'impulse to go *inside* when it just gets too tough and scary *outside*. To pull a shell of safety around yourself, so you're not at the mercy of a mean, unpredictable world.' This was, she explained, the retreat from everything – from the horrors of 'rude waiters' to more serious threats of 'crack-crime, recession and AIDS'. Popcorn's evidence, or what she calls 'indicators' for this trend, were such things as the growth in sales of video recorders, a rising demand for comfort food, a new baby-boom and even an increase of gun ownership among women.

But were we really 'cocooning for our lives' in the 1990s? Did we go in for 'huddling and cuddling' or even the hard-core variety of cocooning she terms 'burrowing'? In his deeply sceptical book *The Fortune Sellers*, William A. Sherden claims simply that 'cocooning is nonsense'. Sherden took a 'quick perusal' of the *1996 Statistical Abstract of the United States* and declared, 'The premise that people are hiding out in their homes is just not happening.' His counter-proof was that from 1989 to 1994 revenue of eating and drinking places has increased by 25 per cent, and that sales of cinema tickets are up by 20 per cent. Richard Slaughter was a little more merciful with Popcorn, and – following his brutal attack on Naisbitt in *Futures* magazine – kindly remarked that she 'covers a lot of useful detail about some of the ways that suburban life in the USA is evolving'.

Naisbitt, however, does not take kindly to be put in the same bag as Popcorn. 'I just don't do consumer trends and fads,' he says emphatically. As Slaughter put it, she is more 'folksy and practical' than Naisbitt, has little to say about the big wide world and offers little in the way of theory. She is also conspicuously absent from most key reference books on futurism. Despite these differences, their methodology is not as different as the results and opinions might suggest. Like Naisbitt, Popcorn's company scans hundreds of newspapers and magazines every month, and she regularly taps the opinions of her TalentBank, a network of around 6,000 experts including, it is rumoured, everything from an Indian chief to an organic farmer and even an acupuncturist.

Another of her key methods of predicting and recognizing trends is so-called TrendTreking. To mere mortals this is window shopping, for Popcorn and her co-workers it is 'a field trip to cutting-edge locations in order to stimulate fresh thinking about new products and services'. As Popcorn herself admits, her work is all about capturing the mood of the times and the trends, something she also calls 'brailing the culture'. 'What always amazes me the most,' she declares like the Queen in Wonderland, 'are the companies that think they don't need to heed consumer trends. That it's only today, and not to-morrow that counts.' She also believes, contrary to common opinion, that you cannot 'make' a trend. 'The thing about a trend is that you cannot look for it,' she told Richard Johnson in an interview for the *Sunday Times*. 'It's like finding a wife or husband. They just appear.' (Her track record with trends is, she confided to him, better than with husbands – she was nearly married five times, 'or was it eight?'). One of the ways that the company boils down and pots all this scanned, snipped and shopped information for their customers is by regularly holding so-called BrainJams in the New York office. These meetings take place in an Alice-like Wonderland, 'a magic room where every idea is a good idea'. Here, apparently anything goes – as long as it is positive and you speak in headlines.

As well as talking in headlines, Popcorn is good at writing and grabbing headlines. As Sherden complains, 'If Popcorn is any kind of genius, it is only for marketing and self-promotion, for she has packaged pure fantasy and successfully sold it to some of the highest-level executives in the US industry.' US industry it has to be said, is very grateful and protective, and *The Popcorn Report* is spilling over with trend testimonials and satisfied client lists and stories. In Europe there has been a slightly more mixed reaction to the idea that you are what you buy, and that you can make money from predicting the future. The German futurist Matthias Horx recalls a telling scene about her at a conference in Munich in the 1990s after the publication of her much-anticipated second book, *Clicking*.

Flown over at a vast expense for the big event, Popcorn, in her inimitable, upbeat optimistic American style presented '16 Trends to Future Fit your Life'. 'Clicking', she explained to the curious audience, is about 'being ready to be in synch with what's coming tomorrow', and she talked enthusiastically about how to 'click' (i.e. make money) with trends such as cocooning, pleasure revenge ('our halos have slipped'), ego-nomics (individualization) and, ironically, with cashing out (downshifting). Horx recalls how at the end of the presenta-tion a hard-core left-wing journalist leapt up and barked at Popcorn, 'So how the hell is that going to help the Third World?' Horx, who had the unenviable job of translating the questions for Popcorn, toned it down as much as he dared. The audience smelt blood and there was a dark silence as everyone eagerly awaited her defence, her outrage or her rapid retreat from the stage. Popcorn was, however, unruffled and entirely professional, and shot the question smoothly back, saying 'maybe you would like to share with us some of *your* suggestions . . . ?'

Popcorn is, as they like to say, a tough smart cookie who was always something of an outsider. She was brought up in Shanghai, where her father was posted as a captain in the US Army's Criminal Investigation Division. Her mother, a work-ing lawyer, wasn't exactly delighted about being packed off to the Far East, and nor it seems was little Faith. As the child of Jewish parents in a Catholic convent, she was marked out as a bit of an oddity even then. As Popcorn explains in *Clicking,* 'No matter what, I always felt out-of-step with my own age group. Never in the right crowd, never in the right school.' This strange feeling of being a bystander to the world is also what defined Peter Drucker's early years, and to which his success as an outside observer of society has often been attributed. As a young girl back in New York Popcorn recalls how she once again felt out of place, and honed her talking and thinking skills in order, for example, to distract her piano teacher from the fact that she had not practised. Later she decided she wanted to be an actress, 'because it would put me where I wanted to be – right at center stage'. The profession in which she recalls she first really 'clicked', as she annoyingly insists on calling it, was in advertising, where she ended up in an attempt to impress a boyfriend. Although she was fired from several companies, including once incredulously for wearing a 'rabbit-fur micro-miniskirt to a maxi-client meeting', she had found her *métier*.

When she left the advertising business in 1974 to set up BrainReserve, for 'future supported long-term strategies rather than a series of quick-fix commercials' she barely had a business plan, and even admits to roping in friends to sit at pretend phones in a 'fake' office to impress potential clients. Today she boasts that clients don't choose her. She chooses them. As well as her confidence, enthusiasm and relentless optimism that to European tastes borders on the manic, one of the things that she has capitalized on is being a woman in a very male-dominated field. In another copy-writing coup, she coined the term 'EVEolution' for her book about the 'Eight Truths of Marketing to Women'. Published in 2000, it was her answer to Naisbitt's 'Megatrend Women', and was marketed as a wake-up call to business about the fact that women make an estimated 80 per cent of all purchasing decisions. As in her previous books she offers testimonial-style success stories, and generously throws out tantalizing glimpses of gaps in the market just waiting to be filled in so-called FutureLand. What, she asks, if companies like General Motors could arrange 'test drives where women work?' Or how about, she proffers more bizarrely, a liquor store 'co-parented and run by women'? Five years later, Heidi Fleiss' plans for a brothel for women, a so-called Heidi Stud Farm in Nevada, makes some of Popcorn's suggestions about EVEolving look positively quaint. As Fleiss in the Popcorn spirit of EVEolution said, 'Women make more money these days, they're calling the shots, they're more powerful.'

Ironically, Popcorn was so busy predicting such things as the increased sales of baby clothes that she became 'one of those women who forgot to have a baby'. Parenting first became a personal trend for Popcorn when she was already fifty years old and adopted her Chinese daughter, whom she named Georgica Swan Pond Rose Petal Qi Xin Popcorn (thankfully g.g. for short). Around the same time, Popcorn's best friend and co-writer on the book, Lys Marigold, also adopted a Chinese baby whom she called simply Skye Qi Marigold. Popcorn was cruelly accused at the time of using her child to reposition herself – a sort of trend-making as opposed to baby-making. But becoming a mother not only provided part of the inspiration to write EVEolution, but has also, she hopes, enabled people to see her in a more human way. Bringing her down, some like to joke, from 'superwoman' to a mere 'super-mum'.

The problem with popping Popcorn into the futurist bag is that while she is full of great-sounding suggestions for making a successful business and for zappy naming, she offers little in the way of satisfying and belly-filling theory to get your teeth into. Her time-scale is generally short term – a ten-year range is far in the future for many of her clients, and she clearly likes to leave the examples and the storytelling to speak for themselves. From pointing out the failure of Revlon to initially act on the EVEolution trend to the success of small chic hotels in 'clicking' into the small indulgences trend and to foreseeing the rise of the car as the 'mobile cocoon', she bombards the reader with anecdotes and examples. Furthermore, her books are written for the attention span of someone on a two-and-a-half-hour flight, and particularly in the case of *Clicking* have coined an annoying amount ofwordswrittentogether such as CreativeThink, TrendSalons or even DialPain (apparently nothing more harmful than phoning someone who gives negative feedback). On the other hand, she has popularized the notion of tapping into the potential of 'FutureLand' in a way that no one else has managed with quite so much business bravado. To be merciful, as Sterling says, 'The victorious futurist is not a prophet. He or she does not defeat the future but predicts the present. Futurism doesn't mean predicting an awesome wonder; rather it means recognizing and describing a small apparent oddity that is destined to become a great commonplace.' And Popcorn herself is one such oddity who has succeeded in doing just that.

At the first European Futurists Conference in Lucerne in July 2005 delegates voiced concerns about the dearth of women speakers. There were few big-draw names in the business who sprang to mind beyond Popcorn, but any mention of her name was greeted with a curious mixture of derision, fascination and even envy. If she would come for free to such an event in the future, then naturally she would be more than welcome, suggested some of the participants. If she would demand her usual fee, then perhaps she really is little more than a money-making charlatan, they hastily agreed. 'What we really need here,' offered one fast-talking futurist, 'is someone like Cayce Pollard.'

Cayce Pollard is the epitome of a new brand of trend prophet or 'cool-hunter', as they are also sometimes known, who carved out a niche in the 1990s. The native New Yorker has been called a 'sensitive' of some kind, or stranger still, 'a dowser in the world of global marketing'. In worldwide demand by international companies for her skills, she describes what she does as pattern recognition. 'I try to recognise a pattern before anyone else does,' says Pollard, sounding remarkably like Popcorn, and dangerously like Sterling's comparison of futurists to the special forces. Pollard's colleague Damien calls it more of 'an allergy . . . a morbid and sometimes violent reactivity to the semiotics of the marketplace'. Indeed, Cayce is so highly attuned and hypersensitive that just the sight of a Tommy Hilfiger logo makes her feel sick, and the Michelin Man rather mysteriously causes a total panic attack.

Cayce Pollard is not real. But she could be. She could even, some suspect, be a thinly disguised portrait of Popcorn herself. She is, in fact, the key figure in William Gibson's novel *Pattern Recognition*, who has been flown in to London to evaluate the redesign of a famous corporate logo. While there, dealing with insightfully described insidious marketing and advertising people, she gets drawn into the hunt for the makers of an anonymous video clip that mysteriously appears on the web and is causing a worldwide buzz because it seems to encapsulate something that touches a trend-nerve. Although Gibson is primarily a writer of science fiction, this is his first novel set in the present, and he manages to capture the sensitivity, talents and skills that a trend researcher needs for recognizing 'group behaviour pattern around a particular class of object'. When asked what she does when she has recognized a pattern, Cayce says 'I point a commodifier at it. It gets productized. Turned into units. Marketed.'

As well as taking a swing at the corporate language that is often used in the advertising and trend development business, Gibson uses the novel to explore the more insidious effects of branding and trend creation. In one scene Cayce meets Magda, a woman who is paid to hang out in trendy places and simply namedrop a client's product to suitable looking consumers. Magda explains to Cayce how the process works:

> You're in a bar, having a drink, and someone beside you starts a conversation. Someone you might fancy the look of. All very pleasant, and then you're chatting along and she, or he . . . mentions this great new streetwear label, or this brilliant little film they've just seen. Nothing like a pitch you understand, just a brief favourable mention. And do you know what you do? . . . You say you like it too! You lie!

Cayce sees immediately how and why it works:

> And then they take it away with them. This favourable mention, associated with an attractive member of the opposite sex . . . They don't buy the product, they recycle the information. They try to use it to impress the next person they meet. The model's viral.

While writing *Pattern Recognition* Gibson says that he had heard of such things being done, but assumed it was simply an American urban myth. Then he came across a newspaper article that claimed it was being carried out in Manhattan. Not surprising then that shortly after the appearance of Gibson's book someone felt moved to 'out' themselves on the web. Under an article entitled 'Confessions of a cool-hunter', Catherine Farquharson describes how she 'prostituted' herself 'for a sly marketing scheme to promote the next big product'. She tells how she was paid $15 an hour – by an undisclosed company – to trawl the streets of Toronto for 'cool' people (her best catch was an engineering student with blue hair) and to give them a hand-held computer. For free.

Just like that. The next stage was to get names and phone numbers of people 'in the know'. At that point her conscience caught up with her and she quit. Cayce, too, having finally discovered the secret source of the video-clip, tries to protect the person from becoming a 'product', and the real message throughout the book is not so much about finding the 'future' itself but the sometimes dubious morality behind the methods and means of doing so.

Gibson himself is not immune to the trappings of marketing. 'In my own life I'm much more gleefully complicit than Cayce would ever be happy being,' he admitted in an interview with the *Philadelphia Inquirer*. 'I don't mind the extent to which William Gibson is a brand as well as being me. It makes for an interesting life.' Gibson was born in Conway, South Carolina, but following the sudden death of his father when he was just six years old, he and his mother moved to south-western Virginia. In the 1950s this was, he recalls, 'a place where modernity had arrived to some extent but was deeply distrusted' – a theme that echoes throughout much of his writing. This feeling of being abruptly exiled to what seemed like the past, began his relationship with the future and he grew up in a bookish huddle in his bedroom, on a diet of American science-fiction magazines.

Following the unexpected death of his mother when he was eighteen, 'the descent of an Other Shoe I'd been anticipating since age six', Gibson left boarding school without graduating, drifted about and ended up in Canada to evade the draft, from where he 'watched the hot fat of the Sixties congeal as I earned a desultory bachelor's degree in English'. From this self-imposed exile he later found himself needing to support a family and rediscovered his childhood love of science fiction and his desire to write. In taking up writing professionally, Gibson not only end up sparing himself a lifetime of working in a 'cat food factory' but created a new genre of science-fiction writing known as 'cyberpunk'. As he recalled, 'The art form I loved as a kid had gone completely flat. I realized no one had tried to write a science-fiction novel as if Lou Reed and David Bowie were writing it.'

When his first cyberpunk novel *Neuromancer* was published in 1984, it was an unmitigated success and reaffirmed the importance of fiction in futurism. Hailed as a dystopian masterpiece, it tells the story of Case, a computer cowboy who lives 'for the bodiless exultation of cyberspace'. Gibson defines cyberspace as 'a consensual hallucination experienced daily by billions of legitimate operators, in every nation . . . A graphic representation of data abstracted from the banks of every computer in the human system. Unthinkable complexity. Lines of light ranged in the non-space of the mind, clusters and constellations of data'. Heavily influenced by Stanislaw Lem's synthetic realities published twenty years previously, Gibson went much further than just predicting the far reaches of the Internet, and envisaged a world where you could connect your nervous system directly into it (grossly called 'jacking in'). By now science fiction had moved on from focussing on fears of over-population to fears of over-stimulation. This frightening fable about the dark side of computer-simulated reality was also inspired in part, he told one interviewer, by a rather harmless sounding bus-stop epiphany. 'I remember [in the early 1980s] seeing posters for the small, semi-portable version of the Apple IIc,' he told the *Philadelphia Inquirer*. 'Quite a lot of what I subsequently imagined in my early science fiction simply came from seeing that ad in a bus stop. I didn't know anything about it technologically. I just thought if it's that small and that nicely styled, everything is changing.'

Like many people who grew up with euphoria surrounding the first mass computer hardware, Gibson fuelled the fear in the 1980s that everything was getting faster and out of control, and that machines, corporations and government were taking control Big Brother style. 'I believe that we don't have the luxury of an imagined future in the way that my parents had it in the '50s, or in the way I had it myself as a child in the '50s,' he said in an interview. 'What we had then was, we had a much longer "now". "Now" was maybe even a few years long, because things just didn't change that quickly. And in a world where things change as quickly as they do today, it's impossible to calculate a future. So, in a sense, we don't. There's going to be a future, but it's not predictable in a way that the culture can create a dream of it and *lean* into it. I don't really see how we could, because we don't know what's going to happen.'

This is rather disingenuous of Gibson, whose ideas about the future, both in *Pattern Recognition* and *Neuromancer*, lean very heavily into social criticism and warnings about not just information overload, but also chemical and medical overload. 'Julius Deane was 135 years old, his metabolism assiduously warped by a weekly fortune in serums and hormones. His primary hedge against aging was a yearly pilgrimage to Tokyo, where genetic surgeons re-set the code of his DNA . . .' (from *Neuromancer*).

Despite being dubbed 'The Vasco da Gama of Cyberspace', Gibson is still a reluctant futurist: in fact, he wrote *Neuromancer* on a good old-fashioned portable typewriter (apparently an olive green Hermes 1927 model). Today he admits to using a computer (albeit the slowest in his family), but still finds the accusation that he tries to predict the future rather disarming. 'When you write a science-fiction novel set in some sort of recognizable future, as soon as you finish it you have the dubious pleasure of watching it acquire a patina of quaint technological obsolescence,' he admitted to one interviewer.

'For instance, there are no cell phones in *Neuromancer*. I couldn't have foreseen them. It would have seemed corny, like Dick Tracy wrist radios.' Furthermore, he adds poignantly, 'I always assumed that social-science fiction – anything set on Earth in a not-too-distant future – is just a mutant version of the present. But the easiest hook to hang on me was that I was a futurist. I had always maintained that I was squinting at the present in a certain way.'

While many businesses in the 1980s and early 1990s were starting to put their money on people like Popcorn and real-life equivalents of Cayce Pollard, and the sexy scanning, scouting and squinting methods of predicting the future, the less seductive scenario methods had taken a bit of a back seat. Herman Kahn's dramatic nuclear war scenarios had not done their image any favours in the 1960s, and the technique was henceforth contaminated with associations with the Cold War and strategic military planning. There were also a few little mishaps whereby the scenarios got into the wrong hands and were taken as hard-line strategy rather than a suggestion of how things *might* occur. As Kahn recalled in *Things to Come*, there was an embarrassing incident when 'an article in *Izvestia* accused the Hudson Institute of planning the liberalizing movement in Czechoslovakia for the CIA and "Zionist" elements. Apparently the Russians had seen a scenario written in the mid-1960s which had a remarkable resemblance to the events which occurred in 1967–1968.' Another damaging misunderstanding occurred when in the reporting of the 'Pentagon Papers' in *The New York Times* 'reporters chose to interpret scenarios which were being written in the US government in late 1964 as normative plans for escalation of the Vietnam War.'

*   *   *

The man who is credited with reviving the public popularity of scenarios and their use for business in the 1980s is the American Peter Schwartz. He is also the man said to have 'predicted' the events of 11 September 2001 rather more accurately than Nostradamus ever did or indeed ever could have. As part of a scenario-building exercise for the US Senate in 1990, Schwartz included the possibility of terrorists flying into the World Trade Centre. As he told *Time* magazine in an interview in 2004, 'Somewhere in each scenario exercise – if we've done our homework – is the future.' Schwarz doesn't, however, like to directly define his work as prediction *per se*. 'If you try to predict something,' believes Schwartz, 'you end up with very conventional ideas. Scenarios help you anticipate surprises.'

Put officially by Schwartz, 'A scenario is a tool for ordering one's perceptions about alternative future environments in which today's decisions might play out. In practice, scenarios resemble a set of stories built around carefully constructed plots.' The evolution of the story depends on three factors: the decision to be made, the driving forces such as technology, politics, or social developments, and so-called critical uncertainties. Unofficially, it is like rewriting the story of Little Red Riding Hood for 2020. The outcome hinges on who survives the story according to a combination of successful driving forces, possible personal decisions and – as in any good fairy story or scenario – a few little surprises:

- **Scenario Number 1: New Mobility** Little Red Riding Hood switches on her fourth-generation mobile phone/GPS device, which alerts her to the fact that someone else in the proximity is heading the same way. She takes the recommended short cut and gets to her grandmother's house before the wolf.
- **Scenario Number 2: Forever Young** Grandmother is taking the latest generation of anti-ageing drugs prescribed by her

on-line doctor, and kills the wolf herself with techniques learnt from her personal defence trainer.

- **Scenario Number 3: High-Tech Grandma** The retina-recognition security scan system at grandmother's house identifies an unwelcome visitor at the door and automatically eliminates it.
- **Scenario Number 4: Age of Activism** The wolf meets one of the extreme anti-globalization environmental campaigners hiding out in the forest and agrees to have his DNA tweaked to turn him into a vegetarian.

Scenarios, as Schwartz likes to remind people, are simply a way of rehearsing the future. Superficially, they are simple and effective tools for forecasting, but they are deceptively difficult to work with, as there are so many factors to bring into play. Having set your goal (for example, grandmother surviving to 2021), you then have to find and prioritize all the potential ways to get to this goal via forecasting or backcasting to the present day. In putting the case for scenario thinking Schwartz says, 'Anticipating the future in this volatile environment calls for more than systematic analysis: it demands creativity, insight, and intuition. Scenarios – stories or story outlines about possible futures – combine these elements to create robust strategies. The test of a good scenario is not whether it portrays the future accurately but whether it helps an organisation to learn and adapt.' And to what extent everyone from a grandma to a government can prepare for future surprises. As many a futurist will tell you, their work is not about glamorously and grandly predicting the future Popcorn-style, but simply and unglamorously being prepared for it.

One of the first large organizations outside the military to successfully use scenarios on a large scale was Royal Dutch/

Shell. As far back as in the early 1970s Pierre Wack had set up a new department for its London office and employed a few Cassandra-like scare tactics to shock his bosses into taking the technique seriously. By the time Schwartz took over in the early 1980s the technique was established as a key working tool and Shell had shifted from being a relatively weak player to one of the largest and most profitable oil companies in the world. Nevertheless, Schwartz ran into problems when he proposed a deeply unfashionable study of the future of the Soviet Union that would take into account the possibility that one day it might become a key player in world energy supply. Forget it, 'they're not on the agenda', protested his bosses. But Schwartz stomped down the proverbial futurist foot, insisting, 'they *will* be on the agenda. Their oil and gas reserves are among the largest in the world.' Not only was this still during the Cold War era, but Shell at the time was planning a humungous showpiece gas platform at great expense in the North Sea, which would be severely compromised if a cheaper supplier (i.e. the Soviet Union) were ever allowed a bigger share of the European market. A practitioner of the Kahn school of 'thinking the unthinkable', Schwartz had the experience and the confidence to push for such a study. He also, as he reveals in *The Art of the Long View*, deeply believed that 'What my colleagues and I did together at Shell . . . had enormous consequences – not just for the oil platform, but for the world.'

In 1983 Schwartz and his team proudly presented the Shell managers with their two scenarios, which in terms of story-telling were more of an adventure than a fairy tale. 'By that time,' explains Schwartz, 'we knew enough about the Soviet government to say that if a virtually unknown man named Gorbachev came to power, you'd see massive economic and political restructuring . . . declining tension in the West; and major shifts in international relationships.' Even though dissidents such as Andrej Amalrik had already predicted in 1974 that the Soviet Empire would fall by the year 1990, Shell was still rather surprised by the findings, and asked around (as it often did) for a second opinion. All but one Soviet expert said Schwartz and his team were completely crazy, and the CIA told them off: 'You really don't know what you're talking about,' they barked,' You just don't have the facts.' In fact, as it turned out, they both had access to the same available data, but they had just asked different questions and had decidedly different agendas. While Shell had a policy of various scenarios to consider, the CIA's view on the future of the former Soviet Union was a one-horse race. As a rightly smug Schwartz points out, 'If we had to pick only one, we might have been just as wrong as the CIA.' Slightly less smugly, he adds, 'We ourselves did not know for certain that things were moving toward our "Greening" scenario until Gorbachev was elected. But having more than one scenario allowed us to anticipate his arrival and understand its significance when he ascended to the leadership.' In fact, as he explains, the key to the whole successful prognostic progress was finding and scanning papers by obscure Russian economists and basic statistics such as birth rates. 'Demographics,' he announced, 'made it clear why *perestroika* was inevitable.' In a nutshell, the GNP depended heavily on the size of the labour force, and as it fell, so did productivity, and the economy collapsed. Furthermore, it was predictable that Gorbachev would not be able to jump-start the economy until the number of twenty-one-year-olds rose again after 1991. As Sterling put it, a good scenario, properly handled, will slice through layers of time like a cake knife.

Schwartz not only proved himself as a tenacious and smart 'scenarist' but quickly saw the potential in selling the scenario technique for wider business purposes. In 1986 he left Shell to set up his own consultancy company, the Global Business Network (GBN), which works primarily with scenario techniques. Today, GBN – which was sold in 2000 to another company for an undisclosed seven-figure sum – works for a wide range of large- and middle-sized companies and the US government, and has also provided futuristic visions for such films as *Minority Report* (Schwarz believes retinal security scans as featured in the film will become commonplace by 2012). Membership of the network alone costs $40,000, according to the last rumour; it includes several meetings and access to the network's research and an elite network of movers and shakers. The fee is calculated on the annual wage of a decent research assistant (RA), and in defending it Schwartz often finds himself reminding CEOs, 'If you can get your RA to do a better job, then that person is remarkable – lock him or her up.'

Like many of his species, Schwartz is a shrewd hunter and gatherer of information. He admits to reading and filtering everything that comes his way, scanning statistics, newspapers and books, drilling friends and fellow futurists, and even occasionally taking advice from people who spot him on the street to recommend a book or an idea. One of the crucial things in communicating the scenarios effectively is the 'naming', something that Kahn clearly revelled in, and the new generation of futurists such as Toffler, Popcorn and Naisbitt do with their trends to great and glorious effect. In addition to bringing your work to public attention, a good name helps focus the mind. Schwartz tells how at one GBN meeting they were discussing what might happen if Gorbachev failed. A Sovietologist present spontaneously entitled such a scenario 'Brezhnev Plus', which neatly encapsulated the sense that the Soviet Union would not revert completely to bulky Brezhnev-like bureaucracy, but would be marked by the reduced elements of *glasnost* and *perestroika*. Similarly, a multiracial group that included a GBN member working on the future political scenarios of South Africa in 1991, a year after Nelson Mandela's release, came up with the following.

- **The 'Ostrich' Scenario**: White power structure keeps its head in the sand, and unrest is brutally dealt with by repression.
- **The 'Lame Duck' Scenario**: Negotiations take place but lack decisive and definite action. Everyone is dragging their feet and ends up frustrated.
- **The 'Icarus' Scenario**: Populist government goes on spending spree. Motto, fly now, crash later. All come off worse economically in the end.
- **The 'Flight of the Flamingos' Scenario**: The country takes off slowly but flies high and together (as do flamingos). The happy-ever-after scenario.

'The amazing thing about these scenarios,' wrote journalist and self-confessed GBN member Joel Garreau in *Wired*, 'is not that they were drawn up. The amazing thing is that they had such power – were logical, persuasive, easily understood and com-municated – that to-the-death enemies, all of whom had it in their power to prevent the flamingos from taking off, began to see a feasible, positive path toward a successful national democratic future together.' In futurist terms it is used as a positive example of a self-fulfilling prophecy, in which the narrative power was so compelling that it allowed the multi-racial group to agree on possible future realities (though even Schwartz admits it is rare that the best case is the real outcome). Garreau was in fact so dazzled by the mythology of GBN that when he first heard about these 'mysterious people . . . with far out ideas' he thought immediately of Asimov's science of psychohistory and declared, '*Holy Shit. This is the Foundation.*'

GBN's successes and clients are today the stuff of futurist legend and envy, and Schwartz even goes so far as to claim 'very rarely have we really missed. More often our failure is in getting people to take us seriously.' He does, however, admit to a few spectacular and sobering failures, such as the Iraqi invasion of Kuwait in 1990. The night before it happened, he was dining with a client who asked Schwartz if the reports of an army amassing on the Kuwaiti border were something to worry about. 'Don't think twice about it,' he declared confidently. Another little embarrassment was his comment in *Time* magazine in October 2004 that if Bush won a second term the administration could become more environmentalist, since 'even the auto industry is greener than this administration' (Schwartz was at the time working on scenarios for a second administration). At the climate change talks in 2005, the USA was widely described as 'obstructive' if not entirely destructive.

Despite a few knocks here and there, Schwartz remains an optimist and convinced of the usefulness of the technique for forecasting. He even uses it at home. When he and his wife bought a house they used scenario techniques to help decide whether to go for a fixed- or variable-rate mortgage (he went successfully for the former). Once you have mastered the technique, the real problem and sticking point with scenarios is not usually deciding 'which dinner scenarios shall we consider for tonight darling?' or where the next terrorist attacks could take place, but simple human failure to act on them. A classic example, says Schwartz, was the case of Hurricane Katrina that hit New Orleans in 2005. Writing in *Wired* magazine in November 2005, he soberly reminded us that scenario planners had predicted the disaster practically down to the last death as far back as the 1960s. 'The brutal logic of risk,' he wrote, 'dictates that it's cheaper to pay for the aftermath of a single relatively localized disaster than it is to prepare for the same disaster in every place at every time.' And, he added sagely, 'Turns out there's a huge difference between anticipating disaster and actually being prepared for it.'

Scenarios have sometimes been seen as another way in which futurists scare people about the future. On the one hand, it is claimed that where there is the danger of people falling over a metaphorical cliff it is the futurists' responsibility to warn them how high it is, how bumpy the way down could be, what awaits them at the bottom, and the chance of injuries/ maiming/death/survival. A more pragmatic approach would be to say that their job in revealing the cliff's existence means people can avoid going to the precipice in the first place and 'change' the future. The history of futurism is littered with grotesque and grandiose attempts to predict and change the future of the world, even though that particular 'cliff' is way too high for even the mightiest of futurists' ego and imagination to see right to the bottom. Even in the 1980s and 1990s, when futurism was expanding into a more profitable line in business and political consulting, there were still a few who risked the even bigger bird's-eye view, or a bigger slice of the future cake.

Warren Wagar, who first came to futurist attention in the 1970s, was one such academic. He liked to boast, 'The focus of nearly all my work is the only thing that we can do a damned thing about: the future.' Wagar started out as a history teacher, and after sixteen long years of dredging around in the past, 'the fateful thought' came to him to teach a course about the future. When he got it off the ground in 1974, it was, as he excitedly described it, 'a lightning survey of the last 6,000 and a more leisurely exploration of the next 200 years of world history'. It has been said that good historians have the future in their bones, and this was undoubtedly the case with Wagar. 'I am not a spellbinder,' he once confessed, 'not an evangelist, not even particularly warm or accessible.' But he was a great believer that 'the future can be changed'. So while people like Schwartz were hedging their bets in the 1980s and working on *Seven Tomorrows* (which even Schwartz himself later admitted were a few too many alternatives), Wagar was busy with the mother of all scenarios – a reverse history of the world from 2200. When *A Short History of the Future* was published in 1989 he confessed that the title was purloined from H. G. Wells, who had described *The Shape of Things to Come* as simply that. Just over fifty years later, Wagar had boldly tried to emulate Wells' future history in the form of a transcript from a 'holofilm' as bequeathed to ten-year-old Ingrid Jensen on Earth Festival Day 2200 by her historian grandfather.

Suitable reading for a ten-year-old, however far in the future, it is not. Our future begins dramatically with the collapse of world capitalism, which was set to begin in 1995 ('The depression of those years 2030s and early 2040s was the most brutal in history'), and takes us mercilessly through an apocalyptic landscape of dying forests and eco-systems, fields turning to desert, superheated skies and melting ice caps. The warnings get worse before they get better. 'Compounding the woes of the flesh was the sense of meaninglessness and purposelessness fostered by credicide.' Credicide, which he defines as the 'the killing off or the dying out – it hardly matters which – of the moral, spiritual and metaphysical values that modern civilisation inherited from the immemorial past,' is one of Wagar's bugbears, and his socialist soul puts it down to the pursuit of greedy capitalist goals, and 'the rush and wobble of the global economy'.

Nor are we going to be spared a Third World War, which

occurs in 2044 after a rebellion of Israelis in an autonomous
district of the Jordan Valley is crushed by Soviet forces. By
2045 there is a death toll of 5.8 billion. Also awaiting us (yet
again) is the establishment of a socialist world government, to
be followed by a decentralized utopian world community.
There will also, sadly, still be insurmountable problems with
sending a letter from the post office in Reykjavik in 2044, but
that is really nothing to get excited about when you look at the
rest of what is to come:

- 2020 United Nations lunar base founded
- 2023 First satellite colony ('Moontown') built
- 2036 Lunar colony abandoned
- 2091 Reclamation of coastal Bangladesh concludes world
  program of restoring areas lost to rising sea levels
- 2099 Scientists confirm falling carbon dioxide levels
- 2110 Zero population growth worldwide completed
- 2115 Accident destroys most of Mars colony
- 2200 Detailed radio transmission from third interstellar
  expeditionary ship.

Naturally, you can reassure yourself that none of this will
happen, as Wagar arms himself in the introduction with the
popular futurist proviso that 'scenarios make no predictive
claims'. The point, he reiterates in his later book *The Next
Three Futures*, is 'not to predict what will happen, but to
suggest that the end of the Cold War and the coming of the
liberal democratic bourgeois state do not necessarily spell the
end of major war or the building of a just world peace'. Like
those of many fear-mongering futurists, Wagar's basic belief
(and hope) was that the future can be changed and shaped by
people such as himself and that if you 'think backwards'
about it in shocking-enough terms, perhaps someone, some-

where, can make sure the worst-case scenario doesn't actually happen.

Futurism in the 1990s was to a large extent conditioned by the frenzied build-up to the turn of the millennium. As we lurched towards the year 2000, an embarrassment of futurists hopped out of every closet imaginable, often to be rewarded with fame and fortune for predicting the predictable and, more often than not, the entirely unpredictable. One of the reasons for this is what novelist Michael Crichton calls the 'state of fear'. His much-contested theory is that in the absence of the threat of the Cold War, people still need something to worry about – such as the end of the world, the decline of morals and values, etc. Yet, amid the inevitable voices of global doom and gloom, there were thankfully a few people who concentrated on predictions of more basic matters. In 1999, while everyone else appeared to be whingeing on about the millennium bug, Dr Robin Baker provided some welcome distraction with his controversial book *Sex in the Future*. Written using a seductive combination of science and storytelling, the book was shocking not for the sex scenes, but for the notion of what will happen when 'ancient urges meet future technology'. Using a combination of dramatized scenarios, sprinkled with a bit of gratuitous detail, Baker takes us through a world of reproductive possibilities that are all the more disturbing and fascinating for being seemingly only *just* out of our reach.

A biologist by profession and a writer by choice, Baker goes boldly where most science fiction and futurists have not yet dared to go – into graphic and gritty detail of how in just a few short decades it will become common practice rather than a scandalous exception to visit 'reproduction restaurants' in order to choose our ideal baby-making partner from the Internet. One scene, set around the year 2075, is rendered all the more surprising for the fact that what he describes is not a couple, but a mother and son who visit the restaurant. She is fifty-four and wants grandchildren and he, a star tennis player, is just twenty-four, and really not yet very interested. 'It's not your age that matters. It's mine,' says the grandmother-to-be. After their meal they settle comfortably down at a computer terminal. 'Double click on "Eggs",' his mother says, 'and type "Tennis Players" into the keyword box.' As he peruses the thumbnail portraits of women selling their eggs he realizes to his amusement that he has already slept with some of them. His mother has her eye on the number-one ranked player, who is asking more than most per egg ('not even per baby'), but he protests as she's 'too big, too ugly and has a bad attitude'. His mother is getting impatient and points out, 'You're not going to have to have sex with her. It's her genes you're after.' She reminds her son that she never even met *his* father, she just received the sperm along with a promotional (as opposed to emotional) six-hour-long biographical CD. As they appear to reach a decision on one of the women, the mother worries about getting the egg in time so that baby will be born before the Wimbledon season starts. 'I do want to be there when you win your first major. You know,' she reminds him, 'It would be just my luck if you did it while I'm giving birth.'

One of the devious things about Baker's controversial vision of the future is that it unravels quite unexpectedly. Just when you have been coaxed into thinking that you could probably, maybe, just begin to cope with the idea that one day in the indeterminate future it may be commonplace to buy and sell eggs and sperm like must-have designer dresses he chucks you into another conceptual and moral maze. Moving backwards, reproductively speaking, from the à la carte baby-making scenario, he also gives us a view into the 'contraceptive cafeteria' of the future. This, he believes, will be based on a so-called BlockBank system, or BB for short. So as well as blocking your tubes, in the future it will be normal to freeze sperm and eggs and place them in a bank until you (or, indeed, someone else) need them. This is, of course, he points out well within the stretches of the imagination of the near future, but Baker uses it simply as a platform for asking what he sees as the real everyday questions that will arise in the future of reproduction and family. 'Should a couple use sperm and eggs to reproduce? If so, should they be freshly collected or banked? Or should they use manufactured gametes, derived from cell lines they banked at puberty . . . Should they reproduce with somebody of the same sex as themselves or should they commission a surrogate?'

In one of the scenes, Baker, clearly an intellectual product of the liberal 1960s, describes a foursome living happily together in a kind of cosy reproductive collective. The lesbian couple are both pregnant, one with their child they have 'made' together, and the other one carrying the male couple's child. With his subtle shock tactics, and solid scientific background, what Baker is trying to point out is that thanks to techno-logical advances, in the future there will be a totally new landscape of reproductive possibilities, sexual behaviour and family structures. Choosing the sex of your child will be as easy as choosing which colour socks to wear in the morning, bereaved mothers will commission clones of their dead chil-dren, and infertile men will be able to conceive with their partner. What Baker essentially predicts is that advances in technology will free us from reproductive stress rather than increase it. His other key claim is that in the first half of the twenty-first century 'the divorce of sex from reproduction – which is currently nisi – is expected to become absolute'. This, he believes, means that future populations will be more pro-miscuous, a sort of return to the 1960s without the worries.

'There will be *no* diminution in sexual activity, adventure, emotion or fun,' writes the proud father of five. 'In fact with the BB scheme in full swing combined with child support legislations and paternity testing, people will be liberated sexually far more than was ever the case in the past.' Asking unromantic political and moral questions about the future of sex, relationships and reproduction is a theme that most futurists skirt sheepishly around. Stanislaw Lem, for one, kept well away, while H. G. Wells and Charlotte Perkins Gilman made bold attempts that revealed as much about them as it did about fears for the future. As one futurist gleefully pointed out, it's a dirty job, but someone's got to do it.

CHAPTER 8

THE 800-LB GORILLA

What is it like working in politics and big companies? Put simply, you don't argue with an 800-lb gorilla . . .
        Futurist who would rather remain anonymous

Thomas Huber shuffled nervously along the street trying to think about sex. Facing him were the first signs of a reluctant morning. Dustmen were resignedly sweeping up the used condoms, smashed beer bottles and splatterings of vomit on the pavement. Flyers for porno cinemas and live sex shows littered the gutters, and the first clatter of shutters being raised could be heard from the World of Sex and Sexorama. A few neon signs flickered into life. It was his first day in his dream job at Trendbüro, one of Germany's leading trend and future research consultancies.

Proud to have landed the position of researcher against over thirty applicants, he was determined to do his best. He arrived punctually at the office at 10am on the grey Monday morning, and by 11am he was out in Hamburg's notorious red-light district, the Reeperbahn. His briefing was to find material and ideas for 'The Future of Sex', a study commissioned by a major publisher in the German soft-porn-magazine market. He not only felt slightly sick at the thought, but also desperately out of place in the suit that he had put on especially for his first day. But Huber was not in a position to argue. 'Beyond the facts everybody at the age of twenty-eight knew,' he confesses, 'I had no scientific interest in sex, and to be honest I hadn't a clue where to start with my research. I didn't know much about "the sex scene", even less about trend researching and nothing about how to present such studies to clients.' Despite the fact that he thought the subject of the future of sex might be a 'bit big' for him, he heroically dragged himself from sex shop to sex supermarket, from customer to salesman, and, as he got a little bolder, from prostitute to client. He asked what he hoped were the right questions about who was buying what, who liked doing what, what was the most popular buy, and all the time wondering in the back of his mind what he was going to tell his mum and envious friends about his first day of his new job. Some of the interviewees chatted away openly and enthusiastically, while others treated him like some strange new species of voyeur. They were used to people pretending to be journalists to chat about what the hottest new sex toy or perversion is, but claiming to be a trend researcher, studying the future of sex, well, that was something very perverted.

Back in the safety of the clean, minimalist office, he skirted past the smirks and sniggers from his colleagues, sat down on his designer chair at his desk, and tried to make some sense of his findings. His brief was to combine this information hot off the red-light district with expertise and knowledge about changing images of women in the media, the shifting demo-

graphics and buying patterns, and studies on changing attitudes to sexuality. His next port of call was the infamous
Trendbüro archive, which consisted of a huge collection of
brown cardboard boxes filled with a muddle of cuttings,
magazines and press releases. Back in the early 1990s there
was virtually no Internet, so the main source of his research
was printed matter. 'There was masses of bizarre stuff about
sex in nappies, the SM-scene, sex with fatties or pregnant
women and similar stuff,' he recalls with a shudder. 'But there
was also evidence that the gay revolution was going to become
a mainstream culture, and many articles by cutting-edge
columnists writing in explicit detail about all kinds of things
which today, since *Sex in the City*, are common knowledge.'

The results that were assembled for the client included the
following 'predictions'.

- **Gourmet Sex:** Increasingly, the middle classes would be
  playing 'games', buying 'toys' and would be indulging in
  more experiments such as 'S&M light'.
- **The Sexual Paradox:** The more sexualized the media becomes, the less sex there would be at home.
- **Female Power:** Women would in the future play an increasingly active role in the buying decisions of bedroom toys, and
  in bed.

A week later, when Huber and Trendbüro director Matthias
Horx arrived at the drab brown offices of the publishing
house, they were well prepared. Or so they thought. For
instead of a boardroom full of chain-smoking journalists
dripping in testosterone, they were confronted with a room
full of chain-smoking, cynical, middle-aged women. Apart
from the Trendbüro team, there was only one other man
present, and that was a thin, pale secretary. They made their

presentation, there were a few perfunctory nods here and there as if to say 'what the hell can you tell us about what men want', and after ninety minutes it was all over. Huber was relieved and delighted. 'I had passed the first hurdle to becoming a trend researcher and didn't fall flat on my face.' The job was in fact a bit of a disaster. The client basically wanted to know how to raise sales of trucker porn to truckers and too-long-single men, and the researchers were telling them about subtle shifts among the sexual predilections of middle-class, middle-aged ladies. As the growing market for designer sex toys and high-class naughty knickers by companies such as Agent Provocateur reveals, their findings were not the result of wishful thinking (or the fatal futurists' monkey trap) but a case of right trends, wrong client.

At the time Trendbüro was a prime example of one of the new, ultra-hip European agencies for trend consulting, monitoring and research, which in the 1990s based its success on the increasing popularity of the Faith Popcorn-approach to looking at the future. The cool open-plan offices overlook the Elbe river in the up-and-coming area around Hamburg harbour, which back then was beginning to get a reputation as interesting rather than simply seedy. If as a visitor you were lucky enough to get a glimpse past the pretty secretary with her must-have Prada handbag slung over her swivel chair, you could just see the sweep of shelves brimming over with 'trendy' new objects brought back from shopping/scouting trips from all corners of the globe (mostly London, New York and Tokyo). There was a peculiar collection of around sixty toothbrushes that illustrated the evolution of teeth-cleaning utensils – from a basic, wooden, streamlined one-headed version, to a monstrous three-headed beast of a thing that was supposedly the ultimate in quick and efficient teeth care from America. On a glass shelf were several objects of questionable use (loo-roll holder, bird house, no one was ever completely sure), and at least a hundred different vessels containing everything from designer drinks to bathroom unguents which one of the directors collected with a passion that bordered on fetishism. On his return from business trips his suitcase would spill forth with items, each lovingly rolled up in a shirt or stuck into a sock or two. Office favourites included the 'Déjà Shoe' (a recycled boot), bottled glacial water (guaranteed a few thousand years old) and ladies' tights with in-built mosquito repellent.

The team of researchers all had elegant designer desks, handmade to perfection by a rough-looking local carpenter with a bent for minimalism, and all permanently covered in a blasphemous scattering of colourful magazines and cuttings. There were piles of Japanese comics, scientific abstracts, specialized statistical analysis, market research reports, *Vogue* from every country imaginable, and yes, occasionally a *Playboy*, all naturally in the interests of research. Wielding a large pair of scissors – the key working tool apart from the brain – the researchers had to slice their way through the pile and 'find' trends. To scan the surfaces and look for patterns, interesting titbits, something with a bit of trend potential, symbolic pictures or simply something that dished up differently might spark the imaginative hunger of the clients.

The main customers at the time I worked there as a researcher were Unilever, Philip Morris and Beiersdorf, for whom Trend-büro produced regular trend reports and dossiers. *Line-up* for Philip Morris was a monthly affair; its brief was to look at short-term consumer, marketing and advertising trends, especially those relevant to youth culture. On the one hand Trendbüro was careful not to put in anything about children under the legal age of buying cigarettes, but on the other hand there was never any mention of what the future would bring in an increasingly regulated and lambasted industry. What these kind of jobs reveal is not only the expanding market for selling the future commercially, but the credibility gap that grew in futurism – between the future in terms of the next consumer or marketing trend and those futurists looking at the bigger and deeper geo-socio-political megatrends. So while a hard-core long-term planning futurist would say advise the cigarette industry on how to plan for a future in which their product might be illegal in twenty years' time, soft-core trend research is often aimed at shorter-term marketing and advertising strategy (or, more cynically put, how to get on and sell more now before it is too late). Trends that were 'identified' for Philip Morris included such things as 'Soft-Philosophy'. The evidence that people were increasingly interested in philosophy was found in everything from ninety-minute books on philosophy, to fashion labels, pictures of ladies with letters scattered over their legs, lamps decorated in poetry, and invitations to underground poetry slams. Another typical example was the 'relationship marketing' trend that showed how firms were increasingly building strong ties to their customers, making their products into a trusted 'friend' of the family through clubs, networking and exclusive parties. The problem is not to find such trends, but to find out why they occur, to back them up with the deeper social-economic forces driving them, and then to decide if they will last beyond the sell-by-date of the latest marketing campaign.

The real craftsmanship and fun was in the wording and naming of the trends, sitting around over a cappuccino and bouncing words around until you could bundle the sense of it all into a single word or pithy phrase. This is what Popcorn did so effectively, and at Trendbüro we were well aware that if you could coin a word that entered the common language such as 'cocooning', your reputation was made. I did my best, but came up rather meekly with trends such as the 'Renaissance of the Housewife', which I produced for Unilever and Beiersdorf with ironic advertisements for sexy washing-up gloves and ladies in hotpants pushing shopping trolleys with babies casually tucked under their arms. Beyond the eye-catching ironic illustrations, statistics and surveys revealed a generation of overworked American women who were dying for some time out, and a European post-feminist generation who were trying to re-invent and repair the image of the housewife. Not entirely coincidentally, I had just had a baby, and was desperately trying to find ways to convince myself that it could be hip, glamorous and maybe even trendy to be a mum and work only part time. Another attempt at an inspired naming was 'Nouveau Aristocracy', a trend that manifested itself almost exclusively in advertisements for fashion and interior design. The trend of 'My Home is My Castle' was a form of cocooning, driven by the fin-de-siècle feeling of the 1990s. My husband and I had just bought a cheap chunk of a crumbling castle in the Bohemian woods and were dreaming of turning it into a modern retreat from the madding crowds. Looking back, the identification of these and many other trends was based on a mixture of personal projection (a sort of monkey trap-lite) and casual polls of the researcher's peer group (chats with other desperate mums over endless cups of tea), but they were also soundly and professionally backed up where possible by statistics and market research.

Huber, who like Horx, has since left Trendbüro and set up his own company, also quickly came to the conclusion that trend research is often about proving what you already sensed might be a trend, and that a good solid trend can never be based on advertising or media images alone. 'More important than searching for trends is thinking about trends and then finding the proof for what you thought and the longer you work on trends the better your instinct becomes.'

Organizations that want to know about the driving trends and megatrends will often commission or buy studies from companies such as Trendbüro or one of the many that now exist worldwide. They may also look to academic institutions such as the college in Pennsylvania where researchers set out to determine a link between the type and shape of women pictured in *Playboy* and the state of the US economy. John Casti in his forthcoming book, provisionally entitled *Destiny's Design* calls it a 'they-got-paid-for-this?' kind of study, but joking aside reminds us that the researchers came to the serious and possibly significant conclusion that, 'In boom economic times (optimistic social mood), men prefer softer, more vulnerable women. When the economy goes bust, those same men prefer stronger-looking gals.'

But many firms today rely on their own in-house futurists. Corporate and company futurism is a thriving branch that disguises itself under such titles as 'insight and foresight', 'strategic visioning' or even the strangely old-fashioned sounding 'moderning'. Despite the lure, to be employed as a corporate futurist is not always a thankful, rewarding or even well-received task. At the 2005 European Futurists Conference in Lucerne, one such employee from a large company stood up and confessed he didn't know whether to call himself a consultant or an 'insultant'. At best you are the envy of your colleagues, you have your own buzzing department and someone in top management listens regularly and eagerly to you. But catching the ear of busy directors dealing with the urgent day-to-day running of a business is an art in itself. About once a month, Anja Kober, of Corporate Foresight at Deutsche Telecom, manages to corner her boss in the elevator and delivers a well-prepared and perfectly rehearsed twenty-second speech on the hot future issues of the moment to a small but entirely captive audience.

According to Patrick Sallner, ex-head of foresight at Nokia, most companies do not prepare proactively for the future but adapt through disruptive change. In non-corporate speak, this means they don't have a proper budget for a future research department – instead they suddenly notice that all the competitors are on to a good thing, rush to catch up and hope and pray it is not too late. Seen in terms of Kondratieff's waves, the innovative, future-thinking companies are helping drive the wave of innovation, and the latecomers surf in on the wane. Sallner also believes that very few companies today actually gain tangible benefits from working with external futurists, though they occasionally pay for people such as Horx to give an affirmatory pre-dinner speech. 'The truth is,' agrees Horx, 'the really innovative companies don't actually need to work with external futurists like myself. They can look to us, our studies and our ideas for reassurance, information and occasional inspiration, but are largely driven by their own visions and visionaries.' Siemens, despite having a small official futures department, believes that 'the future works best when you create and shape it yourself'; hence its optimistic company motto, 'Inventing the Future'. Meanwhile, at Microsoft, Bill Gates is said to get his big ideas by locking himself away in a remote cottage for a 'think week' twice a year with nothing more than a pile of papers, reports and the generous contents of the company suggestion box.

Nokia's futures department admit that it prefers instead to send out its scouts Delphi-like to conferences, buy in publications from research and trend agencies, and then set its own people to work with the material. One of Nokia's eagerly anticipated products for 2006 was the 7380 mobile phone for women, developed using all the latest trend intelligence and research. Clearly made with the design-conscious modern working woman on the move in mind, it combines eye-catching elegance with modern electronics, and the screen smartly doubles as a mirror for lipstick application. There are no unsightly number or letter buttons, and indeed it looks so unusual that I was even asked by one friend if it was a vibrator! Despite appearances it has all the functions a state-of-the-art mobile phone should have. Looking at it, I can almost hear the satisfied voices of the development team ticking the boxes of the trends that it satisfies. But in all the excitement there was one little thing they forgot. Practicality. The silver screen reflects so much it is impossible to read in sunlight, and the wheel system means writing a number or an SMS takes five times as long as on a conventional mobile.

Such things do not surprise Ernst Beinstein, who has worked for a range of international companies on future products and planning. Back in the 1980s, in the pre-Popcorn era, Beinstein was employed in the small innovation department of Unilever in Vienna. At the time the company was aware of a small and modestly growing trend in men's skin-care products and decided to see if it could find a way for the company to benefit from it. It had noted that there were several such products out on the market doing well in the upmarket segment, among the 'gentlemen' consumers, but there was as yet little for the Tom, Dick and Harrys, who were probably in the supermarket only to buy a frozen meal and some beer. What, wondered Unilever, would entice the ordinary man to the much-dreaded and frighteningly feminine beauty product shelves and, more importantly, to buy hair and skin products?

Today, AXE is a successful worldwide brand, but when the concept for these male personal-care products first landed on

Beinstein's desk in Vienna the team's first challenge was to find the Naisbitt-style megatrends – the big socio-economic trends that would back up the concept and ensure its future success. In this case, recalls Beinstein, it was what they called the 'democratisation of consumption', and the changing role and shifting self-image of men, both of which translated in company terms to bringing products such as aftershave and deodorant to the male masses. They looked at their own example of Denim, aimed at what Beinstein and his colleagues in the innovation department regarded as a more 'primitive' consumer. With the advertising image of an open denim shirt revealing an anonymous bronzed chest, it was targeted, as Beinstein puts it, 'at men who have it easy with women, or would like to think they can'. Unilever saw the opportunity with AXE to launch another, softer, sector for male grooming and beauty products. It recognized the trend for men to take more care of their appearance; they were beginning to groom themselves more consciously and conscientiously. It was the birth, says Beinstein, of what we now know as the 'new man'.

What happened next, explains Beinstein, was, however, completely unexpected. Unilever had decided to product-test the new AXE product range in Austria because it has a big capital city and relatively cheap advertising. What it found to its amazement and amusement was that AXE products were bought by women almost as much as by men. Nearly 40 per cent of sales were to women – not for their partners as was first assumed, but for their own personal use. Unwittingly, Unilever had also cashed in on another big up-and-coming trend. Not only had it catered to the 'feminization' of men with AXE but also to the 'masculinization' of women. 'Now if you look back it seems obvious,' says Beinstein. 'It was a time where women really had started wearing the shirts and trousers and they wanted the masculine smell to go with it.'

Today, Beinstein has a better nose for what women want. His latest project at a small Austrian-based company has even earned him the nickname Bernst Einstein. It all began with a simple question. Why isn't there a non-alcoholic drink designed specifically for women? With this simple thought, a small, unknown company set about developing a brand-new product from scratch using trend research. The company, whose name Evalution was inspired by Popcorn's term *EVEolution*, had an unusual team that included a gynaecologist, Waris Dirie (Somali ex-supermodel, UN special ambassador and author), Beinstein and me as occasional trend consultant. The challenge was to produce something not just for 'me' but every other 'me' around, typically an educated thirty-to-fifty-five-year-old woman, living in a city, trying to cope with work-life balance. To fit with 'my' lifestyle it should be healthy, but fun. None of that self-knitted carrot juice or chalky-tasting soya. And it has to have a tangible effect on the mind and body. Long term as well as short term. Now *and* in the future.

The socio-economic trends to shore up the product were well documented. 'Megatrend Women' showed that increasing levels of female education and working women mean more financial independence and purchasing power, but more stress. 'Megatrend Health' research revealed the demand for wellness products that have a health benefit and are free of additives. And the trend towards a 'New Morality' meant the drink also had to have a dash of political correctness. After wading through my demands and those of around 15,000 other women, Evalution found out that women 'wanted it all'. They wanted to be spoilt, but to have a clear moral conscience (a percentage of profit would go to Waris Dirie's foundation against genital mutilation in Africa). The drink should give them self-confidence, energy (without the calories) and a general sense of well-being. As for the bottle design, it should be small, sexy and not compromise the shape and style of a designer handbag. And one more thing; no pear-shaped bottles that remind anyone of big bottoms or failed diets.

The final result was called Very, and there were three variations, all with 'Dong Quai', a Chinese root reputed to have a positive effect on women's hormone balance. 'Very High' was to be sipped ice-cold like Prosecco to give women a boost of self-confidence and a caffeine kick. 'Very Strong' was for energy, and 'Very Well' was for relaxing and enjoying like a good burgundy. When the product was test launched in Austria in 2004, it was tipped to be the hot trend product of the new millennium. Women loved it, men were obsessed as to what it would do to their testosterone levels, and it was generally predicted that it would become a huge international success. Until, that is, the man in charge of financing the product mysteriously disappeared and the whole project collapsed. The moral of this tale, warns Beinstein, who is going to re-launch it in London, is that however perfectly you plan the future and however many trends you faithfully follow, you cannot predict everything.

Ian Pearson, the resident futurist at British Telecom's development unit, is one of the more outspoken and controversial of his breed. Bucking the trend, he flamboyantly – and even rather unfashionably – calls himself a futurologist. Others whisper that he is a kind of modern-day court jester. He even likes to jokingly advertise himself on his personal website as, 'much more accurate than Mystic Meg, much cheaper, but about the same dress sense'. When he is being serious, Pearson claims that using a mixture of trend analysis, common sense, listening to the right people and reasonable business acumen, he is right around 85 per cent of the time. 'I make no claim to be able to predict the future with absolute accuracy,' he declares, 'but I think of it as like driving a car through fog. You can't see a very clear picture of what is ahead, and sometimes you will misinterpret an apparent shape in the distance, but few of us would drive through fog without bothering to look out the window. Blurred vision is a lot better than none at all! The same is true for business, which is why BT employs me.'

One of the real reasons that BT employs him is said to be because back in 1992 Pearson recommended that the company put their money on SMS technology. According to Pearson, he predicted it would be a huge success, but his bosses simply laughed, and asked why on earth anyone would want to send a message when they could just make a call. 'Today they listen to me a little more carefully,' he boasts. More modestly, he claims to be 'just an engineer making logical deductions for tomorrow based on things we can already see happening.' Among the things he can see happening in the future are active contact lenses enabling you to watch films projected directly on to the eye or that can highlight the particular shops you are looking for on a high street. Even more far out is his peculiar proposal that a woman's breast implants could 'house electronic gadgetry such as an MP3 player and her entire music collection'. He even goes so far as to call this concept 'mammary memory', and points out that 'God provides her with two beautifully designed control knobs to select the track and adjust the volume . . . A plastic mobile phone and PDA could be implanted too.'

The equivalent extremity where men will in the future store their digital data and mobile phone memory is, disappointingly, not predicted by Pearson. He claims to believe that by the end of the century we will be able to download our brain into a computer. As he patiently explained to a German newspaper, when our body is worn out we will just pop the information into a replica body, rather like moving house. Or even, it could be said, like putting your SIM card into a new mobile phone. If that idea interests his bosses at BT, they might not be so happy at Pearson's belief that there is only a 30 to 40 per cent likelihood that mankind will survive the next hundred years. Rather disingenuously he also claims that the great thing about his job is not only that it is fun, but also that it doesn't matter if he is wrong because, 'by the time anyone can test my predictions, I will have long since retired'.

Some companies are a little more cautious as to who they entrust with the future. Josephine Green, Director of Trends and Strategy at Philips Design in the Netherlands, calls herself a futurist for want of a better word. In fact, Green, who studied and taught history, says her biggest frustration about working with the future is that she consumes it too quickly. Although she works for an electronics company, Green is not a technological determinist. In fact her approach to the future is driven by a predominantly human focus, as illustrated by her reaction to BT research that concluded you could save a few seconds a day and eventually a few hours a year if you use mobile electronic displays for all your reading material in the future. Instead of counting the saved seconds, Green's approach would be to think about the tactile experience of turning newspaper pages and even rolling it up and throwing it in the bin, and asking what aspect of that is it that people like and need. 'And ok,' says Green, 'you could maybe save a few hours, but the really interesting question is, what are you actually going to do with those hours?'

Green feels privileged to live in what she believes is a period of intense change, but more importantly she sees it is a golden opportunity to rethink the future in ways that bring a better quality of life. 'By the time we look back to today from 2030 things will look seriously different,' she says. In fact from

there, some of the past may even look like the Philips Home
Lab. From the outside, this is an unassuming brick building on
the High Tech Campus in Eindhoven. Inside, it is a playground
of prototypes, some of which induce spontaneous jaw-drop-
ping among even the most hardened of futurists. Here, under
the scrutiny of social scientists, researchers, anthropologists
and ethnographers, products and developments are tested for
their feasibility, usability and acceptability. From an inbuilt
observation tower the researchers watch via hidden cameras
how real families in real time cope with living in the future.
One of the first things that stands out about the interior is that
nothing stands out as being strange or futuristic. Technology
here is discreet and unobtrusive – so-called Ambient Intelligence. As CEO of Philips Design Stefano Marzano says, 'this is
surely what we want: knowledge, excitement, entertainment,
education, productivity, social contact – without the obtrusive
prominence of the technology that delivers them.' Indeed, the
television screens of the future will be so discreet that you
won't even notice them when you enter the room – they could
by 2015 be embedded in all or some of the window panes
instead of cluttering up your living room.

The use of anthropologists and social scientists at Philips
Design means that much of the innovation is driven by people
who are passionate about how society and culture are changing while they still keep a beady eye on the megatrends and
the business case. Design, believes Green, is the crucial link
between people and technology. She gives the simple example
of what happened when her team was asked to develop a new
alarm clock. 'Oh no,' groaned one of the design team, 'the last
thing I want is to be woken in the future by a damn noisy alarm
clock.' So instead the designers decided to ask people how they
would like to be woken. This led to the development of
Nebula, a device that projects images of your choosing onto

the ceiling, gently waking you as it gets brighter. Although this was never made commercially available, Philips instead saw a way to use it for children who were terrified of MRI scans. Using this technology, children can customize the hospital environment by having their favourite images of toys or cartoons projected on to the walls of the MRI room. Overnight, bottlenecks in hospitals where they tested it out were gone, and the business case was sold.

Green believes that the best futures work is not about looking at what you can predict, but what you can imagine. Furthermore, she does not believe that futurists can or should make the future. 'I don't trust any futurist or group of futurists to predict the future,' she says, 'That would be dangerous. Futurists are simply experts who can bring in their knowledge and insight.' And the future of corporate futurism, she believes, will be even more multidisciplinary, with firms in the future bringing in such people as electronic artists, historians, ethicists and philosophers.' And perhaps even a few more women like Green.

While it has become fashionable for companies to have in-house or 'pet' futurists, there are not many governments which have an official futures department. Basic and essential statistical and specialized research for such things as demographic change, the potential spread of diseases like bird flu, or city planning, can be farmed out to any number of think tanks, research agencies, consultancies and quangos. The think tank Demos in London gained notoriety as the engineer behind Blair's Third Way politics, and the Henley Centre for research and consultancy has worked on such projects as the future of the British army. But when it comes to the kind of bold thinking and mindset that really sets futurism apart from basic future planning, there are not many in-house political advisors who would willingly 'out' themselves as futurists. Rare exceptions are people such as the gentleman from the Principality of Liechtenstein who bravely stood up at the 2005 European Futurists Conference to ask for advice from the assembled and rather startled guests. His country – with a reputation as one of the richest tax havens in the world – needed help, and he asked if anyone would like to come to a workshop to discuss the problems of the principality. After a bit of prodding he admitted that he was actually the sole employee of the government's shiny new futures department and that he would be grateful for any input as at the moment it was a bit strapped for cash and ideas.

Most futurists working closely with governments and in politics would, I assume, much rather be laughed at than disposed of like Thomas More, Kondratieff and Condorcet. But even today many don't have much free choice about what they can say or do. As one futurist (who would understandably like to remain anonymous) said about his formative experiences employed in government, 'you don't argue with an 800-lb gorilla.' The underlying problem comes down to concurrence. The former Austrian Chancellor Wolfgang Schüssel once commented in a tête-à-tête with a futurist that to be an effective leader you also have to know a lot more and a lot better about everything than everyone else around you. This means nothing less than being a universalist, and this is indeed what Flechtheim, who coined the term futurology, recommended back in the 1950s. 'There are only really two groups of people who have the right to call themselves universalists,' says Horx, 'good political leaders and futurists. The problem is if a prime minister or president works openly and publicly with a futurist, they can put their own reputation and competence into question.' Horx, who is occasionally asked to write speeches for cabinet ministers and politicians in Europe, calls it the Rasputin syndrome. 'Unless you are invited into the court as a harmless but informed specialist, there is the danger you will be seen as having too much power and influence,' he says.

There are still those rare and satisfying occasions that futurists look forward to when they are not at the beck and call of corporate or governmental '800-lb gorillas', nor are they in danger of their life or reputation. These are the moments they really live and work for, when they get to say what they really think, in front of the people who profess to have the power to change things. One of the few futurists who can get away with this big time is John Naisbitt, who, when asked to speak to leaders at the European Union, Latin America and the Caribbean (EU-LAC) conference in Vienna in May 2006, said he would agree on one condition: that he could say whatever he wanted (which is not always the case at conferences). Oh yes, the organizers reassured him, of course you can. Naisbitt asked them again if they were sure. Yes, they were really sure, but they were also rather surprised when Naisbitt gave his speech and directly accused the Latin American countries present of having 'strong leadership but going in the wrong direction', and the European Union leaders there as having 'weak leadership and no direction'. He caused not only a scandal but succeeded in doing what futurism does best – to boldly sum up what many people fear and hope for the future but are powerless to express.

CHAPTER 9

A WEEK IN THE LIFE OF A FUTURIST

The very best way to become a futurist is to hang around until tomorrow shows up. Of course, once tomorrow becomes now, other people will probably dismiss that wonderful day as being merely 'the present'.

Bruce Sterling

Looking at the profession from the outside, there is undoubtedly something rather glamorous and exciting about being a futurist. One of the things that make it such a seemingly exclusive club is that you cannot apply for it as you would for, say, a job as an accountant or a lawyer. There is no regulating futurist body which decides who is or is not qualified to become a member, and nor do children tell their teachers they would like to become one when they grow up. It is one of those mysterious professions to which some people belong accidentally, many unintentionally grow into, while others casually try out the title like a suit in a shop. Looking at the profession from the inside, things are not always as easy or enticing as they may appear. So what is it *really* like to be a futurist?

Matthias Horx is a modern-day futurist in the good old-fashioned sense of the word. In his formative years he read the works of Verne, Lem, Marx and Asimov, and at the age of fifteen he enthusiastically emptied his piggy bank and sent 100 Deutschmarks off to Pan Am to reserve his place on the first commercial rocket to the moon. In the early 1990s he founded Trendbüro (see previous chapter), but became dissatisfied with the limitations of Popcorn-style future research and left to set up his own independent think tank, the Zukunftsinstitut in Frankfurt and Vienna. Here is a peek into a 'typical' week in the life and mind of a busy European futurist.

MONDAY
9am, Vienna. A young female journalist arrives from a major news magazine and walks blindly past the icy glare of the Delphic neon artwork in the entrance hall that reads 'know thyself' in Greek. That is always a test of whether an interview is going to be good, mumbles Horx to his assistant as the woman settles down to fiddle nervously with her tape recorder. Trying ineffectively to mask his irritation, Horx asks her if she has, as instructed per email, read the infamous 'list of questions I refuse to answer'. Not only that, he warns half-jokingly, if you ask him any of them, he will stop the interview. Horx does not mean to be arrogant or even a prima donna. He is, he claims, just fed up with having to answer the same stupid questions day in day out. But he is learning to be more patient, and since, no, she has not had time to read it, he kindly passes

her the list to read while he disappears into the kitchen to get them both a coffee.

1 *Which trends do you predict for the next ten years?*
Future trends cannot be predicted. They are processes of change that are happening here and now, which our job is to describe. This is one of those irritating questions that people ask when they can't think of anything better to do and need to fill space in their papers.

2 *Why do trend researchers and futurists make so many wrong predictions?*
Ask me instead what they have got right, and why no one likes to hear about that.

3 *Can you make trends?*
At the basic level of consumer products of course you can 'make' trends but that is more to do with marketing hype of products and nothing to do with futurism as I see it.

4 *Which are the most important trends?*
That depends entirely on your interests and agenda. There is not a simple hierarchy. A banker or a businessperson will have a very different perspective on trends and change to a heartbroken teenager.

5 *What do you predict for next year?*
That is the ultimate killer question. First of all I do not predict single events, hurricanes or celebrity divorces/marriages. Second, the future does not think in 'years'. And third, I suggest you go to a fairground palm reader where you might have more luck.

Horx reappears and a somewhat disheartened journalist discreetly turns to her *second* page of questions.

Mr Horx, could you please tell me then what the job of a futurist actually is?
It is certainly *not* his task to predict the future. This is a frequent misunderstanding in which the futurist is mistaken for a 'prophet'.

And why do we need futurists then?
To tell stories.

Stories? Are you joking?
In a certain sense I am serious. A storyteller begins with 'Once upon a time there was . . .' and the futurist says, 'in time there will be . . .' But this does not mean that he predicts the future in terms of outcomes – in the same way that one does not expect the storyteller to be telling 'the truth'. We are talking about metaphors. About knowledge and change processes which we need to understand better and about concepts that explain and clarify things. As colleagues like the American futurologist Bruce Sterling have said, the most noble task is to predict the present.

This sounds more like therapy than science.
Futurists focus on the future in order to redirect attention to the present, to create a kind of self-evaluation of society. It is in effect a kind of mirroring process, which has only one aim: to improve our ability to change, our so-called future fitness. It is the job of the futurist to provide images, analysis and 'truths' at a meta-level. That is his or her job and has been for a long time. It is no coincidence that the Delphi oracle had the words 'KNOW YOURSELF!' above its entrance.

Are you not simply talking about creating visions?
The aim is what Shimon Peres at the age of eighty described as 'a taste for the potential of the future'. Without this 'taste' –

this feeling for what is coming – society, a culture, or even a person cannot develop. I prefer this term to 'visions', which has a problematic historical undertone particularly in Germany. Hitler was also in a certain sense a visionary. Visionaries are everywhere. In reality they are often simply selling some marketing trick.

Do people really prefer to hear pessimistic and negative prognoses?

In many societies today – and particularly in Germany – a whole highly profitable 'industry of fear' has developed. If you predict the end of work, the disintegration of morality or the extinction of the daisy, then the whole hysterical media is bound to pounce on it. This is not only depressive, it is also depressing. Global warming, for example, is a huge theme in whose name the most absurd guilt and self-flagellating fantasies can be sold. This is the problem of the trend opportunism of the media. If so-called futurists pop up and articulate what people expect to hear – above all dark, fear-inspiring stories which enable people to abandon responsibility for their lives, they attract more and more attention and are immediately raised to the status of prophets. In time, society becomes addicted to such negative stories and you get a kind of a collective hysteria.

If you are such an optimist about the future, why do the pessimists bother you so much?

It is a fact that far too much of my time and work is devoted to denial. The images many people have of the future are incredibly antiquated and negative. It is almost provocative to say that the world most probably is *not* doomed and that many trends are developing positively. One has to work one's way through great swathes of depression before one comes to the really exciting questions. And asking the right questions is what I consider to be the highest art of my profession.

So what *are* the exciting questions?

For a start, can we as futurists create the tools and methods for conscious evolution? Or put in simpler terms, can we help change and influence the future in a meaningful way? The Delphic Oracle, for example, was instrumental in helping end blood feuds and creating democracy in Greece. Today we need to ask how to rewrite the social contracts in our society in the knowledge economy. How to create world citizenship rights in a globalized world. How to free work from the claws of its old dependency on salary. How to redefine the relationship between men and women in a world where women are an increasing driving force both economically and emotionally.

Isn't it easy to just ask questions?

Any good futurist will tell you that asking the right questions is both the hardest and most important thing of all. The right answers can only be found if we ask the right questions. Denis Healey once famously said that if Margaret Thatcher was the answer, someone must have been asking the wrong questions. Joking aside, the future is an open process and asking questions is one of the crucial elements of the production of the future. Philosopher Karl Popper hit the nail on the head when he said the future is a situation for which the recipe is not yet fixed but of which the driving forces, the 'trends', can very well be analysed.

That sounds more like therapy.

Just as a therapist 'takes on' the fears and neuroses of his patients in order to facilitate the process of dealing with them, the futurist takes on people's questions about the future.

Together we look for a solution. This is how the future is created, out of a consciousness and a process of clarification. The unconscious is transformed into the conscious. And acts. Freud really, at another level.

What do people want to know about the future?

At least twice a week someone rings and says their business is in trouble, or they want to start a company, and asks if I could please give them a trend which will make them rich quick. I tell them – nicely of course – no I can't, but go away and read my books. Funnily enough, someone really did, then rang me a year later to say he had opened a new sort of baroque-theme disco-cum-diner and invited me to come and take a look.

But if you don't tell people what they want to hear, why do they listen to you?

For honesty, I hope. Take the example of a convention of clothing retailers. The atmosphere is one of despair because the old retail concept of selling clothing no longer works. If I hold a speech there, the audience expects a motivating pep talk containing a host of clichés – words like 'vision', 'future', 'success' and 'innovation' are very popular and, needless to say from my point of view, completely redundant. What would happen, however, if I described the situation as it really is? If I tell them that the textile sector will never be the same again? That too many retailers sell the same boring old rags and that the service and shopping experience they offer are out of date. That many of those in the room would do better to close down their shops, and that future market success does not lie in running after trends but in *astute differentiation*. If I said that I would, of course, radically *disappoint* their expectations and risk my fee. But this is exactly what I have to do in order to do my job well. I call it creative upward disappointment.

So they pay you to provoke and disappoint them?
I hope so. And I try to do it as best I can! I also want to give
hope. I want to create a yearning. I see myself as an evolution
agent and prognosis as a system for communicating ideas
about the future.

So you are a sort of guru then?
Certainly not. A guru would sell the clothing retailers some
easy solutions, breathing techniques for power-selling or three
steps over burning coals to guaranteed sales success. I guide
them, if anything, towards increased, and I hope constructive,
self-doubt. You can't build up a sect on that basis, believe me!

So how does change in society take place?
There are two possibilities. Either mental learning (conscious
evolution, adaptation of the intellect). Or catharsis (collapse
and a new start, depression). Both will repeatedly come about
in the course of history and both are equally probable. The
futurist tries to shift things a millimetre towards adaptation.
No more than that. But that is possible. And it is a lot.

**I am sorry, but everything about futurism seems rather para-
doxical and confusing to me.**
    That is exactly what it is.

TUESDAY
Horx flies to Switzerland to give a speech on the megatrends of
the future for the annual meeting of a top Swiss bank. As usual
the PR company which has organized the event is nervous that
Horx is going to upset the assembled directors and bankers too
much. Will he be late? Will he live up to his reputation as one
of the most sought-after European futurists? And, more worryingly, will he be any better received than the famous fitness

motivation trainer who suddenly broke off his speech at the same event the previous year when he realized no one was listening? Horx is used to calming such customers. He warns them well in advance not to expect any quick trend recipes, nor a speech specifically about their particular field of business, and he point blank refuses to make a PR speech or plug a product.

If the customers are worried the future is unpredictable they also seem to believe that futurists are unpredictable too. This particular event is, however, for Horx entirely predictable. The podium is elevated forebodingly at the head of a large gloomy room in a plush hotel. Dark, conservative and smelling of money, it is filled with 300 white men, with an average age of fifty-plus, all in suits. 'It is one of those occasions where in my welcoming address I don't need to bother with the word ladies,' says Horx, who points out that the only woman in the room is a waitress, and even she makes a rapid exit as the lights dim. In his allotted time of forty minutes, he takes the assembled bank managers, directors and employees though a multimedia presentation of five megatrends, all of which go smoothly until he reaches his pet favourite, 'Megatrend Women'. At this point he notices there is a certain amount of undignified sniggering from the men in suits and the audience has become distinctly restless at the evidence that women are going to be the driving force in the economy of the future. Far from being unsettled, Horx has anticipated the reaction, and much to their delight announces that to conclude his presentation he is going to do something he rarely ever does – make a real live prediction with dates and figures. After a dramatic pause, he announces to the sudden silence, 'At such an event in the year 2020, there will be at least 20 per cent women in the audience.' In most Western countries this would not be shocking, but in Switzerland, says Horx, it almost amounts to treason. He also confesses he would really like to have said that it would be 50 per cent, but given the deeply conservative nature of the audience decided to be a little more gentle with them. Nevertheless, during the buffet lunch after the talk the managing director takes him discreetly aside, and says, 'Very interesting and amusing, Mr Horx. But that bit about women, ha ha, that will never happen. Not in your lifetime, nor mine.' Undeterred, Horx wagers 1,000 Swiss francs that he will be right, but as yet no one in Switzerland has dared take him up on the offer.

WEDNESDAY
10am, Wiesbaden, Germany. Meeting with the Federal Criminal Investigation Agency (the Bundeskriminalamt), which has invited Horx, along with professors and sociologists from a variety of fields, to discuss the possibility of predicting terrorist attacks. Horx, who as a young hippy spent most of his time trying to avoid or annoy the police, believes that the tried-and-tested techniques of futurism can offer some help. The temptation to mention *Minority Report*, the sci-fi film in which crime is portrayed as predictable and preventable, is too good to resist, and Horx warms up the audience with a few of the philosophical and paradoxical questions such as whether a potential future crime can still be classified as a crime if it is prevented. Future crime, like future anything, says Horx, has its clues in the present, and the key to helping prevent it is in the gathering and structuring of information with established methods such as Delphic forecasting, scenario planning or war gaming methods. Terrorist attacks like 9/11, he reminds the audience, do not show up the failures of forecasting but failures in information-gathering and communication. To conclude, he proposes setting up a Cassandra Committee – a sort of terrorist think tank for worst-case scenarios, worthy

of Kahn's thinking the unthinkable. But as with Cassandra, no-one takes him seriously.

4pm, Frankfurt, Germany. Meeting with his assistants about strategy for the speech bookings and consultancy jobs for the coming season, which also reveals large communication gaps. 'I will never again appear with, before or after dancing girls or flame throwers,' groans Horx, looking at the list of requests for speeches which includes the fiftieth anniversary of a toilet bowl manufacturer, the annual meeting of an association of brass bands, a hairdressers' congress in Lisbon and the esteemed association of tyre makers, next to whose request someone has scribbled 'party atmosphere, not too intellectual'. Horx wonders fleetingly if the glamour and intellectual challenge has somehow faded from futurism, then pulls himself together. 'The whole future of mobility is interesting for the tyre manufacturers. The hairdressers might take me seriously because I am bald,' he jokes, 'but what on earth does an oompah oompah club want with me?' Meanwhile, he rather hopes that the annual plumbers' convention can't afford both him *and* the go-go girls, and happily accepts an unpaid invitation to discuss the future over tea with the President of Austria.

'The job is sometimes frustrating, always demanding, but best of all never boring,' says Horx, who over the last five years has consulted and given speeches about the future to the most unlikely people and in the most bizarre places. From cafés on snow-swept Austrian mountaintops, where much to his surprise the CEOs of a slick, luxury, modern designer-kitchen company heartily swigged beer, to a flock of faithful future followers in a barren church on a windswept plain in northern Germany. 'The problem is that a lot of people still think the future is about people prancing around in silver suits and about revealing newfangled gadgets they will have in 2020.' The other problem, he reminds his assistants as they go through the list, is that a lot of companies expect futurists to get up and say that *their* product is the way for the future. At a gala gathering in Berlin of a large pharmaceutical company which produces cholesterol-reducing drugs, Horx made a point of criticizing the butter- and cream-laden dishes on the dinner tables, asking if they weren't just trying to increase their potential customers with such a spread. As he recounts to his assistants, there were a few nervous laughs among the salesmen when he went on to suggest that the main work in the future should be a preventative health policy, to promote a healthy lifestyle rather than to just deal with the fallout from such dinners. As Horx likes to remind them, he is paid to provoke not to predict.

THURSDAY

9am, Zukunftsinstitut, Vienna. A fat pile of post arrives, including, hot off the press, a copy of a large-circulation magazine for which Horx has written an article on 'Technolution', the evolution of technology. It looks fine at first, but on closer inspection he notices that the editor has inexplicably removed the section in which he argues that the picture/video phone will never become a mass communication medium. This is one of Horx's favourite examples of a 'future flop' – his argument being that such devices fail to look at fundamental communication habits. People, he says, do not always want to be seen while phoning, because the phone is about creating distance, not closeness (hence the unexpected success of texting). There will naturally be a small niche market for flirting teenagers, but he argues that most people today and in the future will like to hide behind the visual anonymity of the phone – with their hangover, bad hair day, or just to pick their nose in peace. Perplexed, he rings the magazine editor, who after ten minutes of discussion admits that it was not because of lack of space but because one of the biggest sponsors of the magazine has for the last ten years been pouring money into the idea and still believes it will be the killer application for the future. Lucky there wasn't a videophone in the office or he would have seen the wry smile on Horx's face when he reminded the editor that you cannot 'make' the future that way either.

FRIDAY

10am, Berlin. Horx has been invited by an interior design magazine to test the 'house of the future': an electronically controlled living and working space for the creative class in the heart of trendy Berlin. This is one of Horx's personal favourite subjects, not least for the fact that he currently lives and works in a high-tech-infested hundred-year-old house that creaks and groans and where the TV satellite wobbles in the wind and the Internet connection goes down when it snows. But the real reason goes further back, to the stories he heard as a boy about his father's attempts to construct a living space of the future. Werner Horx was an inventor at heart – an engineering student who at the weekends and evenings disappeared into the cellar to fiddle and experiment with creating his dream of a fully automatic household. In 1950 Werner was twenty-eight years old and living in a half-bombed-out apartment block in Berlin which he ingeniously wired up with panels of flashing lights that showed if the communal loo was occupied, if the occupant of a flat didn't want to be disturbed, and even if the post had arrived. In his own flat the stove started warming water for breakfast and shaving shortly before the ventilator wafted a gentle wake-up breeze over his face. Later, he proudly recalled to his son how his dinner would be cooked by the time he got back from college. Matthias' mother, whom Werner was wooing at the time, told a rather different story – of the smell of burnt porridge and blackened pans and the constant fear of fatal electric shocks.

Such postwar visions and experiments of the house of the future were fuelled by a desire to gain back control over everyday life. Today, says Horx, technology is still in many ways a prosthesis and the question is how will people adapt in the future to what is essentially a loss of control in their home. Take that running future gag, the intelligent fridge, which promises faithfully to re-order everything directly from the supermarket as soon as it is used up or is out of date. This, groans Horx, is simply a misguided attempt by male engineers to replace that dying species, the housewife. A great Stepford Wife-style fantasy, he smiles, but what happens if you really want red wine instead of white, or the kids have been messing around with the chocolate milkshake cartons and a lorry load is rumbling its way to your house. Or better still imagine that one day the fridge is reprogrammed by your partner, who has decided you are taking too many midnight snacks and it remains locked until 7am. And sorry, blinks the control panel, your on-line doctor has prescribed that 'if you try to remove any more of that 60 per cent fat French cheese, or death-by-chocolate mousse, the Smart Garlic Press and I will erase your latest digital TV download as punishment'. The principle of a totalitarian technology, warns Horx, is completely incompatible with a modern, mobile and individualistic society.

As Horx enters the showcase Berlin apartment with its 200 state-of-the-art controllable electronic devices, he warns the assembled journalists and photographers that he believes one of the classic mistakes is in thinking that technology should be more intelligent in the future. It should, he says, essentially be stupid. It should be smart but redundant, leaving the intelligent and creative things to humans. His attention is swiftly drawn to the elegant control panel at the entrance which tells the inhabitant how many messages are awaiting them (fax/mailbox/answerphone) and if anyone has called by while they were out. It can also tell you how warm the bathwater is that you activated on your way home via your personal digital assistant (PDA) or mobile phone. If you have changed your mind about the music and lighting that you 'ordered' for your arrival, you can also change it from here. Or indeed by using the large and not-so-portable control panel. While Horx sees sense in some of the functions for the future, he critically questions the social engineering behind the idea that people want to be permanently reachable. Most people, he points out, want to relax when they come home, and a list of messages and things to do can be counterproductive and stressful. Furthermore, isn't luxury today about being unreachable? Only slaves, as he likes to point out, are permanently on call.

The bathroom here is an oasis of discreetly designed digital delights. The mirror houses a TV so that you can watch the news while you shave or put on make-up. My dentist would be delighted, remarks Horx, as he realizes that you clean your teeth for longer without even noticing. The intelligent fridge is conspicuously absent from the kitchen but there is the strange addition of a serving hatch leading to the dining room that folds up to reveal a large TV screen. The fact that the kitchen is cut off from the main living and dining space is very much against the trend to put the hearth at the heart of the home, says Horx. As Judy Wajcman writes in *TechnoFeminism*: 'Even the most visionary futurists have us living in households that, in social rather than technological terms, resemble the household of today. Democracy in the kitchen is not part of the package.'

Back in the early 1960s when Horx was a young boy, he

collected the free future cards for children from noodle packets and was fascinated by the futurist fantasies of how we would live in the future. There were, he fondly recalls, robots as chess partners, self-driving cars and, there at the helm of a high-tech kitchen, was always a woman poised to prepare the perfect meal in a starched white apron, with pert bosoms and a perfect hairdo. Both that and the Berlin designer apartment where Horx would happily live for the rest of his life are a long way from even this futurist's reality.

CHAPTER 10

THE FUTURE OF THE FUTURE

Brains are for anticipating the future, so that timely steps can be taken in better directions.

Daniel C. Dennett, philosopher

When the Millau Bridge over the River Tarn in France opened in 2004 it was celebrated as a masterpiece of modern engineering and technology. Taller than the Eiffel Tower, it was designed to float up out of the morning mist with the 'delicacy of a butterfly'. If the structural symbolism of the seven pillars was abundantly clear, what was less obvious at first was why the bridge needed to curve as it reaches across the valley. The reason, explained the architect Norman Foster, was simple. People driving across it should be able to look at the design of the bridge. If you head directly in a straight line to the other side, you cannot properly see or appreciate what is supporting you. Looking and travelling into the future is much the same.

The more you bring into your field of vision as you journey, the better the understanding you have of what it is that is taking you there.

At their best, futurists drive us over some of the best bridges to the future. At their worst, they take us on a woolly pig chase miles from where many of us may actually want to go. The truth is that not even universalists can ever see all the paths and possibilities, which is why futurism will need to embrace an increasingly peculiar pot-pourri of people from all sorts of fields and fancies from theoretical physicists, psychologists and neuroscientists, to mathematicians, evolutionary experts and fiction writers. As attention turns towards wider-reaching and less traditional fields, fear-mongering science fiction, futuristic literature and utopias are being slowly squeezed out of the limelight. As science-fiction-writer-cum-futurist Bruce Sterling sulkily remarked in *Tomorrow Now*, 'Science fiction can manage just fine without the future. Quite often the future is a drag on our market.' Despite this trend there are always a few surprises in store, such as housewife science fiction, tipped to be the hot new thing replacing macho doomsday disasters. As one might imagine, these are about desperate housewives driven to distraction by their demanding families, and written by, well, desperate (ex-) housewives. As Nostradamus discovered, there is nothing like a nice bit of doomsaying to boost book sales, and even the provocateur of French literature Michel Houellebecq has been getting familiar with the future in *The Possibility of an Island*, in which he depicts the life of clones 1,000 years on, where there is no sex, love nor laughter.

As the field of futurism widens its reach and reputation it is not perhaps surprising that more and more people are willing to out themselves as not just plain boring old physicists or even part time porno-writers with a kink for the future but as full-time, bona fide futurists. One of the most proudly and loudly self-confessed futurists around today is the American inventor Ray Kurzweil. Over the last twenty years he has made great and provocative contributions to the discourse and development of the future, particularly in the field of artificial intelligence (AI). He has also, unlike many futurists, actively produced many of the things he has foreseen would be possible, such as print-to-speech reading machines for the blind. His most recent book, *The Singularity is Near*, which was published in 2005, is the culmination of decades of bold, practical (and some rather impractical) prediction about how technology will play an increasingly integrated and important role in our lives. He controversially celebrates the idea that in the near future humans will ' transcend biology', and merge with technology. Furthermore, Kurzweil predicts that by as early as 2020 we will have computers that equal the processing power of the human brain, and that by 2030 they will exceed human intelligence. The rate at which technology is moving is still being hopelessly underestimated, according to Kurzweil. Most mistakes in predicting scientific progress, he says, have come about because people think in terms of linear expansion as opposed to exponential increase. His own successes include predicting in the 1980s that by 1998 a computer would defeat the world chess champion (it actually happened in 1997), and that a worldwide information network would emerge in the 1990s. 'The future will be far more surprising than most people realize,' he wrote in 2006, 'because few observers have truly internalised the implications of the fact that the rate of change is itself accelerating' The point, he emphasizes, will not be to compete with this new computer capacity, but to combine with it. In the spirit of why waste it all on robots when you can use it yourself, he believes that we will soon be inserting machines into our bodies via nano-technology. It will, he tried to reassure one interviewer, be more than a prosthesis, 'not a prosthetic device that just fixes problems, like a wooden leg, but something that allows us to expand our capabilities'. This merger of man and machine is a major factor in what he foresees as the 'quantum leap in evolution' that will take us to a state of 'Singularity', a time when we will be able to live as long as we want, free from disease, poverty and hunger.

Kurzweil is, meanwhile, busily trying to expand his own capabilities and capacity with (relatively) old-fashioned methods – trying to reprogramme his biochemistry by taking over 200 dietary supplements every day. According to his longevity doctor, Terry Grossman, Kurzweil is now almost twenty years younger than his chronological age (he was born in 1948). But if he doesn't live to see immortality, he claims, there is a good chance that he can download the contents of his brain before he dies. Should such a thing ever be possible there would undoubtedly be a long queue of potential takers for his enhanced grey matter. While not everyone in the futures field is so sold on Kurzweil's upbeat technological determinism, what many, such as neuroscientist Susan Greenfield, agree is that in the time-honoured way of futurism, his work raises interesting questions. Some would argue that it raises more questions than it answers, though in the book Kurzweil skilfully pre-empts that accusation with neat dialogues such as the one between himself, Darwin, Molly (a friend from the future) and Ned Ludd (of the Luddites). Darwin is a bit unsettled at the idea that machines are evolving at an accelerating pace, and asks, 'Biological evolution is presumably continuing is it not?' Ray (Kurzweil) disappoints him by telling him that it is evolving so slowly that it hardly counts. The Luddite chips in and somewhat predictably demands to know what happens if not everyone wants to go along with progress, and what we can do about the digital divide.

For those who are not devoted technological determinists, or interested in the ins and outs of quantum computing, Kurzweil's books also provide light and much-welcomed entertainment in the form of his signature dialogues from the future. In one such scene in *The Singularity is Near*, Futurist Bacterium and Friend of Futurist Bacterium of 2 billion BC are having a cosy chat about their destiny, and decide that since they won't be endangered for a couple of billion years, go off for lunch instead. In an earlier book, *The Age of Spiritual Machines*, Kurzweil also describes some bizarre future uses of virtual reality under the motto 'I can predict the future by assuming that money and male hormones are the driving force of new technology'. As with a lot of futurists, it lands him right splat in the middle of the temptation to write about sex in the future. Thanks to a wonderful and reliable technological invention called 'poetic licence', Kurzweil (in the present) has a long-running dialogue with Molly, his platonic friend from the future, and can ask her such things as whether in 2009 she is indulging in the virtual or video phone sex that he predicted would become popular. Molly is rather shy, but she explains that her fiancé is not so reluctant to use the new image transformer that allows you to alter someone's clothes, face or body while you are talking to them. She doesn't speak to him for a week after catching him out 'virtually' undressing his old girlfriend while talking to her. From 2029 Molly reports back that schoolchildren are being reprimanded for undressing their virtual teachers when bored of doing their homework, and by 2099 she is describing the nanobot swarms that can recreate living bodies and hug people for you. As one happily married futurist likes to remind his audience, such things will never catch on for one simple sociological and highly underestimated reason – if you need virtual sex or have a virtual relationship in the future, people will think you can't afford or get the real thing.

One of the eternal delights and difficulties of futurism is that it is all too easy to be seduced by high-tech toys and wild leaps of the imagination. What, one asks, would the fun for futurists be without a few woolly pig chases through the fictional forest of the future, or even the odd monkey trap to indulge in? However, as writer Tim Harford once said, 'Good futurology is the art of telling a good story. The story must be new, and it must be persuasive; the scenarios need to be plausible as well as provocative.'

Maybe – just possibly – it is something to do with futurists' egos, but another of those themes that still refuses to die is immortality. While Kurzweil is one of those lineal thinkers who are actively striving for it, Houellebecq asks wickedly 'Who, among you, deserves eternal life?', and there are those such as futurist Freeman Dyson, who claims that one of the worst things he can imagine is that we will find a cure for death. But for all the diversions and projections, the BIG question that still keeps ambitious futurists awake at night and underlines much of the serious hard-core futures work, is 'where are we going in evolutionary terms?' Dyson, a renowned physicist, may never agree with Kurzweil on some things, but he does also believe that, 'compared with the slow pace of natural evolution, our technological evolution is like an explosion. We are tearing apart the static world of our ancestors and replacing it with a new world that spins a thousand times faster.' Dyson predicts that biotechnology will dominate our lives during the next fifty years at least as much as the domestication of computers has dominated our lives during the past fifty. In a lecture at the University of California in autumn 2005 he gave a graphic example from the field of biotechnology. 'Domesticated biotechnology will mean that many objects of daily life, such as beds and sofas and houses and roads, will be grown rather than manufactured.' He envisages a world where biotech games will become as popular as computer games today. Why, he asks, would children play with boring screen images, when in the future they could hatch a real cute dinosaur or grow an ultra-mean prickly cactus. It is not such a leap of the futurist imagination from there to envisage a world in which kids will one day breed their own Barbies or Ninja Turtles. Strangely enough, when a group of British children was asked recently to draw their visions of the future, the results included talking cats, flowers that can do anything you want, and animals such as the 'Eletiger' (be warned, when a specimen of a duckbill platypus was first discovered and sent to a museum they thought it was a hoax too!). Rather more predictable were the children's pictures of trees growing money, huge walking sweets and, naturally, homework-writing machines! As Dyson warns, when children start to play with real genes, evolution as we know it will change forever.

When it comes to a meta-theory of change, futurists are also looking expectantly to people such as the eminent evolutionary biologist Richard Dawkins for inspiration and ideas. Dawkins first rose to fame with his book *The Selfish Gene*, which he said should be read almost as though it were science fiction, since the truth about evolution as he sees it, is anyway 'stranger than fiction'. Dawkins is not only a prolific and poetic explicator of Darwinism but is probably the closest thing to a celebrity that living evolutionary scientists will ever get. He is a captivating speaker and writer, and it is not surprising that his lectures attract not only futurists from far and wide, but philosophers, historians, and even novelists such as A. S. Byatt and Ian McEwan. At a jam-packed talk at the London School of Economics in 2005 Dawkins confessed that he enjoyed indulging in a little futuristic purple prose occasionally. In his book *The Ancestor's Tale*, he toys with the idea of a 'Ratkind' taking over from mankind. 'If nuclear war destroys humanity and most of the rest of life, a good bet for survival in the short term, and for evolutionary ancestry in the long term, is rats . . . Given enough time will a species of intelligent, cultivated rats emerge? Will rodent historians and scientists eventually organise careful archaeological digs (gnaws) through the strata of our long-compacted cities. And reconstruct the peculiar and temporarily tragic circumstances that gave ratkind its big break?'

Evolution is predictable, believes Dawkins. Not in detail, but in certain repeated patterns. If everything was to start again, it is very likely that we would find similar development patterns – such as eyes and bipeds. As Mark Twain once said, and Dawkins likes to quote, 'history doesn't repeat itself, but it rhymes'. Dawkins also believes that for the first time in history we are able to make real long-term predictions and our advantage is that we have a unique ability to look altruistically at the future (unlike the selfish gene). Although he is coming from a completely different direction to, say, Kurzweil, Dawkins also believes that evolution is now essentially technology-driven. It is interesting, he remarked in his lecture, that metal has never featured in the bodily evolution of humans – though now with pace-makers and metal hip-replacement pins it does, and to some extent he believes this will be the direction of future evolution.

Whether he likes it or not, Dawkins is one of futurism's new best friends. In a world that is perceived to be increasingly complex there is a compulsion to understand everything in evolutionary terms – from the development of the lowly toothbrush and mobile phone to the future of war and wildlife. So how will people like Dawkins and evolutionary theory help futurists understand and predict cultural processes and change? If, as he asks, 'the gene, the DNA molecule, happens to be the replicating entity which prevails on our own planet . . . Do we have to go to distant worlds to find other kinds of replicator and other consequent kinds of evolution?' In fact, says a triumphant Dawkins in *The Selfish Gene*, there is a new kind of replicator emerging out of the 'soup of human culture' on our planet that 'is achieving evolutionary change at a rate which leaves the old gene panting far behind'. This is the so-called meme (pronounced to rhyme with cream). Simply put, this is the cultural equivalent of a gene – and memetics is the study of how and why they spread. 'Examples of memes are tunes, ideas, catch-phrases, clothes, fashions, ways of making pots or building arches,' writes Dawkins. 'Just as genes propagate themselves in the gene pool by leaping from body to body via sperms or eggs, so memes propagate them- selves in the meme pool by leaping from brain to brain via a process which, in the broad sense, can be called imitation.'

To illustrate the ability of memes to spread through society Dawkins often uses the simple example of how the word 'gay' has come to be synonymous with homosexual instead of its original meaning. The big question for the futurists is can you create and spread a meme, or do they just occur? In an experiment to 'launch' a meme in 2004, a group in California released the word 'bright' as a new word for 'atheist' into the meme pool. If you have not yet used bright in this context, then the 'virus' has not yet spread or been successful. A devout atheist, Dawkins is hopeful that one day this meme will have established itself, but it could be, warn Dawkins and the philosopher Daniel Dennett, that religious memes are still more powerful.

What makes the concept of memes so irresistible is the thought that if one can unlock the 'DNA' of a successful meme such as you can with a gene, you can then supposedly identify the secret of what makes a successful product or an idea. 'Why do we have fax machines? Why Coca-Cola cans and wheelybins?' asks psychologist Susan Blackmore. 'If we want to understand how the fantastic complexity of our technological world came about it is not enough just to say that technology evolves, without providing a mechanism.' Some people dismiss memetics as pure redundant metaphor, but others such as Blackmore have been infected by the meme meme. In her book *The Meme Machine*, she expands effusively on Dawkins' idea, and asks, 'Imagine a world full of hosts for memes (e.g. brains) and far more memes that can possibly find homes. Now ask which memes are more likely to find a safe home and get passed on again?' You only need to think of jingles, Suduko puzzles, urban myths or pyramid schemes to understand the tenaciousness, selfishness and infectiousness of some memes.

But if we are really, as it has been solemnly suggested by Dennett, just apes infested with memes, can the theory of memetics really help with predicting the future? One of the key things to remember, says Blackmore, is that memes are blind. They are essentially selfish, caring only about replication and not whether they are for the good or bad of the world or the recipient. The significance of this point is applicable on many levels – from the basic levels of products, ideas, or marketing (how many 'fashionable' items do you have hidden unworn at the back of your clothes cupboard?), right up to the global and political consequences of infectious religious 'memeplexes'. Interestingly, she also sees the whole UFO phenomenon as a typical long-lived meme which has in effect disappeared but which Blackmore expects will return again some time in the far future. One theory as to its relatively sudden and mysterious disappearance over the last few years is that the 'alien spotters' have all abandoned their telescopes and have their noses pressed to their computer screens and into the weird happenings on the Internet instead.

Given the power and persuasion of memes it is not surprising that finding the key to understanding which memes will replicate successfully is something that firms will pay handsomely for. As Blackmore writes, 'Memes evolve as memes build on memes; new tools emerge; new clothes are made, new ways of doing things are invented. As these memes spread the most successful people are those who can acquire the currently most important memes.' Evolutionary psychologist Paul Marsden already has a company called Brand Genetics to help firms identify and clone strong memes, and is much in demand. But another factor of great interest to companies is how to find and infect the actual people who 'spread' memes. This is the process that William Gibson fictionalized in *Pattern Recognition*, and something that Malcolm Gladwell describes in his bestseller *The Tipping Point*. The word meme is conspicuously absent from Gladwell's book, but he nevertheless describes the same process by which social epidemics and trends spread with the help of three main groups. The first of these are 'connectors', people in touch with different groups of people who are crucial because 'the closer an idea or a product comes to a Connector, the more power and opportunity it has as well'. The second is 'mavens', who are experts or knowledge carriers – 'if marketplaces depend on information, the people with the most information must be the most important'. The third is 'salesmen', who can win over the customers (i.e. sell the idea of the product or meme). While his theories are admittedly not original, Gladwell's great strength and interest to future thinkers is that he looks at systems through symbolic storytelling. As one journalist put it, he has helped create a 'contagious hybrid gene of non-fiction'. Or, perhaps more accurately put, a hybrid meme of non-fiction.

Like memes, futurism is opportunistic, and will gladly be a best friend to everyone who can help it spread and grow. As well as infecting popular-science writers and evolutionary psychologists, another much underrated and underestimated friend for the future is anthropology. As anthropologist Robert B. Textor put it in *The World Ahead*, anthropology is a natural partner to futurism. 'Futurists . . . have a professional vested interest in identifying and counteracting tempocentrism, as anthropologists have with respect to ethnocentrism.' Stripped of jargon, what he simply means is that futurists can help anthropologists think more about the future and, more crucially here, anthropologists can help futurists think and find inspiration and ideas outside their own cultural box. As Textor bluntly puts it, 'Developing a certain amount of anthropological sophistication would be useful to futurists, the majority of whom are upper- or middle-class urban residents of economically advanced Western industrial nations.'

A certain anthropological sophistication is something that some companies are consciously starting to develop and that others are just starting to consider. One of the legendary but deceptively banal examples of anthropological contributions to technology is the big green button on photocopier machines. Anthropologist Lucy Suchman is famously reported to have suggested it to Xerox back in the 1980s, when she noticed how annoyed people were becoming while trying to figure out how to use the machines. The rest, as they say, is history. Today, companies are increasingly employing anthropologists to complement and work with futurists. As Andrew Herbert, the managing director of research at Microsoft's Cambridge lab, told the *New Scientist*, 'Having an anthropologist on the staff can give software engineers a better perspective on what will appeal to ordinary users.' The habits of less ordinary users can also give valuable insights to computer companies, as anthropologist John Sherry found out when he was sent to Alaska to study mobile professionals for Intel. Here he observed the way salmon fishermen casually strap their laptops to the outside of their trucks, and suggested that the company develop more rugged, weatherproof equipment.

Given the nature of the job, it is not surprising that ideas for future products and services come from unusual sources when anthropologists are involved. One of the popular examples is a postcard service offered by Vodafone that was apparently inspired by a social ritual of the people of the Trobriand Islands near Papua New Guinea. Every year the people exchange gifts made of seashells in a chain system that ensures no community receives something from the one it gives to. This ritual was first discovered by a social anthropologist back in 1922 and was found to cement social bonds between the island populations. Vodafone modernized this ritual to enable phone-users to send a multimedia messaging service (MMS) picture/text message to the company which is then printed out and sent to the recipient in the form of a postcard. This, it hoped, would have the dual function of creating a 'gift' (it turns a temporary MMS into a permanent object) and create new loyalty and exchange bonds between the customers and customer and provider.

Like anyone else involved in the futures business today and tomorrow, evolutionary agents and anthropologists can in the end only make intelligent guesses, ask clever questions and tell inspiring stories. They cannot guarantee a particular future any more than they can guarantee the success of a product, a government policy or a marketing methodology (although there are a suspicious amount of trend-spotting agencies and charlatans out there who would like you to believe they can). The fact that there is no regulating body to tell you who is a good or a bad futurist is both one of the disadvantages and delights of futurism. On the plus side it allows in ideas and people who might not otherwise get a look in (philandering mathematicians and pessimistic porno writers, to name just two who would probably be the first to fail a strict suitability test). On the downside, the absence of a *Which?* guide to futurists means that it is largely a self-regulating body (get something right and you are 'in') that will always attract its share of both dodgy and delightful characters with their various tricks and tics. It also naturally leaves the door wide open to the questionable wisdom of people such as Donald Rumsfeld, who, when asked in 2002 about weapons of mass destruction in Iraq, noted in flamboyant futurist fashion, 'There are things we know we know. There are known unknowns . . . things we know we don't know. But there are also unknown unknowns – things we don't know we don't know.'

The lack of a unified view of the future and a cosy futurist community also means that it can still be a dangerous business. Bruce Sterling rightly pointed out that 'someone who could give you a detailed, fully accurate portrait of tomorrow would not be human but a wizard. Such a prophet would also be extremely dangerous and very uncanny, and would have to be arrested.' As one poor man writing in 2005 to his fellow futurists in a plea from a mental institution deep in the Bavarian woods said, 'Futures research is always risky . . . It's easy to call a futurist non-realistic, utopian and crazy – no profession is more suited to feed that image and the necessity for psychiatric interventions.'

Risk-taking has always been both a hazard and an attraction of the job, and as far back as in the 1970s there was an attempt by the World Future Studies Federation to circumvent potential problems and ward off lunatics and charlatans by establishing a code of ethics for futurists. Like Asimov's Three Laws of Robotics, most of the demands were common sense, and included a general obligation to do no harm, to search for the truth, and not to 'spoil the opportunities for other futurists who may want to collect data in the future'. Last but not least was a plea not to cheat on your expenses with clients. There was, however, an embarrassing and overwhelming lack of interest and the whole idea was discreetly dropped from the society's agenda. Some futurists would, however, like to see it revived in some form or another, and an informal poll of suggestions for a code of conduct included the following golden rules and recommendations:

- Never ever put a specific date to a prediction (unless you are willing and likely to be alive and answerable on that date)
- Avoid predicting the end of the world (ditto)
- Know what you don't know (or what you can't know)
- Warn but do not scare people witless (lesson from Cassandra and *Limits to Growth*)
- Know thyself (in the spirit of Freud, Delphi and the monkey trap)
- Don't talk with your greedy mouth full (with deference to the second slogan at Delphi 'nothing in excess', and there is still that small matter of cheating expenses . . .)

History has shown that it is generally unwise to underestimate the power and influence of futurists on the future. 'Life will,' as writer Charles Handy has soberly noted, 'never be easy, nor perfectible, nor completely predictable. It will be best understood backwards, but we have to live it forwards.' So for as long as there is a foreseeable future we will always need futurists whose main task should not be to predict the future, but to help prepare us for it. As Bruce Sterling succinctly put it, 'At its best, futurism does what history can do. It suggests better decisions about our own actions in the context of the passage of time. Futurism teaches how to recognize profoundly changing circumstances. It offers paths forward that might have reasonable prospects of success. It offers humanity some fresh mistakes.'

BACKWORD

A few words of thanks to all those without whom this book would not have been possible, imaginable, or ever even written . . .

Best supporting male roles: My husband Matthias for the past, the present, the future, and for sometimes even looking after the children while I worked in the British Library. Saul David for liking the paradoxical title and making this book possible in the first place. My father Paul Strathern for all the memes and constant encouragement. John Naisbitt for his valuable time, insights and optimism.

Best supporting female roles: Becky Hardie, my editor at Constable and Robinson, and Sofia Reich and Isabel Naylon for their enthusiasm. My mother Patricia Strathern in Paris for the hotline to French queries, Adele Steiner for keeping the office in Vienna going in my 'absence', and Nithya Rae, my copy-editor.

Most reluctant supporting roles: Tristan and Julian, who dream of a future with sweets growing on trees and home-work-writing machines.

Best musical accompaniment: Julian's trumpet from below and Yunus' piano from above.

And many thanks to all those who willingly and sometimes even a little unwillingly (or even unwittingly) talked to me for this book including: Ernst Beinstein, Josephine Green, Thomas Huber and the board and attendees of the European Futurists Conference.

A BRIEF GUIDE TO FURTHER READING

I do not want to bog you down with endless footnotes and sources, or bore you by repeating all of the titles described in text, so here is simply a reminder of some of the most interesting or influential sources for further reading readily available in bookshops, via the Internet or in a good library. I have also omitted tedious details of publisher and date of publication as all you really need to find a book today is a title, a name and the will.

Introduction
Sterling, Bruce. *Tomorrow Now*. A lively introduction to the dilemmas and difficulties of modern-day futurism, and a look at how we live today by a science-fiction writer with his futurist hat on.

Chapter 1 Sex, Drugs and Heads that Roll
Bacon, Francis. *The New Atlantis*. Free to read at www.classic-literature.co.uk. For a good introductory biography of Roger Bacon, read *The First Scientist A Life of Roger Bacon* by Brian Clegg.

Carey, John (Editor). *The Faber Book of Utopias*. Carefully chosen extracts and short sharp analysis from all the strangest, best and nastiest utopias you could ever wish to read or dream about.

Clarke, I. F. *The Pattern of Expectation*. Dense, yet highly readable, history of futures from 1644 to 2001. One of John Naisbitt's favourite books on futurism. Out of print but worth tracking down, this or any of his other works.

Mercier, Louis Sebastian. A translation of *L'An 2440* entitled *Astraea's Return; or the Halcyon Days of France in the Year 2440: A Dream*, by Harriot Augusta Freeman, London 1797. Available in the British Library.

Nicholl, Charles. *Leonardo da Vinci: The Flights of the Mind*. If you have time for just one biography of Leonardo this could be the one.

Strathern, Paul. *Plato in 90 minutes*. Informative, entertaining – and yes it really only takes ninety minutes to read. Ditto *Marx in 90 minutes*.

Wood, Michael. *The Road to Delphi, The Life and Afterlife of Oracles*. Poetic and almost painterly look at the history of oracles.

Chapter 2: Fancy's Seven-Leagued Boots

Cabet, Etienne. *Travels in Icaria*. Dip into Cabet's stilted romantic story with its stodgy writing and dull detail, but savour the splendid introduction by Robert Sutton on the history and sufferings of the copycat utopian communities.

Strathern, Paul. *Mendeleyev's Dream*. Everything you never thought you would want to know about the history of chemistry.

Verne, Jules. Most of the author's books are available to read free online. See www.jv.gilead.org.il and www.classic-literature.co.uk

Chapter 3: In Next Week To-morrow

Lynn, Andrea. *Shadow Lovers*. Here lie the clues to some of Wells' monkey puzzles.

Marinetti. *The Futurist Cookbook*. Nothing really to do with futurism or cooking as we know it, but great for dinner-party conversation.

Taylor, D. J. *Orwell, The Life*. Comprehensive and compelling reading.

Wells, H.G. *Journalism and Prophecy, 1893–1946*. An Anthology by W. Warren Wagar. Excellent selection of Wells' writings, rantings and predictions. Another alternative to the classics is *The Discovery of the Future*, which outs him as a futurist, edited and introduced by Patrick Parrinder.

Chapter 4 : Here Live Lions

Asimov, Issac. *I, Robot*. A classic, to be read with a large pinch of predictive salt.

Flechtheim, Ossip. *History and Futurology*, with a foreword by Robert Jungk. A selection of his early papers and ideas.

Strathern, Paul. *Dr Strangelove's Game, A Brief History of Economic Genius*. For more on John von Neumann I recommend the chapter entitled 'The Game to End All Games'. For more detail try the excellent *John von Neumann* by Norman Macrae.

White, Michael. *Asimov, The Unauthorised Life*. Highly enjoyable general introduction to his life and works, plus some good juicy gossip.

Wolfe, Bernard. *Limbo '90*. Read it if you dare, care, or can find it.

Jungk, Robert. *Tomorrow Is Already Here, Scenes from a Man-Made World*. Pessimistic but fascinating and highly readable snapshot of the zeitgeist of 1950s America.

Gorn, Michael H. *The Universal Man, Theodore von Kármán's Life in Aeronautics*. Even if you are not moved by rocket science, a great biography of an extraordinary character.

Chapter 5: Surprise-Free Futures

Fuller, Buckminster. *Utopia or Oblivion, Prospects for Humanity*. Epilogue provides a wonderfully fantastic vision of life in a domed (as opposed to doomed) future.

Ghamari-Tabrizi, Sharon. *The Worlds of Herman Kahn*. First stop for an intense look at some parts of Kahn's life and influence.

Kahn, Herman. *On Thermonuclear War*. A stark reminder of the (in)sensibilities of the Cold War. Worth reading just to remind yourself it wasn't a hoax.

Lem, Stanislaw. Take a look at his official website, www.lem.pl. Peter Swirski's *A Stanislaw Lem Reader* includes rare interviews and the revengeful essay *Thirty Years Later*.

McLuhan, Marshall. *The Medium is the Massage*. A heady reminder of how the 1960s were (in case you missed or slept through them). See also the official website, www.marshallmcluhan.com

Mead, Margaret. *The World Ahead, An Anthropologist Anticipates the Future*. Little-known collection of her essays and speeches on anticipatory anthropology.

Toffler, Alvin. *The Futurists*. A great overview of the thinking of the key futurists of the 1950s and 1960s.

Chapter 6 : Fast Forward

Clarke, Arthur C. *Profiles of the Future*. Originally published in 1962, but read the millennium edition as it has his updated comments and apologies. www.clarkefoundation.org/ is his official website where you can read the original 1945 article proposing satellites.

Drucker, Peter F. *Adventures of a Bystander*. Entertaining and enlightening autobiography. See also www.peterdrucker.at

Frewin, Antony. *Are We Alone?* Rediscovered transcripts of interviews with twenty-one futurists for Kubrick's film *2001: A Space Odyssey*. Lots of repetition, but also a few pleasant and some less-pleasant surprises.

Chapter 7: Jam Tomorrow . . .

Naisbitt, John. If you read anything, go for his classic *Megatrends* to see what all the fuss was about and his most recent, *Mind Set!* www.naisbitt.com

Sherden, William A. *The Fortune Sellers*. A cynical and disturbing look at the business of buying and selling predictions.

Cornish, Edward. *Futuring*. The ex-president of the World Future Society (www.wfs.com) and the 'official' angle on futurism.

Schwartz, Peter. *The Art of the Long View*. Good, readable examples of scenario planning. For the Global Business Network see www.gbn.com.

Wagar, Warren. *A Short History of the Future*. Part sci-fi, part prediction (though both tendencies hotly denied).
Baker, Robin. *Sex in the Future*. Not for the squeamish, sensitive or the incurably romantic.

Chapter 8: The 800-lb Gorilla

Casti, John. *Destiny's Design: Why the Future Happens – and How You Can Anticipate It*. A mathematician's gripping and informative book about the rhythm of history.

Chapter 9: A Week in the Life of a Futurist

Horx, Matthias. *How We Will Live: A Synthesis of Life in the Future*. www.horx.com and www.zukunftsinstitut.de

Chapter 10: The Future of the Future

Bell, Wendell. *Foundations of Future Studies, Vol 2*. 'Sedate' but worthy basic reading if you are really thinking of becoming a futurist in the future.
Dawkins, Richard. Read everything you can, including *Unweaving the Rainbow*, the ultimate cure for woolliness.
Dennett, Daniel. *Breaking the Spell: Religion as a Natural Phenomenon*.
Dixon, Dougal. *The Future is Wild*. From a 'future evolutionist', a vision of the world millions of years from now where humans are extinct and kangaroo-sized rabbits roam.
Gladwell, Malcolm. *The Tipping Point* and *Blink*. Good storytelling rather than future-telling, but nevertheless oft quoted by futurists.
Greenfield, Susan. *Tomorrow's People* is a technological trip into the future from a neuroscientist.
Kurzweil, Ray. If you can face it, read *The Singularity is Near*. For a briefer dip into his future, look at www.KurzweilAI.net

INDEX